Introduction to the Theory
of Grammar

D0075241

Current Studies in Linguistics Series
Samuel Jay Keyser, general editor

Introduction to the Theory
of Grammar

Henk van Riemsdijk and
Edwin Williams

The MIT Press
Cambridge, Massachusetts
London, England

This book was set in VIP Times by Village Typographers, Inc., and printed and bound by Halliday Lithograph Corporation in the United States of America.

Library of Congress Cataloging in Publication Data

Riemsdijk, Henk C. van.
  Introduction to the theory of grammar.

  (Current studies in linguistics series ; 12)
  Bibliography: p.
  Includes index.
  1. Grammar, Comparative and general—Syntax.
2. Generative grammar. I. Williams, Edwin.
II. Title. III. Series.
P291.R48 1986   415   85-11339
ISBN 0-262-22028-8 (hard)
        0-262-72009-4 (paper)

To pasta

The character of a cuisine is determined more by basic approach than by ingredients.

—Marcella Hazan, *The Classic Italian Cookbook*

Contents

Contents

Contents

Contents

Contents

Preface

The past thirty years have seen an explosive development in the study of the grammatical structure of languages. For centuries, linguistic thinking was essentially limited to compiling inventories of grammatical categories and to largely unempirical philosophizing. Nineteenth-century historical and comparative linguistics made it possible to achieve scientific results. Structuralism has contributed greatly by stressing the systematic nature of syntactic relations. But the true breakthrough came in the mid-1950s when Noam Chomsky introduced the innovative concept of *generative grammar*. This concept has given the field a new and exciting direction and has defined its position with respect to neighboring disciplines such as philosophy, psychology, biology, and mathematics. The development and characteristics of generative grammar—that is, of generative syntax, for generative grammar also includes a theory of sound structure or phonology, which we will not cover—will be the subject of this book.

In the past twenty-five years generative grammarians have come to understand enough about the workings of language that it is difficult to become acquainted with the principal results in a relatively short time by reading the original literature. In this book we try to convey an impression of these results and how they were achieved. Along with so many others we have been drawn into linguistics by the realization that "the grammar is in the mind," that by studying grammatical structure we may find out something about human cognition, and that it is possible to develop a theory of Universal Grammar about properties of the human brain that can account for the fact that we are able to acquire the grammar of our native language at an age when we are still considered too young to go to school and learn the alphabet. This realization has given the field the impetus that is indispensable if it is to become a truly scientific enterprise: the ability to ask significant, far-reaching, and difficult questions combined with an approach that makes answering these questions seem feasible. These questions and answers are central to this book. Each answer breeds new questions that in turn require answers.

Our main goal will be to show why these questions have been asked, and we will try to convey how it is possible that some of the answers have been enlightening and at the same time frustrating because they show very clearly how much more work is needed. In doing so, we will not give a faithful history of "how it actually happened." Instead we will trace the logical development of present-day grammatical theory, avoiding the sidetracks, dead ends, and shortcuts that have characterized the actual course of events. The vicissitudes of the field are interesting in their own right, and they are insightfully reported and analyzed in Frederick Newmeyer's *Linguistic Theory in America* (1980).

In outlining the major phases and breakthroughs in linguistics since the mid sixties, our history also covers what is presently understood about the theory of grammar. In that sense, this is an introductory book, addressed to teachers and students as well as to anyone interested in what grammatical theory is and why people are excited about it.

However, it is not a textbook of the usual sort. It is not a full-fledged account of the present state of the art, nor does it codify a precise and complete set of principles that can be accepted and learned as immutable linguistic facts. Linguistics is very much a dynamic science, and principles are continually being discovered, modified, even discarded. Thus, we have not attempted to present the full intricacy of today's version of "the best theory," and we have forsaken some points of formalization and of how details are resolved, in favor of stressing important ideas and questions and how they have developed. As a result, the reader will become acquainted with the history and general content of generative grammar and—most important in an ever-changing field—with how linguists actually develop their theories.

The exposition presupposes little. An introductory textbook or an "Introduction to Linguistics" course that delves into syntax will give sufficient background on such basics as constituent structure, how to write a linguistic rule, how to apply it, and so on. Useful general introductions to linguistics are Neil Smith and Deirdre Wilson's *Modern Linguistics* (1979) and Adrian Akmajian, Richard Demers, and Robert Harnish's *Linguistics* (1984). Reading C. L. Baker's *Introduction to*

Generative-Transformational Syntax (1978) will provide the information about syntax that is presupposed here.

The book is organized as follows. The introduction considers why we study grammar and why we go about it as we do. It also covers the early history of generative grammar, from Chomsky's *Syntactic Structures* (1957) to his *Aspects of the Theory of Syntax* (1965). This introduction is followed by four parts consisting of several chapters each. Part I discusses how the rule systems of the 1950s and 1960s, which provided an excessively rich descriptive framework, were gradually replaced by simpler, more constrained rule systems. Much of the work originally done by stipulations in the rules themselves was progressively taken over by general, universal principles governing the form and functioning of these rules and the properties of their inputs and outputs. The establishment of such a theory of principles is the main topic of part II. Part III considers how semantics fits into grammar and how the syntactic properties of logical representations can be integrated into the overall theory of grammar. The rules and principles of grammar developed in these parts account for grammatical phenomena in an essentially modular way in that they constitute autonomous subparts of the grammar that interact with each other in determining the properties of syntactic representations. This system of modules, which constitutes the state of the art of the early 1980s, is established in part IV. As more and more new languages are studied from this theoretical point of view, new questions arise, promising ideas abound, and new perspectives animate the field. The epilogue (chapter 19) gives a necessarily dated and eclectic picture of this activity in order to convey a sense of how much remains to be done and of where the field might be going.

So as not to clutter the chapters with credits and bibliographical information, we have ended each chapter (except chapter 19) with a bibliographical section attributing the main ideas discussed in the chapter to their authors and providing selective suggestions for additional reading.

In a text of this length it is unavoidable to simplify many formulations, to select from existing alternatives, to ignore potential objections. The bibliographical sections will make up for some of these deficiencies but not all of them. The reader who wishes to go from the broad outline provided here to a truly detailed discussion should next study the main exposition of modern grammatical theory, Chomsky's *Lectures on Government and Binding* (1981c). We believe that our text provides a good introduction to that book, not so much in supplying the reader with the precise definitions that appear there but rather in giving some feel for the goals of the theorizing that led to the stage of the theory that book represents.

Grammatical theory, as presented here, would not exist without Noam Chomsky. Without the changes that he has brought about in linguistics, neither of us would be linguists today. We have benefited greatly from discussions with and suggestions from Terry Dibble, Morris Halle, Jan Koster, Pieter Muysken, Adam Wyner, and Richard Zatorsky. We are particularly grateful to Sylvain Bromberger, Noam Chomsky, Roger Higgins, Riny Huybregts, Howard Lasnik, and Anna Szabolcsi for reading an earlier draft and commenting on it. We owe much to several groups of students who have been exposed to earlier and partial drafts in syntax courses in Amherst, Salzburg, and Tilburg. The secretarial assistance by Annemieke de Winter and Janneke Timmermans and the editorial assistance by Anne Mark have been invaluable. Many thanks are also due to Clemens Bennink, Norbert Corver, Angeliek van Hout, and Willy Kraan for doing most of the work on the index. Finally, we gratefully acknowledge financial support from Tilburg University, the Netherlands Organization for the Advancement of Pure Scientific Research (ZWO), and Michael Arbib and the Computer and Information Science (COINS) Department of the University of Massachusetts, Amherst.

Introduction to the Theory
of Grammar

Chapter 1
Introduction

1.1 The Assumptions and Goals of Grammatical Theorizing

The study of grammar (specifically, syntax) is a part of the study of language, that part concerned with the rules of sentence construction. By calling grammar a part of general language study, we mean that it is a "coherent" self-contained part. It is distinct from the study of language as a vehicle for communication, from the study of the history of languages, and from the study of the human neurology that subserves language—distinct in having its own internally general laws and primitive elements and in not being reducible in any interesting sense to any of these other disciplines.

It is by no means obvious that the study of grammar is not an arbitrarily defined subdiscipline most properly dissolved in favor of some combination of studies. Perhaps the most general point that this book will make is that there is a significant domain of fact and explanation that can be approached through grammatical theorizing.

The material in this book constitutes a detailed and specific theory of grammar. As such it naturally rests on strong assumptions about the domain of phenomena that the theory of grammar is about, and about the role of the theory of grammar in the general theory of language. These assumptions are supported to the extent that the resulting theory of grammar gives satisfying explanations, and to the extent that it supports or "meshes with" theories concerning other aspects of language. In this book we will be concerned exclusively with the first of these kinds of support.

For instance, it is assumed that many factors interfere with the direct perception of the object of study itself (grammar) and that the greatest obstacle to progress is often the very richness of the available facts.

Thus, the study of grammar rests on an idealization of the world: linguists must factor out the interfering elements in order to study the grammar itself. For example, in this book we will not take into account data involving "mean utterance length" of speakers of various ages or backgrounds, or other data involving memory capacity, slips of the tongue, and so forth. This is because it is our hunch, and the hunch of grammarians at large, that although such data may have something to say about the use of grammar, they have nothing to say about its form. (This hunch could certainly be wrong; all that remains is for someone to show how. No kind of data is excluded in principle, only as a matter of practice—judicious practice, we think, but not irrefutable.) Instead, grammarians use data like "such and such a string of words is a sentence in such and such a language" or "such and such a string of words means such and such," where such facts are determined by native speakers of the languages in question. Data of this kind vary enormously in quality—ranging from the clear fact that *He are sick* is not grammatical in English to the rather subtle judgments involved in determining whether *John* and *his* can refer to the same person in *His mother likes John*. Despite this variation in quality and despite the fact that linguists have not formulated a "methodology of sentence judgments," such data remain the principal source of information about grammar, again, not as a matter of principle, but because they have so far provided successful insights.

Thus, the study of grammar is not the study of sentence judgments; rather, sentence judgments are our best current avenue to the study of grammar. In other words, the grammar is a real thing, not an artifact erected on top of an arbitrarily demarcated set of facts or types of facts. Therefore, it is often difficult to determine whether a given fact bears on grammar or not; this is not an arbitrary decision, but ultimately an empirical question about how the world divides up. For example, actives and passives bear a certain formal (grammatical) relation to each other:

(1)
a. John gave the answer
b. The answer was given by John

Despite the formal relation between these sentences, they are functionally and conversationally dissimilar; for example, either could be used to answer the question *Who gave the answer*, but only the first could be used to answer *What did John do*. It is not a priori clear whether this observation is to be explained within the theory of grammar proper (along with the ungrammaticality of *John are tired*) or within the larger containing theory, the general theory of language or of language use. Therefore, the grammarian must proceed tentatively, ready to revise even basic assumptions about what the theory is about; but of course no work would be done at all without some assumptions, and the best work has been done under very strong idealizations.

1.2 What Is a Grammar?

What, precisely, is a grammar? Linguists routinely use the word *grammar* in an ambiguous way, and though the ambiguity is actually useful, it is nevertheless worthwhile to examine the two meanings. In its most important sense, the grammar of a language is the knowledge that we say a person has who "knows" the language—it is something in the head. The study of grammar is *the* study of this specialized kind of knowledge—how it is constituted, how it is acquired, how it is used.

In its other sense, a grammar is a linguist's account of the "structure" of a language, or a "definition" of a language. For example, definition (2a) could be considered the "grammar" of the language shown in (2b):

(2)
a. $\{S: S = cX, X = a, X = aX\}$
b. $\{ca, caa, caaa, caaaa, caaaaa, \ldots\}$

Of course, linguists are interested only in grammars of natural human languages, but the sense of the word *grammar* is the same: a formal "definition" of the language.

It is important to note that this use of the notion "language" is quite different from the commonsense idea of language—here we are talking about language as a set of objects, and the grammar (in either sense under discussion) is a "criterion for membership" in that set, or a definition of that set. It is for this reason that grammars of the sort we are discussing are called "generative": the grammar is a definition (or "device") that "generates" all of the members of the set, in the sense that (2a) can be said to "generate" the language indicated in (2b).

There is no tension between these two senses of the word *grammar* as long as one regards the linguist's formal definition as a model not of a language per se, but rather of a speaker's knowledge of that language. With this assumption, it will always be possible to determine which of two different grammars of a language is the "right" one: it is the one that reflects a speaker's knowledge of the language, a determination that can always be made, at least in principle. We will constantly refer to a grammar as "a system of rules" or "a definition of a language," but we will always have in mind that it is nothing if it is not a model of a speaker's actual knowledge.

A language, then, is a set of objects that we call *sentences*. What, then, is a sentence?

Human languages are richer in structure than the artificial language in (2), and their grammars are accordingly more highly structured. For the artificial language, it was sufficient to regard a sentence as simply a string of items. But very little about an English sentence can be explained if it is regarded as simply a string of words. A sentence has a meaning that is more than the set of meanings of the words, and it has a "sound" that is not simply the stringing together of the sounds of individual words. Thus, it appears that each sentence has a structure that mediates the connection between its sound and its meaning. For example, it appears that each sentence is divided into a subject noun phrase and a verb phrase:

(3)
John – bit the dog   (S = NP VP)

This aspect of syntactic structure affects not only how the sentence can sound (for example, the most natural place to pause is at this juncture) but also what the sentence means—the subject is the "agent" of the verb, so that the meaning of this sentence is different from that of *The dog – bit John*. We may thus regard a sentence as consisting of three things: its sound, its meaning, and its syntactic structure. A grammar, then, is the rules for the formation of syntactic structures and associated sounds and meanings, and a language is the set of all such triples defined by the grammar:

(4)
L = {... (sound, syntactic structure, meaning) ...}

The main goal of modern linguistics has been to formulate some contentful theory of "grammar," and in particular to discover and study universal properties of grammar, or *Universal Grammar*.

Like *grammar*, the term *Universal Grammar* (*linguistic theory*) is ambiguous. On the one hand, it refers to the linguist's account of the notion "possible grammar of a human language"—a notion to be defined by studying grammars with an eye for their general properties. On the other hand, *Universal Grammar* can be viewed as an account of the human language faculty in general, apart from any particular language—in other words, the general human ability to learn and use language.

Again, there is no conflict between these two views as long as one takes a "realist" view of linguistic theory, that it really is about something. The general properties of the human language ability will determine the notion "possible grammar": a possible grammar will be a grammar that can be constructed by the human language faculty on the basis of some exposure to a particular language.

What is impressive about Universal Grammar, to the extent that it is currently understood, is that it is remarkably specific about the notion "possible grammar." Of the huge number of rule systems that we can imagine, only a minute fraction appear to be used as the grammars of human languages. This is not so surprising when we consider the speed and uniformity with which humans learn their various native languages; perhaps at each juncture in the learning of a language, Universal Grammar permits only a few options for the further elaboration of the grammar of that particular language.

In a sense this book is a synopsis of one current view about the nature of Universal Grammar. In the remainder of this chapter we will briefly examine two important early stages in the development of this view: the versions of Universal Grammar in Chomsky's *Syntactic Structures* (1957) and *Aspects of the Theory of Syntax* (1965).

1.3 *Syntactic Structures* **and** *Aspects of the Theory of Syntax*

In *Syntactic Structures* Chomsky formalized a type of grammatical description, which we would now call a *phrase structure rule system,* and showed that it was not adequate for the general description of language. He proposed that another type of rule was needed as well, namely *transformational* rules, and he suggested how the grammar of a language might be composed of both types. In *Aspects of the Theory of Syntax* he refined this picture of grammar, but maintained the view that the grammars of languages were composed, in a specific way, of these two major types of rules, phrase structure rules and transformations.

1.3.1 The Phrase Structure Rules

The words in a sentence group together in *phrases*. For example, the sentence *The man in the road spoke to Mary* breaks down into two phrases, a noun phrase (NP) and a verb phrase (VP):

(5)
The man in the road – spoke to Mary
      NP   VP

This division of the sentence into two phrases is a part of its structure, and knowing this is a part of our knowledge of English. We cannot adequately defend this claim here, though it will amass overwhelming support in the course of the book. For example, the break between *road* and *spoke* is the most natural place to pause in (5); moreover, *the man in the road* is a recognizable unit that occurs with the same meaning in many different sentences in fixed positions (as subject, as object, etc.), whereas other sequences of words in (5), such as *road spoke to,* do not.

If all sentences are composed of an NP and a VP, we can represent the relationship between a sentence and its constituent parts in terms of the following rule:

(6)
S → NP VP

The NP and the VP can themselves be further decomposed into constituent phrases:

(7)
a. the man in the road

   Art N   PP
b. spoke to Mary

     V   PP

There are many NPs of the form "Art N PP" (*a picture of Bill,* etc.) and many VPs of the form "V PP" (*look at the sky,* etc.), so each of these also represents a general pattern. In rule form:

(8)
NP → Art N PP
VP → V PP

Rules of this type, called *phrase structure rules,* have the following general form,

(9)
X → Y Z W ...

where X is the name of the phrase defined, and Y Z W, etc., are either phrases (and therefore in need of definitions themselves) or the names of lexical categories (Noun, Verb, etc.). A set of such rules defines a set of structures known as the *phrase structures* of the language described. We may represent a phrase structure by means of a phrase marker (or phrase structure tree), which shows graphically how the phrase structure rules determine the form of the structure:

(10)

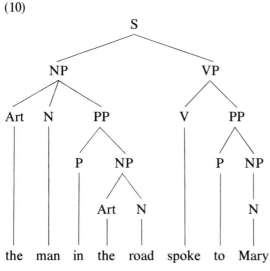

the   man   in   the   road   spoke   to   Mary

Might rules of this type be the only ones needed to describe natural human language? This is not an idle question, since not all "languages" in the formal sense can be so described. One inherent limitation of these rules is that given two subphrases, the composition of each must be completely independent of the composition of the other (hence, these rules are called *context free*).

Phrase structure rules are a part of the grammar of both *Syntactic Structures* and *Aspects.* An important feature of this type of rule system is that it is capable of describing languages with infinitely many sentences, because the rules are *recursive,* or "circular" in a certain harmless but important sense. Given the rules in (11),

(11)
S → NP VP
VP → V S

an S can contain an S (via VP); furthermore, the contained S may itself contain an S, and so on, with no limit.

This recursive property was realized in different ways in *Syntactic Structures* and *Aspects*. In *Syntactic Structures* the phrase structure rules themselves defined only a finite number of structures, called *kernel sentences*, each of which was a simple S (with no Ss contained in it). Instead of the rules in (11), this system might have the rules in (12), which would generate sentences like (13a–b):

(12)
S → NP VP
VP → V NP

(13)

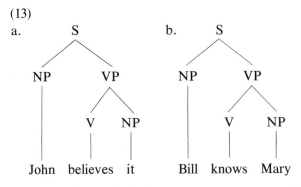

A different type of rule (not a phrase structure rule) could then embed one kernel sentence inside the other, to give, for this pair, *John believes Bill knows Mary,* thus producing the recursive effect. In *Aspects* recursion is realized essentially as shown in (11); that is, the phrase structure rules themselves have the recursive property. A strong reason to prefer the *Aspects* version is that the *Syntactic Structures* version permits derivations in which the embedding (or matrix) S is transformed before the embedding takes place; since such derivations seem never to be needed, a theory that permits them is less highly valued than one that does not. We will assume the *Aspects* version throughout.

We will also assume the *Aspects* mechanism of *subcategorization.* Different verbs fit into different types of VPs, and not others; for example, *believe,* but not *eat,* fits into a VP that contains an S (*John *eats/ believes that Bill left*). Phrase structure rules can call both *eat* and *be-*

lieve verbs, but cannot further specify their required context; hence, they cannot make this distinction. *Aspects* allows a limited kind of context sensitivity for this kind of context dependence. The "dictionary" lists with each verb a specification of the contexts in which it can appear, and for a phrase structure tree to be well-formed, all such context specifications must be met:

(14)
hit, ＿＿ NP   (can appear before an NP)
believe, ＿＿ NP, ＿＿ S   (can appear before an NP or an S)

The phrase structure rules together with the lexicon (or dictionary) are often called the *base component*.

1.3.2 Transformations

Syntactic Structures demonstrated that phrase structure rules are not sufficient to describe human language, because they cannot encode certain dependencies between parts of sentences. A phrase structure rule can express dependencies between "sisters" (nodes all immediately dominated by the same node) but not between subparts of sisters. Given the rules in (15),

(15)
$A \rightarrow (b)\ C$
$C \rightarrow (d)\ e$

the grammar expresses the dependency "If b appears in the sentence, then C appears"; however, it cannot express the dependency "If b appears, then d appears," since d is a subpart not of A but of C.

Consider the following sentences:

(16)
a. John thinks that Bill saw Mary
b. ?John thinks that Bill saw
c. Who does John think that Bill saw
d. *Who does John think that Bill saw Mary

These sentences illustrate just this kind of dependency. (16a–b) show that the verb *see* normally has a direct object. However, when the entire sentence is prefixed by *who,* this requirement is suspended; in fact, as (16d) shows, the direct object is impossible. Thus, there is a dependency between whether the direct object appears and whether *who* appears. Phrase structure rules cannot describe this dependency, since *who* and the direct object of the embedded clause are not sisters. For example, writing the VP rule so that objects are optionally present and the S rule so that *who* is optionally prefixed does not express the fact that these options, for these sentences, are connected:

(17)
a. VP → V (NP)
b. S → (who) NP VP

To express such dependencies, then, another kind of rule is needed.

In some sense, *who* in (16c) "is" the direct object of *saw,* even though it does not appear in direct object position. We might regard it as having been displaced from this position; in fact, in a special kind of question (an "echo" question) the *who* can appear there:

(18)
John thinks that Bill saw who?

Given this sentence, we may derive (16c) by "moving" the direct object of *see* to the front of the sentence; we may call this a *transformation* of (18) to give (16c), and the type of rule that accomplishes it a *transformational rule* (or simply a *transformation*). We consequently do not need the phrase structure rule (17b), but instead can make do with *S → NP VP,* assuming that all prefixed occurrences of *who* (and similar words) result from applying a particular transformation to a structure like (18). This transformation expresses the relevant dependency: a sentence with prefixed *who* can only result from transforming a structure with *who* in direct object position, which explains why prefixed *who* and a direct object are mutually exclusive in constructions like (16c–d).

The structure to be transformed—(18)—is often called the *underlying structure* or *deep structure,* and the result of applying the transformation—(16c)—is often called the *surface structure.* The terms *deep* and *surface* are used in a purely technical sense here. Nevertheless, they have given rise to a certain confusion over the years because of some unwanted connotations (deep = fundamental, profound, meaningful, etc.; surface = superficial, unimportant, etc.). Following current practice, we find it useful to replace *deep structure* by *D-Structure* and *surface structure* by *S-Structure;* however, the reader should be aware of the terminological variation. Given this terminology, then, a transformational derivation can be represented as follows:

(19)

D-Structure ——————————→ S-Structure
                    transformation(s)

The addition of transformations to the kinds of rules used in writing grammars raises many questions. What is the general form of transformations? What principles govern their application in the derivation of sentences? What relation do they have to the phrase structure rules? How can the presence of a transformation in the grammar of a language be detected by a child learning the language? *Syntactic Structures* and *Aspects* offer preliminary answers, which we will sketch here (though with little or none of the justification given for them in those two works).

Both *Syntactic Structures* and *Aspects* suggest that a transformation consists of two parts, a description of the structures to which the transformation is applicable and a description of the resulting structure. Furthermore, in this version of the theory these descriptions are of a very elementary form, consisting simply of a string of "terms," each of which is simply a category label (such as "NP" or "VP") or a variable. For example, the rule just discussed, *Wh*-Movement, might be written as follows (where *wh-phrase* refers to a phrase that contains a *wh*-word):

(20)

a. *Structural description (SD)*: X *wh*-phrase Y
b. *Structural change (SC)*: *wh*-phrase X Y

This simply means "Any structure that can be segmented into three parts, the first of which (X) can be anything, the second of which is a *wh*-phrase, and the third of which (Y) can be anything, can be transformed into a structure with these three parts arranged in the order *wh-phrase X Y*":

(21)

	Mary saw	who	yesterday
SD:	X	*wh*-phrase	Y
	who	Mary saw	yesterday
SC:	*wh*-phrase	X	Y

This restriction on the form of transformations—that they can consist of nothing more than a string of category labels and variables—is quite severe, given all the different types of rules one could imagine; in fact, linguistic practice subsequent to *Syntactic Structures* and *Aspects* went well beyond this restriction, in general.

In complex sentences, a transformation may apply more than once. For example, (22a) is derived from (22b) by two applications of *Wh*-Movement:

(22)
a. Who did Bill tell [who Mary saw]
b. Bill told who [Mary saw who]

Here the direct object of *saw* moves not to the front of the entire sentence, but only to the front of the embedded sentence. This shows that an embedded S is taken as a domain for the application of transformations apart from the S it is embedded in. But if more than one transformation can apply, questions again arise. In what order do the rules apply? Simultaneously? Sequentially? If the latter, which rule applies first? Indeed, does it matter which applies first? *Syntactic Structures* established that all derivations can be done under the restriction that all transformations apply in sequence, none simultaneously, and furthermore that the application of each transformation does not depend on which transformations have applied previously, but strictly on the structure to be transformed. Compared to what one can imagine, this is a very simple notion of derivation; such derivations are called *Markovian,* and this notion of derivation underlies all current work.

Aspects established that the notion "derivation" can be further restricted. The order of application of transformations to a deep structure can be said to always obey the following principle:

(23)
Principle of the Cycle
Given two domains (Ss) in which transformations are applicable,
one contained in the other, all transformations apply in the smaller
domain before any transformations apply in the larger domain.

1.4 Evaluation and "Expressive Power"

Both *Syntactic Structures* and *Aspects* present general formalisms for writing two types of rules, phrase structure rules and transformations. The grammar of a language then consists of two sets of rules, each of which conforms to one of these formalisms. The very generality of the formalisms means that the theory defines a vast number of grammars. How does a language learner (or for that matter a linguist) sort out the correct one, given some finite range of data from the language?

The linguist can make progress in answering this question in two distinct ways. One is by revising the theory so as to permit fewer overall grammars. The smaller the number of grammars a theory permits, the less "expressive power" the theory has. Expressive power can be reduced either by constraining the types of rules that can be written or by devising entirely new and "more restrictive" (less "expressive") rule-writing systems.

The other way to make progress on this question is not to reduce the number of grammars available under the given rule formalism, but to "rank" the grammars in some way; this formal ranking of grammars may be called the *evaluation measure*. We may then refer to the highly ranked grammars as the "simple" ones. Under this ranking analysis, adopted in both *Syntactic Structures* and *Aspects,* the child acquires language (constructs the grammar of his or her language) by testing various rule formulations against the innate instruction "Pick the simplest grammar compatible with the data." Of course, *simple* is a technical term to be defined in the theory, but if it is correctly defined, it could in principle give the result that for any finite range of data, the theory determines a unique grammar of a language, and that for a substantial (but finite) range of data, it determines the "correct" grammar. Clearly, "shortness" is one component of simplicity—all else being equal, short grammars are preferred over longer ones—but it was quite clear from the start that "shortness" did not exhaust the technical notion of simplicity.

This approach, including development of general rule-writing systems and formal evaluation of grammars, has largely been abandoned in favor of less formal and more "substantive" ideas about how grammars are composed. This has happened largely because nothing of interest emerged beyond the initial idea of "shortness" that helped to define how the language learner or the linguist is to determine the correct grammar from finite data. The shift in emphasis from general rule-writing systems with formal evaluation to universal substantive specifications of large parts of grammars has been a main theme of linguistic research over the last 10 or 15 years and is a main theme of this book.

1.5 Bibliographical Comments

The first complete discussion of the philosophical and methodological underpinnings of the study of formal grammar can be found in chapter 1 of *Aspects* (Chomsky (1965)). This book is a classic that has lost none of its relevance despite the fact that it has given rise to numerous misunderstandings, misinterpretations, and misrepresentations. Newmeyer (1983) provides a good overview in this regard. Some of these issues are also discussed in a more informal setting in Chomsky (1982b).

Certain more philosophical questions (in particular, the epistemological question of what we mean when we say that humans "know" a grammar) have given rise to their own literature. Chomsky (1980a) represents the most recent important contribution from the linguist's point of view to this domain of inquiry. For a more philosophically oriented text, see Fodor (1983). A background of philosophical history is provided in Chomsky (1966).

Syntactic Structures (Chomsky (1957)) and *Aspects* are the major landmarks in the early history of generative grammar. *Syntactic Structures* is particularly valuable, especially in view of its discussion of generative capacity and the hierarchy of grammars, which, though somewhat tangential to the development of modern generative grammar and frequently misconstrued (again see Chomsky (1982b)), nevertheless constitutes important background information. Peters and Ritchie (1971) and Lasnik and Kupin (1977) also contain useful information on this issue. In addition, *Syntactic Structures* provides the first accessible analysis of numerous phenomena of English syntax, most of which have lost little or none of their relevance for current theorizing. The book is largely based on Chomsky's 1955 Doctoral dissertation, a much more technical and difficult text that appeared 20 years later as Chomsky (1975). To bridge the gap, Chomsky wrote an introduction to the 1975 publication that contains a great deal of interesting information about the early history of generative grammar. Heny (1979) is an insightful review article of Chomsky (1975).

Beyond its important first chapter, *Aspects* contains a long discussion of the structure of the lexicon, necessitated by the separation between the context-free phrase structure rule system and the lexical insertion rules (the rules responsible for the insertion of dictionary entries in syntactic structures). The basic mechanisms introduced there are still valid, though they occupy a relatively marginal position in current linguistic theory. *Aspects* incorporates the new conception of embedding by recursive phrase structure rules, which was largely due to Fillmore (1963). But the discussion is somewhat overshadowed by the struggle to come to grips with the delimitation of syntax and (lexical) semantics. To that end a version of Katzian semantics (Katz and Fodor (1963)) was incorporated. That the struggle was not, at the time, entirely successful is shown by the meteoric rise of so-called Generative Semantics in the late 1960s. Newmeyer (1980) provides a good discussion of the ensuing "linguistic wars."

In addition to the component of syntax delimited in this chapter, the grammar as a whole is thought to consist of a phonology, a semantics, and a lexicon (including morphology). For generative phonology, the seminal work is Chomsky and Halle (1968). Good introductory textbooks are Hyman (1975) and Kenstowicz and Kisseberth (1979). Articles dealing with recent developments, supplemented with a useful introduction, are to be found in Van der Hulst and Smith (1982). For discussions of morphology and the lexicon, we recommend Aronoff (1976) and Selkirk (1982). Good overviews of semantics are presented in Kempson (1977) and Fodor (1979).

Other important subdisciplines are historical linguistics (Lightfoot (1979)) and mathematical linguistics (Wall (1972), Partee (1975a)). Since the study of grammar is the study of one aspect of human cognition, it is embedded in the context of a wide variety of subfields dealing with related aspects of cognition. Today these subfields are often collectively referred to as *cognitive science*. Though no overview of cognitive science has yet appeared, we recommend Newmeyer (1983) for some discussion of (at least part of) this domain.

Part I
_____

TOWARD A THEORY
OF RULES

Chapter 2
Toward a Theory of Conditions on Transformations

2.1 The A-over-A Principle

Chomsky's *Current Issues in Linguistic Theory* (1964) marks the first important step toward establishing a general theory of conditions on transformations. Perhaps the most appealing constraint proposed in that book is the *A-over-A Principle*. Consider (1a–c):

(1)
a. Mary saw the boy walking toward the railroad station
b. This is the railroad station which Mary saw the boy walking toward □
c. Which railroad station did Mary see the boy walking toward □

"□" indicates the position from which the *wh*-phrase was moved, by Relative Clause Formation in (1b) and by Question Formation in (1c). In the remainder of this chapter we will refrain, however, from indicating this "gap."

(1a) is ambiguous between the readings (2a) and (2b):

(2)
a. Mary saw [$_S$ the boy walk toward [$_{NP}$ the railroad station]$_{NP}$]$_S$
b. Mary saw [$_{NP}$ the boy [$_S$ who was walking toward [$_{NP}$ the railroad station]$_{NP}$]$_S$]$_{NP}$

Both (1b) and (1c) are unambiguous, however: they can only be understood in the sense of (2a). The A-over-A Principle accounts for this fact by requiring that a transformation that could apply to two NPs, one of which is embedded in the other and both of which match its structural description, can only apply to the higher (more inclusive) one. More formally:

(3)

A-over-A Principle

In a structure ... [$_A$ ... [$_A$ ...]$_A$ ...]$_A$ ..., if a structural description refers to A ambiguously, then that structural description can only analyze the higher, more inclusive, node A.

This principle will correctly prevent Relative Clause Formation and Question Formation from applying to (1a) when it has the structure of (2b).

In *Current Issues* this proposal was simply a more or less plausible and elegant-looking solution to the descriptive problem posed by (1a–c), and it was hidden in a footnote. Furthermore, in the same footnote, Chomsky pointed out several potential counterexamples:

(4)

a. Who would you approve of my seeing

b. What are you uncertain about giving to John

c. What would you be surprised by his reading

But what started out as an interesting attempt at solving the descriptive problem associated with processes of *wh*-movement (processes that move *wh*-phrases—phrases consisting of or containing *who, what, which,* etc.) in examples like (1a–c) was to become the germ for the construction of a general theory of constraints on transformations, which has constituted the main research program throughout the 1970s. Though the idea still remained unexplored in *Aspects,* it was taken up again, more or less simultaneously, by Chomsky in *Language and Mind* (Chomsky (1968)) and by John R. Ross in "Constraints on Variables in Syntax" (Ross (1967)). Chomsky stresses the fact that, despite many empirical problems, the A-over-A Principle has "a certain explanatory force." Ross, on the other hand, concentrates on the empirical problems raised by the principle and tries to formulate more adequate alternatives. This chapter presents the most influential of Ross's proposals, their shortcomings, and their significance.

2.2 A-over-A Phenomena

Among the phenomena that are potentially relevant to the A-over-A Principle are the following.

(i) An NP that is a conjunct of a coordinate structure cannot be questioned or relativized:

(5)

a. We have to read some books and some papers
b. *Which books do we have to read and some papers
c. *Those are the papers that we have to read some books and

Since the coordinate structure *some books and some papers* in (5a) has the form (6), the A-over-A Principle prevents transformations from applying to the circled NPs and thereby accounts for the ungrammaticality of (5b) and (5c):

(6)

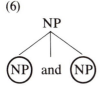

(ii) An NP that is part of a subject NP cannot be questioned or relativized:

(7)

a. For John to win a medal is easy
b. *What is for John to win easy
c. *It is the gold medal that for John to win is easy

(8)

a. My letter to a friend in Italy got lost
b. *Who did my letter to get lost
c. *Gianni is the friend who my letter to got lost

Here the A-over-A Principle straightforwardly prevents transformations from applying to the NPs *a medal* and *a friend,* contained in the subject NPs *for John to win a medal* and *my letter to a friend.*

(iii) An NP that is contained in the sentential complement to a noun cannot be questioned or relativized:

(9)

a. He refuted the proof that you can't square an ellipse
b. *What did he refute the proof that you can't square
c. *The figure that he refuted the proof that you can't square looks a
    bit like an egg

Again, the grammaticality judgments on these constructions follow directly from the A-over-A Principle, since (9a) is of the following form:

(10)

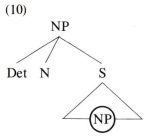

(iv) An NP that is part of a relative clause cannot be questioned or relativized:

(11)
a.   Bill found a principle which solves the problem
b.   *Which problem did Bill find a principle which solves
c.   *The problem that Bill found a principle which solves was very recalcitrant

These cases also have the typical A-over-A structure:

(12)

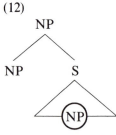

However, Chomsky (1964) notes that there may be another explanation for the facts in (11). Observe that Relative Clause Formation has applied twice to elements of the most deeply embedded relative clause: the subject and the object. Suppose now that this is ruled out as a matter of principle. This principle will then account for the ungrammaticality of (11c). Furthermore, if the principle is extended to exclude more than one application of either Relative Clause Formation or Question Formation, (11b) is also accounted for. This analysis also explains the following facts:

(13)
a.   Who saw what
b.   *Who what saw (*What who saw)

This restriction also accounts for a fifth set of facts, which does not fall under the A-over-A Principle in any obvious way.

(v) The *Wh-Island Constraint:* An NP that is part of an indirect question cannot be questioned or relativized:

(14)
a.   John wondered who would win a gold medal
b.   *What did John wonder who would win
c.   *The medal that John wondered who would win was the gold medal

These facts, to which we will return in chapter 4, have come to be known as *wh-island phenomena*.

Since Relative Clause Formation and Question Formation consistently pattern together with respect to these phenomena, they have been identified under the heading *Wh-Movement*. We will therefore often exemplify arguments with instances of one or the other, but not both.

In the next sections we will discuss first some problems with the A-over-A explanation of the facts in (i) through (iv) and then Ross's alternative accounts for them: the Complex NP Constraint for (iii) and (iv), the Sentential Subject Constraint for (ii), and the Coordinate Structure Constraint for (i).

2.3 The Inadequacy of the A-over-A Principle

The A-over-A Principle is both too strong and too weak; that is, it excludes certain grammatical sentences and fails to exclude certain ungrammatical ones. We have already seen examples of the former problem in (4). The latter, however, appears to be much more serious. In fact, it appears that most cases where a phrase of type B is extracted from a phrase of type A are ungrammatical too, and consequently an A-over-B Principle would seem to have at least as much chance to be correct as the intuitively more appealing and plausible A-over-A Principle. To illustrate:

(i) An adjective phrase cannot be extracted from an NP:

(15)
a.   You have a very intelligent sister
b.   How intelligent a sister do you have
c.   *How intelligent do you have a sister

(ii) A PP cannot be extracted from the contexts given in section 2.2:

(16)

a. Bill rejected the suggestion that he should talk to someone

b. *To whom did Bill reject the suggestion that he should talk

(17)

a. He has [an ID which is valid until tomorrow]

b. *Until when does he have an ID which is valid

   (iii) In many languages, such as French and German, an NP cannot be extracted from a PP:

(18)

a. Ils   ont   voté   pour de Gaulle
    they have voted for   de Gaulle
    'They voted for de Gaulle'

b. *Qui ont-ils   voté   pour
    who have they   voted for

(19)

a. Sie sollte   mit   ihrem Bruder spielen
    she should with her   brother play
    'She should play with her brother'

b. *Wem sollte   sie mit   spielen
    who should she   with play

   There are other problems as well, but it is clear even from these examples that the A-over-A Principle is far from adequate. An alternative conclusion is that the constructions listed in (i) through (v) in section 2.2 will not permit the extraction of any kind of phrase. This is what Ross realized. In Ross (1967) he studied large portions of English syntax in this light to discover the properties of these constructions, giving them the name *islands*.

   Ross proceeded to impose a number of constraints on transformations in order to account for such island phenomena. Viewing these as constraints on the variables in the structural descriptions of transformations, he assigned them the following general format:

(20)

No rule can involve X and Y (move Y to X, for example) in the structure

$\quad ... X ... W_1\ Y\ W_2 ...$

if ...

What follows *if* is the characterization of the island structures.

2.4 The Complex NP Constraint

The main idea behind Ross's approach to constraints on transformations is that the class of moved items to which they apply must be strongly generalized, in view of the observations in section 2.3, but that some generality with regard to characterization of the island contexts must be sacrificed. In other words, there is no one principle that will cover all the extraction contexts in section 2.2; instead, it is necessary to formulate several constraints, each of which captures only part of the phenomena in section 2.2. However, each one will apply to a wider class of phrases, as required by the data in section 2.3. The first of these, the Complex NP Constraint (CNPC), covers the phenomena of (iii) and (iv), which obviously look quite similar; however, it applies not only to NPs but to any phrase:

(21)

Complex NP Constraint (CNPC)
No element contained in an S dominated by an NP with a lexical head noun may be moved out of that NP by a transformation.
(Ross's (4.20))

The CNPC is not limited to *Wh*-Movement of NPs, as in (9) or (11), but applies to PPs as well, as in (16) and (17). APs also fall under the restriction:

(22)
*How intelligent are you looking for an au pair who is

Other movement processes seem to be subject to the CNPC as well. Consider the processes of VP-preposing and *though*-inversion:

(23)
a. They all argued that Bill would leave the country, and leave the country I must conclude that he did
b. *They all argued that Bill would leave the country, and leave the country I resent the conclusion that he did

(24)
a. Intelligent though I agree that your au pair is, I still don't like him
b. *Intelligent though you have an au pair who is, I still would have preferred a girl

2.5 The Sentential Subject Constraint

Ross limits his account of the phenomena in (ii) of section 2.2 to sentential examples of type (7) (for the generalization to all subject NPs, see chapter 4). Again, however, the constraint he proposes applies to any element to be moved out of the island configuration:

(25)
Sentential Subject Constraint (SSC)
No element dominated by an S may be moved out of that S if that node S is dominated by an NP which itself is immediately dominated by S. (Ross's (4.254))

The SSC applies not only to *for*-clauses, as in (7), but also to *that*-clauses:

(26)
*Who did that Mary was going out with bother you

And again, the constraint applies to other processes as well:

(27)
*They said that John would win the race, and win the race that he did was evident to everyone

(28)
*Intelligent though for an au pair to be is unlikely, one shouldn't be prejudiced

It is clear that these facts depend on more general questions regarding the distribution of sentential substructures, which may be governed via base-generation or some process of extraposition (see chapter 3 for discussion). In any event, though we will not pursue the matter here, it appears that *that*-clauses, and also to some extent *for*-clauses, cannot easily occur in sentence-internal positions, an observation often referred to as the *Internal S Constraint*. This constraint would also account for most of the facts handled by the SSC.

2.6 The Coordinate Structure Constraint

The phenomena in (i) of section 2.2 are also accounted for in Ross's framework by a separate constraint that defines conjuncts of coordinate structures as islands. The main generalization achieved here with respect to the A-over-A Principle is that the new constraint also applies to the extraction of parts of a conjunct, which the A-over-A Principle would not cover in any obvious way:

(29)
Coordinate Structure Constraint (CSC)
In a coordinate structure, no conjunct may be moved, nor may any element contained in a conjunct be moved out of that conjunct.
(Ross's (4.84))

The CSC easily accounts not only for (5) but also for sentences like (30a–b):

(30)
a.   Bill is [AP proud of [NP his father]NP]AP and [AP tired of [NP his mother]NP]AP
b.   *Who is Bill [AP proud of [NP his father]NP]AP and [AP tired of]AP

It also improves on the A-over-A Principle by preventing (31b) from being generated from (31a):

(31)
a.   Mary wondered [S (whether) John would come]S and [S who would bring what]S
b.   *Mary wondered [S what John would come]S and [S who would bring]S

In (31b) the *wh*-phrase has been moved from the second conjunct to the initial position of the first.

A final observation concerning coordinate structures and the CSC is that *Wh*-Movement can extract parallel *wh*-phrases out of conjuncts when *all* conjuncts of a coordinate structure are affected this way, as in

(32). This property of *Wh*-Movement (and certain other transformations, including Subject-Aux Inversion) is called *across-the-board rule application*.

(32)

I wonder which books Mary hates and Sam likes

These, then, are the beginnings of the theory of constraints. All the principles discussed here have since been modified, generalized, or replaced. The fate of the CSC has been somewhat different, however, because it has not interacted with the other constraints under these revisions. Instead, there have been essentially very few proposals to derive the CSC from specific formalizations of the way transformations apply to syntactic structures that are primarily designed to capture the across-the-board property.

2.7 Pied Piping, the Left Branch Condition, and Upward Boundedness

Ross formulated constraints to account for two more important phenomena: cases involving (i) pied piping and the Left Branch Condition and (ii) the upward boundedness of rightward movement rules. Again, these proposals deserve to be mentioned not so much because they offer real explanations for the phenomena in question as because they define standard problems that continue to be highly relevant for present-day research.

The Pied Piping Convention emerged from the observation that the A-over-A Principle is too strong in certain cases. Consider, for example, (33a–b):

(33)

a. This is the book $[_{NP}$ which$]_{NP}$ I have proofread $[_{NP}$ the preface $[_{NP}$ of$]_{NP}]_{NP}$

b. This is the book $[_{NP}$ the preface $[_{NP}$ of $[_{NP}$ which$]_{NP}]_{NP}]_{NP}$ I have proofread

(Note that Ross regards PPs as NPs, hence as structures of the form $[_{NP}$ P $[_{NP}$ *wh*-word$]_{NP}]_{NP}$.) Here the *wh*-word, which is an NP, is contained within a larger NP, a paradigmatic A-over-A situation. Nevertheless, *Wh*-Movement can move the smaller NP as well as the larger one. Ross suggests that in such a situation the more inclusive structure may optionally be carried along in the movement of the *wh*-word. Following a suggestion of Robin Lakoff, he calls this phenomenon *pied*

piping ("... just as the children of Hamlin followed the Pied Piper out
of town, so the constituents of larger noun phrases follow the specified
noun phrase when it is reordered" (p. 263)). He formulates the Pied
Piping Convention as follows:

(34)
Pied Piping Convention
Any transformation that is stated in such a way as to move some
specified node NP, where this node is preceded and followed
by variables in the structural description of the rule, may optionally
apply to this NP or to any noncoordinate NP that dominates it,
as long as there are no occurrences of any coordinate node, or of the
node S, on the branch connecting the higher node and the specified
node. (Paraphrasing Ross's (4.180))

(Adopting the more standard view that PP is distinct from NP would
require modifying this formulation.)

   The main feature of this principle is its optionality. Consequently,
auxiliary principles must be formulated to account for cases where pied
piping is either prohibited or obligatory. Preposition stranding (as in
(33a)) provides instances of both. On the one hand, when *Wh*-Move-
ment applies to an NP that is the object of a certain type of preposition
in Danish, then pied piping cannot occur; in other words, preposition
stranding is obligatory. On the other hand, in German, French, Russian, and other languages preposition stranding is impossible. For these
languages, then, pied piping of prepositions is obligatory. Finally, in
English, where pied piping of prepositions appears to be essentially
optional, several additional constraints are nevertheless involved. The
only one of these that reaches a fair generality is the Left Branch
Condition:

(35)
Left Branch Condition (LBC)
No NP that is the leftmost constituent of a larger NP can be moved
out of this NP. (Paraphrasing Ross's (4.181))

This principle will account for facts such as the following:

(36)
a. You saw the president's wife's guard
b. *Whose did you see wife's guard
c. *Whose wife's did you see guard
d. Whose wife's guard did you see

In other words, the LBC imposes obligatory pied piping in such structures. Although some interesting ideas have been raised in the literature in this regard, the LBC remains largely a mystery for which no truly satisfactory explanation has been found.

Ross also formulated the Upward Boundedness Constraint to account for the type of paradigm shown in (38):

(37)

Upward Boundedness Constraint
No element that is moved rightward by a transformation may be moved out of the next higher node S. (Paraphrasing Ross's (5.58))

(38)
a. [$_S$[$_S$ That a serious discussion *of this topic* could arise here]$_S$ was quite unexpected]$_S$
b. [$_S$[$_S$ That a serious discussion could arise here *of this topic*]$_S$ was quite unexpected]$_S$
c. *[$_S$[$_S$ That a serious discussion could arise here]$_S$ was quite unexpected *of this topic*]$_S$

The extraposition of the PP yields an ungrammatical result when it goes out of the first S-node up.

More recent proposals have been made to deal with examples like (38c), but they remain inconclusive in view of the possibility of successive cyclic movement (see section 4.1). Thus, the upward boundedness issue is currently one of the standard unsolved problems.

2.8 The Domain of Transformations

The primary impact of Ross's proposals concerning island constraints was on rules like *Wh*-Movement. Such rules are typically unbounded in their domain of application, and the fact that the variable that covers this unbounded domain of application is subject to the island constraints does not alter this. The question then arises whether all transformations can apply over unbounded domains. Ross partially answered this question: only transformations with a "crucial" variable have this property (that is, transformations with a structural description of the form $X - A - Y - B - Z$, where A and B are constant terms of the structural description, X, Y, and Z are variable terms, and Y is the "crucial" variable—the variable that separates the two constant terms). Rules like Affix Hopping or Subject-AUX Inversion, which lack such a crucial variable, cannot apply over unbounded domains. They are local. Subject-AUX Inversion, for example, moves the first auxiliary verb in a sentence to the position immediately to the left of the subject; the structural description of the rule can therefore be written without an essential medial variable, as in (39a):

(39)

a. X NP V_{AUX} Y

b. George can leave → Can George leave?

More or less simultaneously with Ross's work on island constraints, Peter Rosenbaum was exploring the syntax of complement clauses in English (Rosenbaum (1967)). Rosenbaum proposed transformations such as Extraposition and Equi-NP-Deletion (his Identity Erasure). Equi-NP-Deletion accounted for the phenomena of subject control that we will discuss in chapter 8. Curiously, this rule was neither unbounded nor local. In fact, it operated in general exactly across one (cyclic) S-node. In view of this, linguists began to wonder about what we might call the typology of transformations. The following basic typology emerged with respect to domain of application:

(40)

a. Monocyclic transformations: transformations that operate within one clause (S-domain), including the local transformations Passive, Reflexivization, etc.

b. Bicyclic transformations: transformations that operate across exactly one S-boundary, such as Equi-NP-Deletion and Raising-to-Object

c. Unbounded transformations: transformations that operate across arbitrarily many S-boundaries, such as *Wh*-Movement

This typology was quite popular for a while, even though it had two important weaknesses. First, it imposed a heavy burden on the language learner, who was now thought to learn not only the particulars of each transformation (its structural description, its structural change, whether it was obligatory or optional, etc.) but also its domain type. (It might be possible to circumvent this objection by positing a learning strategy based on the assumption that all rules are monoclausal unless evidence is found to the contrary, much as in our discussion of Emonds's typology in the next chapter. In the present case, however, a much more elegant solution is available, which we will present in chapter 4.) The second weakness was that (40) presupposes that a given transformation belongs to the same type in all its applications. This is not obviously true, given the behavior of Passive, for example:

(41)
a. I believe [$_S$(that) John left]$_S$
b. *John is believed [$_S$(that) left]$_S$ (by me)

(42)
a. I believe [$_S$ John to have left]$_S$
b. John is believed [$_S$ to have left]$_S$ (by me)

If the ungrammaticality of (41b) follows from the fact that Passive is a monocyclic rule, then how can the grammaticality of (42b) be accounted for? Rosenbaum devised an ad hoc solution for this problem: he proposed that there is a bicyclic transformation that raises the subject of the infinitival complement clause into the VP of the matrix clause. This rule was called *Raising-to-Object,* and it provided the intermediate step (42c) for the derivation of (42b), making it possible to maintain Passive as a purely monocyclic rule:

(42)
c. I believe John [$_S$ to have left]$_S$

Much evidence was adduced to motivate Raising-to-Object, but virtually all of it was of the same type: counterexamples to the typology of (40) that could be eliminated if Raising-to-Object was assumed. Apparently nobody wondered about the correctness of (40) itself.

Raising-to-Object was shortly abandoned. Ross's island constraints, on the other hand, are still partly with us as central problems for linguistic research. Very few of the constraints have been regarded as true solutions because they lack sufficient generality. Most of them mirror in a fairly direct way the structural properties of the island configurations. In that sense they are observational generalizations rather than truly general abstract explanatory principles. Their great importance is in having initiated the systematic quest for such an abstract explanatory theory of conditions on transformations.

2.9 Bibliographical Comments

The A-over-A Principle was first introduced in Chomsky's (1964) *Current Issues in Linguistic Theory.* The first part of that book is devoted to largely methodological matters (in a way a precursor of the first chapter of *Aspects*), and the second part deals with phonology. The A-over-A Principle is hidden in footnote 10 on page 46. (Interestingly, the proposal appears in the main text of Chomsky (1962), an earlier version in article form of the same monograph.) The A-over-A proposal first takes real shape in Chomsky (1968) and is simultaneously attacked in Ross (1967), a very important piece of work that regrettably has remained unpublished.

The proposal regarding across-the-board rule application referred to in section 2.6 appears in Williams (1978). More recent proposals concerning the across-the-board property can be found in Gazdar (1981) and Pesetsky (1982b).

The Left Branch Condition has given rise to numerous publications. Of particular interest is the proposal in Bresnan (1976a) to derive the LBC from a reformulation of the A-over-A Principle, her "Relativized A-over-A Principle." Among the many counterarguments to the LBC, the most thoroughly documented is Obenauer (1976). Interesting observations with respect to the Upward Boundedness Constraint appear in Akmajian (1975) and Baltin (1981).

The typology of transformations discussed in section 2.8 was first introduced in Rosenbaum (1967). Its most controversial element, the Raising-to-Object transformation, was defended in Postal (1974). In the aftermath of the battle, which basically had already been won with the appearance of Chomsky (1973), Postal's book was reviewed by Bresnan (1976c) and Lightfoot (1976).

Chapter 3
The Role of the Phrase
Structure Component

3.1 Introductory Remarks

We have seen that many facts about the functioning of the rule of *Wh*-Movement need not be stipulated as specific properties of that rule but can instead be made to follow from general constraints on transformations. We can also consider the Passive transformation from the same point of view. (1) is an *Aspects*-style formulation of Passive:

(1)
Passive

	X	– NP –	AUX –	V	– NP –	Y –	*by*	– Z
SD:	1	2	3	4	5	6	7	8 →
SC:	1	5	3+*be*	4+*en*	∅	6	7+2	8

This rule raises many questions:

(2)
a. Should transformations be permitted to refer freely to specified morphological material such as *be, -en,* and *by?*
b. Rule (1) effects two movements (element 2 is adjoined to *by,* and element 5 is moved to position 2). How many movements can a single transformation effect? Or, for that matter, how many operations (insertions, deletions, substitutions, adjunctions) can a single transformation perform?
c. Rule (1) mentions five constant terms in its structural description. Is there any limit on the number of constant terms mentioned in the structural description of a transformation?
d. In rule (1) some of the constant terms are separated by variables (for example, 5 and 7), but others are adjacent to one another. In other

words, structural descriptions can stipulate not only left-to-right relations but also their adjacency. Are both necessary?

e. Rule (1) mentions the verb of the sentence. This is necessary because the structural change of the rule assigns the verb its participial form. But alongside passive sentences there are also passive nominalizations:

(i) The enemy destroyed the city
(ii) The city was destroyed by the enemy
(iii) the enemy's destruction of the city
(iv) the city's destruction by the enemy

Shouldn't rule (1) be revised so as to permit (iv) to be derived from (iii)?

f. The two movement operations of (1) both have the effect of moving an NP to a position where NPs are also generated by the phrase structure rules: the direct object NP (5) moves to the subject NP position (2), and the subject NP moves to the position to the right of the preposition *by*, which, by virtue of the base rule PP → P – NP, is also an NP position. Is this an accident?

We could ask more questions along these lines, but the general strategy should be clear: every stipulation that is employed in the formulation of a rule should be questioned. The range of stipulations that are permitted in the formulations of rules is directly related to the expressive power of these types of rules and hence to the expressive power of the theory of grammar as a whole. Since the ultimate goal is to restrict as tightly as possible the expressive richness of grammars permitted by linguistic theory, one of our main research objectives must be to eliminate as many of these stipulations as possible, either by making their effect follow from general principles or, of course, by simply showing that they are unnecessary in the first place. This is an ambitious research program, and it has not been carried out in its entirety. Consequently, we will only discuss some of the main steps that have so far been taken in the right direction, and in many cases this will involve offering a promissory note about some auxiliary subtheory that must as yet be elaborated before the simplification has been fully achieved.

In this chapter we will address (2e) and (2f) in detail, and in the course of the discussion we will also suggest some tentative answers to questions (2a–d).

3.2 The Status of Nominalizations

Question (2e) was originally answered by saying that (iii)–(iv) (= (3a–b)) are derived from (i)–(ii) (= (4a–b)) by means of a nominalization transformation that operates after Passive (Lees (1960)):

(3)
a. The enemy destroyed the city
b. The city was destroyed by the enemy

(4)
a. the enemy's destruction of the city
b. the city's destruction by the enemy

Consider some of the things this nominalization transformation must be able to do:

(5)
a. Change categories: S becomes NP, V becomes N
b. Introduce a preposition (*of*) in the transitive active case (4a)
c. Assign a genitive -*s* to the prenominal NP
d. Change the morphological shape of the head: *destroy-/destroyed* becomes *destruction,* etc.
e. Delete all auxiliaries

Needless to say, such a rule again prompts many questions. It should be kept in mind, however, that (3) and (4) clearly bear certain systematic relationships to each other that must be expressed in the grammar.

Chomsky took up this issue in "Remarks on Nominalization" (1970). There he argued that the grammar should allow no nominalization transformations, nor any other transformations with similar expressive power, and he proposed that the relationships between (3) and (4) should be captured by other means. But this, of course, meant that another answer would have to be found for the problem mentioned in (2e). We will first review very briefly some of Chomsky's arguments against nominalization transformations, and then consider his reformulation of Passive.

There are three major types of arguments against incorporating a nominalization transformation in the grammar to derive nominalizations, or, as they are often called, derived nominals. The first is, again, that such transformations are an extraordinarily powerful type of device to have in a grammar. Some of the properties of such rules were listed in (5). If ways can be found to eliminate such transformations from the set of descriptive possibilities that a grammar can make use of, then we must in fact eliminate them in view of our goal of reducing the expressive power of grammars. If each of the operations in (5) is considered a possible transformational operation, and if further transformations can be composed of arbitrary numbers of such operations and others, then the sheer variety of types of possible transformations is vastly increased—increased in a way that makes the prospect of a concrete and specific characterization of "possible grammar" very remote.

The second type of argument involves the relationship between derived nominals and other NPs. In fact, it appears that the structure of derived nominals corresponds in every respect to the structure of other types of noun phrases. Chomsky (1970) lists many such NPs, of which we repeat only a few:

(6)
a. the weather in England
b. a symphony by Beethoven
c. the enemy's anguish over his crimes
d. the author of the book

None of these nouns can reasonably be argued to be derived from a corresponding verb. Nevertheless, the head nouns can take *by*-phrases as in (6b), possessive phrases as in (6c), direct object NPs with the preposition *of* as in (6d), etc. Clearly, the phrase structure rules must be able to assign a structure to such NPs. Consequently, those parts of the nominalization transformation that have the task of creating such structures are redundant. It is better, so the argument goes, to generate them via the phrase structure rules, which are independently required to assign nominalizations like (4) their structure.

The third type of argument involves the nature of the relationship between sentences and the corresponding derived nominals. This relationship is highly unsystematic in several ways. First, the morphological relation between a verb and the corresponding derived nominal is to a very large extent unpredictable:

(7)

prove:	proof	*proval	*provement	d.n.a.
refuse:	*refuse	refusal	*refusement	*refusion
amuse:	*amuse	*amusal	amusement	*amusation
destroy:	*destruct	*destroyal	*destroyment	destruction

Semantically, the relation between the verb and the derived nominal is also highly unpredictable. Very often the derived nominal has acquired certain idiosyncratic meaning aspects that are not part of the meaning of the corresponding verb:

(8)
imagine ~ imagination
erect   ~ erection
revolve ~ revolution
reside   ~ residence

In both cases these idiosyncratic, unpredictable properties of individual words must be stated somewhere, and the lexicon appears to be the natural place for stating them. The proposal that emerges from such considerations, then, is that derived nominals must be listed as independent lexical items in the lexicon, and that whatever systematic relationships they have with verbs must be stated there in a nontransformational way by means of redundancy rules in the lexicon. *Lexical redundancy rules* state general relationships among sets of words. For example, the set of nouns ending in *-ion* is related in a systematic way to a certain set of verbs (e.g., *connect-connection, destroy-destruction*). Under this hypothesis, both the nouns and the verbs are lexical items, and the redundancy rules express the commonalities of meaning, form, etc. This proposal defined the *lexicalist hypothesis* of grammar, which now opposed the original *transformationalist hypothesis*.

Another straightforward indication that the lexicalist hypothesis is superior, another argument of the third type, is that many verbs do not have a derived nominal associated with them, and, correspondingly, that many nominals do not have a verb from which they might have been derived:

(9)
a. to speak ~ ∄
   to roam   ~ ∄
   to quash ~ ∄
b. ∄   ~ thesis
   ∄   ~ custom
   ∄   ~ rite

Again, under the lexicalist hypothesis these words should simply be listed in the lexicon, and any redundancy rules that the lexicon might contain will simply not apply to them because they have no corresponding noun or verb. Under the transformational hypothesis the nominalization transformation would have to be blocked for the examples in (9a), presumably by rule features (features of lexical items that state which transformation(s) a given item is an exception to), and abstract, nonexisting verbs would have to be assumed, from which to derive the examples in (9b).

A final consideration along these lines concerns the problem of nominalized passives (or passive nominalizations). In many cases the derived nominal cannot occur in the passive construction even if the corresponding verb can:

(10)
a.   John criticized the book
     The book was criticized by John
b.   Bill refused the offer
     The offer was refused by Bill

(11)
a.   John's criticism of the book
     *the book's criticism by John
b.   Bill's refusal of the offer
     *the offer's refusal by Bill

Such noncorrespondences abound, and they are not limited to passives. Though nouns and verbs often show a certain morphological and semantic similarity, the contexts in which they can appear are often quite different.

We may conclude from these few considerations that the lexicalist hypothesis is well supported, pending the elaboration of a more complete theory of the lexicon. Adopting this hypothesis has the desirable consequence that we can impose a number of strict limitations on what transformations can and cannot do. In particular, we can hypothesize that at least some of the operations listed in (5) can be banned from the transformational component of the grammar altogether.

3.3 The $\overline{\text{X}}$-Theory of Phrase Structure Rules

The nominalization transformation was designed to express certain relationships holding between verb/noun and sentence/nominalization pairs (excluding the above-mentioned problems with passive nominalizations)—namely, (a) that strict subcategorization statements very often carry over from the verb to the noun, and (b) that grammatical relations are very similar in sentences and nominalizations. To consider again our original example:

(12)
a. The enemy destroyed the city
b. the enemy's destruction of the city

The NP *the enemy* is the subject and the actor in both (12a) and (12b), and *the city* is the object and the theme in both (12a) and (12b). How can this generalization be accounted for in the lexicalist framework? The answer must be that the internal structure of noun phrases is sufficiently similar to that of sentences to permit a generalized formulation of grammatical functions and the rules of subcategorization that will apply to sentence and phrase alike. This is in fact what Chomsky (1970) proposed.

What was required, in other words, was an elaboration of the theory of phrase structure rules. For a long time, however, generative linguistics concentrated so heavily on transformations that there simply was no theory of phrase structure at all beyond the fact that phrase structure rules must be context-free rules of the form $A \rightarrow B\ C$, that they are unordered with respect to each other, and that they apply before the transformations. Lyons (1968) had already observed that this is not sufficient. There are some facts about the structure of phrasal categories that must be captured by the theory of phrase structure. The most important of these is the notion "head of a phrase." The noun is the head of the noun phrase, the verb is the head of the verb phrase, the adjective is the head of the adjective phrase, and the preposition is the head of the prepositional phrase. The notion "head" is important because it embodies the insight that the head node shares some fundamental properties with the phrasal node containing it. Thus, for example, *boys* is the head of the noun phrase *the big boys,* and since it is a plural noun, the whole noun phrase is a plural noun phrase. However, the general format of phrase structure rules permits the formulation of many rules that do not embody such correspondences and that simply do not occur in natural languages. For example:

(13)
a. NP $\rightarrow$ A VP
b. V $\rightarrow$ PP AP

c. VP → NP V V AP V PP V
d. PP → NP AP VP
e. NP → AP

The mechanism used to express the notion "head of a phrase" must ensure in the first place that the phrasal node and the terminal node (the head) share an essential property. Furthermore, it must express a number of generalizations regarding the categories that precede and follow the head in a phrase.

In "Remarks on Nominalization" Chomsky proposed the following solution, known as the $\bar{X}$-*Convention*. The head of any phrase is termed X, the phrasal category containing X is termed $\bar{X}$, and the phrasal category containing $\bar{X}$ is termed $\bar{\bar{X}}$. ($\bar{X}$ and $\bar{\bar{X}}$ are then known as *projections* of X.) That is, NP corresponds to $\bar{\bar{N}}$, there is an intermediate category $\bar{N}$, and the head of NP is N. Using this terminology, the main phrase structure rules of English are as follows:

(14)
a. $\bar{\bar{N}}$ → Det(erminer) $\bar{N}$
   $\bar{N}$ → N $\bar{\bar{P}}$ S
b. $\bar{\bar{A}}$ → Q(uantifier) P(hrase) $\bar{A}$
   $\bar{A}$ → A $\bar{\bar{P}}$ S
c. $\bar{\bar{P}}$ → Spec(ifier) $\bar{P}$
   $\bar{P}$ → P $\bar{\bar{N}}$
d. S → $\bar{\bar{N}}$ AUX(iliary) $\bar{V}$
   $\bar{V}$ → V $\bar{\bar{N}}$ $\bar{\bar{P}}$ S

Before we show how these rules have been generalized further, two remarks are in order. It is apparent from (14) that further parallelism could be achieved by redefining S as $\bar{\bar{V}}$. This has been proposed, most notably by Jackendoff (1977), but this issue is complex and controversial. Therefore, we will continue to consider S as a separate category that does not participate in the $\bar{X}$-Convention. Second, for typographical reasons, most generative linguists now use primes rather than bars (while still calling them bars). In other words, X″ stands for $\bar{\bar{X}}$, X′ for $\bar{X}$, etc. With the exception of the terms $\bar{X}$-*theory* and $\bar{X}$-*Convention* themselves, we will adopt this usage here.

The most important nodes in terms of the rules and principles of grammar are the *head* (X or X^0) and the *phrasal node* (the X with the maximal number of bars (primes)). It is therefore often useful to refer to the latter as X^{max}. (It should be noted, however, that there is no strong consensus about whether this phrasal node always has two bars.)

The categories that follow the head in (14a–d) are quite similar. Let us assume, therefore—pending verification in chapter 16—that the differences (for example, whether a given head can or cannot be followed by N″) can be made to follow from independent principles of the grammar. Given this assumption, the rules for the head—the second rule in each of (14a–d)—have been generalized by saying simply that (in English) the head (N, V, A, P = X) is followed by its complements, where the complements are an arbitrary string of phrases (Y):

(15)
$X' \rightarrow X \ Y''$ (X, Y = N, V, A, P)

This has been taken to mean in addition that the category on the main projection line (the head X of X′ or the X′ of X″) is the only obligatory category in the expansion, all the other categories being optional.

The structure of the categories that precede the head of a phrase— the determiner of a noun, the quantifier of an adjective, and the specifier of a preposition—is in many cases also remarkably similar:

(16)
a. more potatoes
   more beautiful
   more in the picture
b. so much more water than there that I went for a swim
   so much more beautiful than me that I feel like an old man
   so much more into ESP than the others that we should invite him for a talk

Following the same strategy, the phrase structure rules that determine these pre-head specifying categories—the first rule in each of (14a–d)— can be generalized as follows:

(17)
$X'' \rightarrow \text{Spec}_{X'} \ X'$

A final element of the $\overline{\text{X}}$-theory of phrase structure concerns the feature analysis of syntactic categories. The four basic syntactic categories can be characterized as follows in terms of the features [±N] (substantive) and [±V] (predicative):

(18)

[+N,+V] = A
[+N,−V] = N
[−N,+V] = V
[−N,−V] = P

This notation allows crosscategorial reference to groups of categories. For example, the two categories that can occur with an NP complement in English, verbs and prepositions, can now be referred to with the single designation [−N]. In other words, it becomes possible to characterize natural classes of syntactic categories.

The theory of phrase structure outlined here adequately characterizes the parallelism of the internal structure of phrases such as N″ and S, the problem that we started out with in this section:

(19)

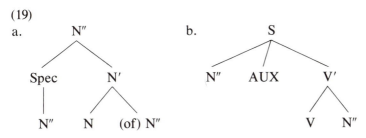

The structural relations in these phrases are sufficiently alike to permit a generalized formulation of grammatical functions and subcategorizational statements for N/V pairs.

Exploiting the possibility that S is equal to V″, that is V^{max}, the notion of "subject of" could be stated in a very general way: "An NP immediately dominated by X^{max} is the subject of that X^{max}." Or, in a somewhat more formal notation: "Subject-of = [NP,X^{max}]."

3.4 A Modular Approach: NP-Preposing and NP-Postposing

We can now return to the problems connected with the Passive transformation, and in particular to the problem of passive nominalizations (2e). Adopting the lexicalist hypothesis requires expressing the relationship between pairs like (3) and (4) in some way other than by transformational rule. The solution to this problem is very simple, yet it has far-reaching consequences. The idea is that Passive must be modified in such a way that it will apply both in sentences like (19b) and in noun phrases like (19a). Clearly, (1) must be drastically revised in order to make this possible. No mention can be made of AUX and V, nor can the morphological changes (the adjunction of *be* and *-en*) be maintained. Note furthermore that the two movements, which we have so far taken to be linked, are really independent. This is important because the preposing of the direct object NP to the subject position appears to be obligatory in sentential passivization but optional in NP:

(20)
a. The enemy destroyed the city
b. *Was destroyed the city by the enemy
c. The city was destroyed by the enemy

(21)
a. the enemy's destruction of the city
b. the destruction of the city by the enemy
c. the city's destruction by the enemy

These facts suggest that the two movements expressed by the Passive transformation (1) should be separate. Moreover, they suggest that a distinction should be maintained between the general process (here, passivization) on the one hand and the specific, construction-bound idiosyncrasies of its manifestation in a given context (like NP vs. S) on the other. In other words, the correct approach to the passive construction is *modular*. Rather than building all the changes brought about during passivization into one component of the grammar (transformational), as in (1) and (5), linguists have assumed that several components, each of which has a fairly general domain, interact in such a way as to determine the basic properties of the passive construction, for example, in both NP and S. The modular analysis of the passive construction will involve (at least) the following modules:

(22)
a. *Transformations*

   NP-Preposing
   $$X - np - Y - NP - Z$$
   SD: 1   2   3   4   5 →
   SC: 1   4   3   ∅   5

   NP-Postposing
   $$X - NP - Y - np - Z$$
   SD: 1   2   3   4   5 →
   SC: 1   ∅   3   2   5

(where *np* stands for a lexically empty (or phonetically unrealized) noun phrase and *NP* for a lexically filled one)

b. *X̄-theory*

c. *Morphology/Lexicon*

   i. Principles accounting for the cooccurrence relationship between the (passive) past participle of the verb and the auxiliary *be* in sentential passives (e.g., Affix Hopping)

   ii. Principles concerning the morphological subregularities involved in such pairs as *destroy* ~ *destruction, criticize* ~ *criticism,* as well as their subcategorizational relatedness

d. *Semantics*

   i. Rules assigning the role of *agent* or *experiencer* to a *by*-phrase

   ii. Rules ensuring that the grammatical subject of passives is interpreted as the underlying ("logical") subject

We will have little to say about the morphology/lexicon and semantics modules in this chapter. As for the transformational module, however, consider the two rules NP-Preposing and NP-Postposing. Clearly, these rules are much simpler and much more general than the Passive transformation that we started out with. This fact has two main consequences, one highly desirable, the other potentially dangerous.

First, it is now possible to offer interesting answers to some of the questions raised in (2). Since the modular analysis allows the rules in (22a) to be formulated without mentioning the specific morphemes that were necessary in (1), question (2a) may be answered by tentatively imposing the restriction that transformations can never refer to, delete, or insert morphological formatives. The rules in (22a) also suggest a restrictive answer to questions (2b) and (2c): it may be possible to limit the number of movements effected by a single transformation to one, and to impose the constraint on the theory of transformations that a structural description may never mention more than two constant terms. As will become clear, some of these answers may well be correct and may even be refined further.

The second, potentially dangerous consequence is that NP-Preposing and NP-Postposing are formulated so generally that they may apply in many contexts where they produce highly ungrammatical, or at least undesirable, results. For example, NP-Preposing may now move the object of a preposition to the direct object position:

(23)

a. The queen sent np for her husband

b. *The queen sent her husband for np

Similarly, NP-Postposing may apply to derive ungrammatical structures in many cases. (The diacritic (*) following an example is used here to indicate that the structure it marks is an underlying structure about which it is technically incorrect to say that it is (un)grammatical but about which it is true that it results in an ungrammatical s-structure when no transformations are applied to it.)

(20)

b. *Was destroyed the city by the enemy

(24)

a. John put the flowers in np   (*)

b. *John put np in the flowers

This phenomenon, which is the direct result of the extreme simplification of the transformations in question, is known as *overgeneration.* Clearly, overgeneration is intolerable. In order to compensate for it, either some of the above generalizations must be sacrificed or additional principles must be found that will rule it out. Since the first strategy is defeatist, linguists have explored the second. In fact, we have already seen this strategy in action in chapter 2, and it will be a major, recurring theme in this book. As far as the NP-movement rules of NP-Preposing and NP-Postposing are concerned, this theme will be picked up again in chapter 7.

3.5 Structure Preservation

Let us now turn to question (2f):

(2)

f. The two movement operations of (1) both have the effect of moving an NP to a position where NPs are also generated by the phrase structure rules: the direct object NP (5) moves to the subject NP position (2), and the subject NP moves to the position to the right of the preposition *by,* which, by virtue of the base rule PP → P NP, is also an NP position. Is this an accident?

This property of NP-movement rules is encoded in the formulations in (22a) by use of the notation *np.* This notation presupposes in fact that lexical insertion at D-Structure is optimal and that nonlexicalized phrase structure positions may serve as receptacles for lexicalized nodes that are moved by transformation. If np is not included in the structural description of NP-Preposing and NP-Postposing, these rules can be reformulated as follows:

(25)

a. *NP-Preposing*

	X	– Y	– Z	– NP	– W	
SD:	1	2	3	4	5	→
SC:	1	4	3	$\emptyset$	5	

b. *NP-Postposing*

	X	– NP	– Y	– Z	– W	
SD:	1	2	3	4	5	→
SC:	1	$\emptyset$	3	2	5	

That is, an NP is moved, either leftward or rightward, to an arbitrary position, either by adjunction or by substitution for an arbitrary empty category. Clearly, this move greatly amplifies the overgeneration problem in that derivations such as the following are no longer excluded by any principle:

(26)

a.   John m has been dating Mary   (*)   (*m* = empty Modal)

b.   *John Mary has been dating

(27)

a.   John may have been dating Mary

b.   *May have been John dating Mary

In (26) an NP is preposed and substituted for an empty modal position; in (27) an NP is postposed and adjoined to the VP or the AUX. It seems reasonable to conclude from this that question (2f) should be answered in the negative: it is *not* an accident that NPs typically move to NP-positions. This phenomenon, known as *structure preservation,* came to light at MIT in the late 1960s and was incorporated into the theory of transformations by Joseph Emonds (1970, 1976). The idea is quite simple: Universal Grammar specifies that certain transformations must be structure preserving. This implies, as noted above, that positions generated by the phrase structure rules need not be filled by lexical insertion but may be filled at a later stage of the derivation by a movement rule. Again, however, a restriction is needed: unwanted proliferation of empty nodes must be excluded. This is achieved by imposing a condition on derivations to the effect that every syntactic position must be filled at least once during a derivation; otherwise, the derivation is filtered out as ungrammatical.

For enlightening discussion of the nature of structure-preserving transformations and for arguments for their existence, see Emonds (1970, 1976). We will assume the structure-preserving character of certain movement transformations here and conclude the discussion with three general remarks.

First, observe that the hypothesis of structure preservation is itself empty if empty positions of the right category can be freely generated by the phrase structure rules in the place where they are needed to receive a moved category. For example, (27) would become a structure-preserving derivation if the phrase structure component of English were allowed to contain the rules in (28):

(28)
a. VP → NP VP
b. AUX → AUX NP

To preserve the explanatory power of the structure-preserving hypothesis, then, such phrase structure rules must be excluded on principled grounds. But we have already seen that there are good reasons for restricting the class of possible phrase structure rules in terms of an $\overline{X}$-theory. The content of the structure-preserving hypothesis will therefore depend on the success of the program outlined in section 2.3.

Second, another answer has been suggested for question (2f). The central observation of that question is that the output configuration of structure-preserving movement transformations is *base-generable* (that is, could actually be generated by the base component of phrase structure rules). Why then, some linguists argue, can we not achieve that result more directly by (a) generating passive sentences and the outputs of other structure-preserving transformations directly by the phrase structure rules and (b) eliminating all (structure-preserving) transformations from the grammar—eliminating, among other things, the transformational module (22a) from our account of the passive construction? The crucial consideration in judging the merit of such a proposal is that all other things being equal, this would indeed be a desirable move toward simplicity and elegance. But all other things do not appear to be equal in this case, since a nontransformational analysis of passive constructions must account for the same facts that the movement analysis was designed to handle, such as the fact that the subject of the passive is interpreted as the logical object of the verb, as well as the other facts that constitute the evidence for the Passive transformation. Thus, whether or not a transformational approach is correct depends on how good its supporting evidence is, or, alternatively, how well this evidence can be accounted for in a nontransformational way that is simpler and more enlightening. This is a complex matter that cannot be decided on the basis of global considerations of simplicity but requires empirical argumentation. The issue is being discussed quite widely, and we have cited the main publications on both sides in the bibliographical commentary. Here we will continue to assume, however, that NP-movement rules are involved in the analysis of passives and other constructions. Part of the reason for doing so will become clear in chapter 7.

Third, linguists have raised the question whether all transformations are structure preserving. If only some transformations are structure preserving, then in the course of language acquisition the child must learn whether each and every newly encountered transformation is structure preserving or not. This amounts to saying that the grammar must stipulate whether each and every transformation is structure preserving or not. This is almost as bad as the stipulation of structure preservation in the structural description of the rules themselves, as in (22a). But in fact it seems clear that not all transformations can be structure preserving. For example, the rule of Subject-AUX Inversion can only be structure preserving if there is an AUX position before the subject NP, an assumption that ought to be excluded by the $\bar{\text{X}}$-theory.

Emonds has proposed a solution to this problem. He suggests that all transformations must conform to one of three types: root, local, or structure preserving. Reduced to its essentials, Emonds's proposal can be summarized as follows:

(29)
a. *The Typology*
    i. Structure-preserving transformations (as defined above)
    ii. Local transformations: transformations whose structural description is limited to mentioning two adjacent constant terms $(X - A - B - Y)$
    iii. Root transformations: transformations that can only apply in main (= root) clauses

b. *Structure-preserving Constraint*
A transformation must be either local or structure preserving. If it can be neither, it is restricted to applying only in root contexts.

Under this typology of transformations, it is still the case, in some sense, that the type of each transformation must be stipulated. Nonetheless, the typology has explanatory value because it is set up in such a way that the inference from the primary linguistic data the child encounters and the hypothetical formulation of a given transformation to the type of the transformation is extremely straightforward. A single instance of an intervening element will suffice to rule out the local formulation of a transformation, and simply checking the effect of a transformation against the phrase structure rules of the grammar will suffice to exclude the possibility of a structure-preserving transformation. If both these simple tests are negative, the transformation must be a root transformation. Starting from the other end, a single application of a transformation in an embedded context will eliminate the possibility that it is a root transformation; hence, it must be local or structure preserving, a decision that can, again, easily be reached.

On the other hand, the typology would be worthless if it did not adequately characterize the transformations that actually occur in natural languages. Emonds's typology is so far the best approximation to such an overall characterization. Although it does not figure prominently in current syntactic research, it has retained most of its validity. We therefore turn next to illustrating the explanatory force of the concepts of local and root transformations.

3.6 Local and Root Transformations

Analysis of the position of the verb in Dutch offers ample opportunity to illustrate the essential properties of local and root transformations. The verb (or verbal cluster) is always VP-final in Dutch, with one exception: the finite verb in a root clause is second in declaratives and first in direct yes/no questions:

(30)
a. Ik geloof   dat Jan dit   boek *kent*
   I   believe that Jan this book knows
   'I believe that Jan knows this book'

b. Jan *kent*   dit   boek
Jan knows this book
'Jan knows this book'

c. *Kent*   Jan dit   boek
knows   Jan this book
'Does Jan know this book'

(31)

a. Jan zei   dat   Piet dit   boek niet *heeft* gelezen
Jan said that Piet this book not   has   read
'Jan said that Piet has not read this book'

b. Piet *heeft* dit   boek niet gelezen
Piet has   this book not   read
'Piet has not read this book'

c. *Heeft* Piet dit   boek niet gelezen
has   Piet this book not   read
'Has Piet not read this book'

Root clauses lacking a finite verb in first or second position are ungrammatical:

(30)
d. *Jan dit boek kent

(31)
d. *Piet dit boek niet gelezen heeft

Correspondingly, in embedded clauses the verb may not appear in first or second position:

(30)
e. *Ik geloof dat Jan kent dit boek

(31)
e. *Jan zei dat Piet heeft dit boek niet gelezen

(32)
*Jan vroeg of heeft Piet dit   boek gelezen
Jan asked if has   Piet this book read

To account for these facts, a verb movement rule must be formulated that either preposes the finite verb in certain contexts or postposes the nonfinite (part of the) verb in the complementary contexts. Whichever is the correct rule, it clearly cannot be local, because material can intervene between the two positions of the verb. But it cannot be structure preserving either, because it would be undesirable to have the phrase structure rules generate two positions for the tensed verb per clause. Hence, we may assume that $\overline{\text{X}}$-theory excludes this possibility. Consequently, Emonds's theory predicts that the process in question must be a root process. This observation is entirely consistent with the pattern illustrated in (30)–(32), and it can be incorporated into the grammar by assuming that the verbal cluster is generated VP-finally in Dutch and moved into place by a root transformation of verb fronting, generally called *Verb Second* or *V2*. This analysis, which correctly makes Dutch an SOV language ("subject - object - verb"), is fully compatible with Emonds's typology, since a single root transformation will account for the distribution of verbs. Moreover, Emonds's theory explains why the split pattern occurs in root clauses; it accounts for the formal similarity of Verb Second and the English rule of Subject-AUX Inversion, also a root transformation; and, more generally, it makes a strong claim about what can and cannot occur in natural languages. For example, given Emonds's typology, there can be no languages that are exactly like Dutch except that Verb Second applies in all clauses, root and embedded alike; nor can there be anti-root languages in which Verb Second applies in all contexts except for root clauses. And in fact no such human languages appear to exist.

Infinitival complement clauses in Dutch may either precede or follow a (VP-final) matrix verb, depending on what the matrix verb is. Thus, Dutch has both "left-hand complements" and "right-hand complements." Consider first the approximate underlying structures:

(33)

a. Ik geloof dat Jan [$_{VP}$[$_S$ *NP Marie voor haar verjaardag een
I believe that Jan   Marie for   her   birthday   a
boek te geven]$_S$ belooft]$_{VP}$
book to give   promises
'I believe that Jan promises to give Marie a book for her birthday'

b. Ik geloof dat Jan [$_{VP}$ belooft   [$_S$ *NP Marie voor haar
I believe that Jan   promises   Marie for   her
verjaardag een boek te geven]$_S$]$_{VP}$
birthday   a   book to give
'I believe that Jan promises to give Marie a book for her birthday'

(*NP stands for the "understood subject" of the infinitival complement clause, which is interpreted as identical with the subject of the superordinate clause. Understood subjects will be discussed in chapter 8.)

A structure like (33b) results directly in a well-formed s-structure. A structure like (33a), however, though perfectly grammatical in its word-for-word German translation (*Ich glaube, daß Johannes Maria zu ihrem Geburtstag ein Buch zu geben verspricht*), is ungrammatical in Dutch. In Dutch the verbs must be inverted:

(34)
Ik geloof dat Jan Marie voor haar verjaardag een boek
$\begin{cases} \text{*te geven belooft} \\ \text{belooft te geven} \end{cases}$

These facts may be accounted for by postulating a rule, Verb Raising (VR), which Chomsky-adjoins the embedded verb to the right of the matrix verb, as in (35a). The term *Chomsky-adjunction* is used to describe the process by which an element X is adjoined to an element Y by creating a new node of type Y to dominate the two. Thus, VR applied to structure (35b) will yield the derived structure (35c), where V_x is the newly created V-node:

(35)

a. *Verb Raising* (VR)

$$X - V - V - Y$$
SD: 1   2   3   4 $\rightarrow$
SC: 1 $\emptyset$ 3+2   4

b.

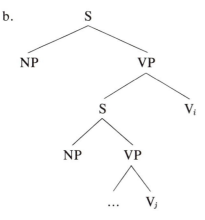

c.

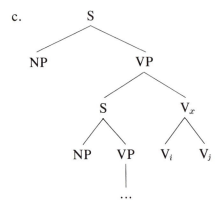

This rule correctly predicts that the mirror image of the D-Structure (and German) verb order results in Dutch when several left-hand infinitival complements are embedded within each other:

(36)

a. Ik geloof   dat   Jan [$_{VP}$[$_S$ *NP [$_{VP}$[$_S$ *NP [$_{VP}$[$_S$ *NP [$_{VP}$ dit   boek
   I   believe that Jan   this book
   lezen$_1$]$_{VP}$]$_S$ leren$_2$]$_{VP}$]$_S$ proberen$_3$]$_{VP}$]$_S$ zal$_4$]$_{VP}$ (*)
   read   learn   try   will
   'I believe that Jan will try to learn to read this book'

b. Ik geloof dat Jan dit boek zal$_4$ proberen$_3$ te leren$_2$ lezen$_1$

VR cannot be a structure-preserving transformation, because it would be undesirable to say that the phrase structure rules can generate arbitrarily many V-positions at the end of the VP. But clearly VR cannot be a root transformation either, because in these examples it applies in complement clauses. Hence, according to Emonds's typology, it must be a local transformation, a fact already implicit in the formulation (35a). This prediction is quite to the point. It can be shown to be correct in several ways, two of which we will briefly illustrate.

In Dutch, particles immediately precede the verb, but they do not (at least underlyingly) form a unit with the verb. Suppose now that a matrix verb took both a particle and a left-hand complement. The following situation would result:

(37)
... [$_S$ ... V]$_S$ Particle V ...

Assuming that VR is local, it cannot apply to such a structure. Thus, it is predicted that whenever a verb has both a particle and a complement clause, the complement clause must be a right-hand one. This is so because VR is in effect an obligatory transformation in Dutch. That is, we cannot simply say that the rule is blocked in (37) and the embedded clause remains in place. The prediction is borne out. Consider, for example, the pair *aanvangen* and *beginnen*. Both mean 'to start', but the first has a particle (*aan*) and the second does not. Thus, they exhibit the following pattern:

(38)
a. Ik geloof   dat   Jan Nederlands begint te leren   (LH–VR)
   I   believe that Jan Dutch   begins to learn
   'I believe that Jan is beginning to learn Dutch'
b. Ik geloof dat Jan begint Nederlands te leren   (RH)

(39)
a. *Ik geloof dat Jan Nederlands aanvangt te leren   (LH–VR)
b. Ik geloof dat Jan aanvangt Nederlands te leren   (RH)

The local nature of VR also manifests itself when a phrase is extraposed inside the left-hand complement clause. Certain PPs, for example, may optionally be extraposed to the end of the clause in which they appear:

(40)
a. Ik geloof   dat   Jan probeert [s *NP de   schuur met een
   I   believe that Jan tries   the barn   with a
   spraydoos groen te schilderen]s
   spray can green to paint
   'I believe that Jan is trying to paint the barn green with a spray can'
b. Ik geloof dat Jan probeert [s *NP de schuur groen te schilderen met een spraydoos]s

When this PP-extraposition occurs in a left-hand complement, a structure like (41) results:

(41)
... [s ... V PP]s V ...

This is again a structure to which VR cannot apply. Hence, it is correctly predicted that extraposition in a left-hand complement leads to ungrammaticality:

(42)

a. Ik geloof dat Jan [s *NP de schuur groen schilderen met een spraydoos]s wil (*)

b. *Ik geloof dat Jan [s *NP de schuur groen met een spraydoos]s wil schilderen

Without pursuing these analyses in any further detail, we may conclude that Emonds's typology of transformations leads to a number of interesting predictions about the possible form and functioning of transformations.

3.7 Concluding Remarks

This chapter has shown ways in which the program initiated in chapter 2 can be extended, in this case with respect to the rules involved in the passive construction. Most significantly, we have seen that it is necessary to analyze such constructions in a modular way by postulating several abstract and general rules or principles that interact to derive the properties of the construction in question (though each rule or principle has a much wider domain of application). The generality of these modules leads to overgeneration, which must be compensated for by the operation of other principles that are (or should be) just as abstract and general.

We have also raised a methodological point: that every stipulation in the formulation of the rules of a particular grammar should prompt a multitude of questions, like those listed in (2). Linguists have found that it is possible to devise (universal) subtheories that answer some of these questions in a principled way, thereby removing the need for the stipulations that gave rise to them. The considerations of this chapter are thus a good example of the overall research program on which this book is based—namely, to develop a rich theory of Universal Grammar by restricting the expressive options available for the formulation of particular grammars, thereby reducing the options the child's mind must consider in searching for hypotheses about the grammar it is in the process of learning.

3.8 Bibliographical Comments

The formulation of the passive transformation that serves as our point of departure in this chapter corresponds roughly to the formulation in Chomsky's *Aspects* (1965, chap. 2).

The classical work on nominalizations, in which the transformationalist theory of these constructions was developed, is Lees (1960). The lexicalist theory, which is currently standard, is presented in Chomsky's "Remarks on Nominalization" (1970). This work lays the foundations for $\bar{\text{X}}$-theory, which is further developed in Emonds (1976, chap. 1) and Jackendoff (1977). A critical discussion of some aspects of $\bar{\text{X}}$-theory can be found in Van Riemsdijk (1978b, chap. 3). A current report on the status of syntactic features is given in Muysken and Van Riemsdijk (1985a).

The structure-preserving hypothesis as presented in sections 3.5 and 3.6 is due to Joseph Emonds. The main reference is Emonds (1976), which is a thoroughly revised version of his (1970) dissertation. The illustrations of local and root transformations are taken from the syntax of Dutch. The main text on Verb Raising (VR) is Evers (1975); the proposal for Verb Second (V2), mentioned in Emonds's own work, is discussed in Koster (1975) and Den Besten (1982). The verb-second analysis as such had already been proposed for German in Bierwisch (1967), which, along with Matthews (1965), is one of the first extensive transformational studies of a language other than English. The only proposal other than Emonds's dealing specifically with the derived structure of movement rules is found in Baltin (1982).

Emonds's observation that some of the major syntactic transformations are structure preserving has led to the formulation of a number of alternatives to his theory. These alternatives differ significantly from one another in various ways, but they all assume that the derived structure of movement rules, in particular NP-movement rules such as Passive and in most cases also Wh-Movement, should in fact be taken as the base-generated underlying structure. Freidin (1975) and Koster (1978a) remain well within the confines of "mainstream" generative syntax. A more radical departure is advocated in Brame (1978, 1979). Two other proposals are Lexical Functional Grammar, a somewhat separate theoretical development arising from work by Bresnan (1978, 1982b), and Generalized Phrase Structure Grammar, arising from work by Gazdar (1982). A discussion of these proposals can be found in Chomsky (1982b).

Chapter 4
Subjacency

Ross's dissertation greatly increased our knowledge of the grammar of English. He studied many new constructions in great detail, brought to light many properties of syntactic rules, and indeed discovered new types of rules. His major contribution, however, was in bringing about the realization that a general explanatory system of conditions on transformations could be formulated. Ross recognized that many properties of individual transformations are common to larger families of transformations, so that it was possible to extract these properties and make them part of Universal Grammar. Before "Constraints on Variables in Syntax" only the most general universals about the form and functioning of transformations had been established: the basic formalism, the elementary operations, the principle of the cycle. More specific properties of transformations, however, had scarcely been approached in terms of universal constraints. The one exception was the A-over-A Principle. Why didn't the discovery of the A-over-A Principle lead immediately to a research program whose central goal was the elaboration of a general system of constraints on transformations? Perhaps it was because the explanatory force of the A-over-A Principle was limited by the relatively small domain of rules and constructions that it applied to, and the overwhelming empirical problems that it was confronted with. Ross's dissertation addressed both of these issues and thereby effectively initiated the strategy that has since guided syntactic research and will undoubtedly continue to guide it in the future. The search for highly general constraints on transformations is at the heart of the central problem that confronts linguistic research: restricting the options for grammars. General conditions permit a sharp reduction in the expressive potential of rules and thereby decrease the class of grammars available to the language learner in view of given data. This is because they make it possible to factor out descriptive details from the formulation of individual rules. That in turn permits formulation of general restrictions on the amount of detail that may be included in structural descriptions of rules.

"Constraints on Variables in Syntax" was also effective in setting a spark to this research program because it constituted not only a great step forward but also, in another sense, a step backward. Both the empirical shortcomings of the A-over-A Principle and linguists' increased knowledge of syntactic constructions made it difficult to find a single very general and simple principle (such as the A-over-A Principle) with sufficient explanatory potential. Consequently, Ross formulated a series of constraints, the scope of each of which is fairly limited. In fact, most of them are by and large construction-specific. The formulation of the Complex NP Constraint, for example, directly mirrors the essential aspects of the constructions in which certain transformations cannot apply. As a result, much subsequent work has concentrated on generalizing and unifying Ross's constraints. The first major step toward such unification is the topic of this chapter.

4.1 Successive Cyclicity and the Strict Cycle Condition

The notion of the transformational cycle, as we have introduced and used it thus far, has been refined in several significant ways. Consider (1a) and (1b), which illustrate the unbounded operation of Ross's rules of Question Formation and Relative Clause Formation, respectively:

(1)
a. Which book did you say that John thinks that Bill should read
b. Is this the book which you said that John thinks that Bill should read

We saw in chapter 2 that these rules pattern together with respect to many phenomena, and indeed they are virtually identical in their essentials: both move a *wh*-phrase to the initial position of some clause. Hence, they have been generalized as a rule called *Wh-Movement*. Let us assume, roughly following Bresnan (1970, 1972), that the initial position of a clause is characterized by a complementizer position COMP, introduced by the following rules:

(2)

a. S' → COMP S

b. S → NP AUX VP

c. COMP → X^{max} $\left\{ \begin{array}{l} \text{that} \\ \text{for} \\ \text{whether} \\ \ldots \end{array} \right\}$

The left-hand portion of the COMP expansion (X^{max}) serves as the target for *Wh*-Movement (that is, the position where the moved *wh*-phrase will land). Thus, *Wh*-Movement can be formulated essentially as follows:

(3)

Wh-Movement

	COMP	X	*wh*-phrase	Y	
SD:	1	2	3	4	→
SC:	3	2	∅	4	

Consider now the phrase marker underlying a sentence like (1a):

(4)

[$_{S_1}$ COMP you said [$_{S_2}$ COMP John thinks [$_{S_3}$ COMP Bill should read [which book]]$_{S_3}$]$_{S_2}$]$_{S_1}$

Given the formulation of *Wh*-Movement and the principle of the transformational cycle, according to which cyclic transformations apply first in an embedded clause and then in a higher clause, there is no reason why the derivation of sentences like (1a–b) should not proceed stepwise on successive cycles, making use of all the intermediate COMP positions, as in (5):

(5)

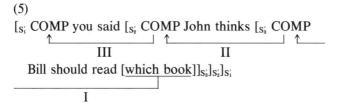

[$_{S_1}$ COMP you said [$_{S_2}$ COMP John thinks [$_{S_3}$ COMP

          III   II

Bill should read [which book]]$_{S_3}$]$_{S_2}$]$_{S_1}$

               I

In fact, this type of *successive cyclic movement* is the null hypothesis: additional machinery would be required to exclude the possibility of such derivations. (Observe in passing that the availability of successive cyclic movement makes it possible to circumvent the Upward Boundedness Constraint discussed in chapter 2. In other words, example (38c) of chapter 2 could be derived successive cyclically without violating the constraint. This problem remains unsolved.)

A noncyclic variant of a derivation like (5) can be constructed if it is assumed that transformations may apply iteratively within one cycle. In order to exclude this possibility, the following refinement of the notion "cycle" has been introduced:

(6)
Strict Cycle Condition (Chomsky (1973, 243))
No rule can apply to a domain dominated by a cyclic node A [i.e., an S-node] in such a way as to affect solely a proper subdomain of A dominated by a node B which is also a cyclic node. (In other words, rules cannot in effect return to earlier stages of the cycle after the derivation has moved to larger, more inclusive domains.)

(6) ensures that step I in (5) can only take place on the S_3' cycle, step II only on S_2', and step III only on S_1'.

With this understanding of how *Wh*-Movement works, consider the phenomena subsumed under the *Wh*-Island Constraint. For example:

(7)
*Which books did you ask John where Bill bought

Successive cyclic *Wh*-Movement and the Strict Cycle Condition make it possible to account for this *wh*-island violation in a very natural way:

(8)

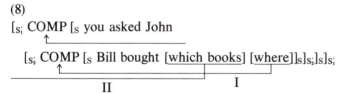

$[_{S_i}$ COMP $[_S$ you asked John

$[_{S_2'}$ COMP $[_S$ Bill bought [which books] [where]$]_S]_{S_2'}]_S]_{S_i}$

        II   I

On the S_2' cycle the COMP is filled by *where;* hence, *which books* can only move directly to the higher COMP on the S_1' cycle. If a principle exists that blocks step II in the derivation, the *wh*-island phenomena are accounted for. Two major proposals have been made to accomplish this. The first, in Chomsky (1973), relied on two constraints, the Specified Subject Condition and the Tensed-S Condition, which will be discussed in chapter 7. The second, in Chomsky (1977a) and Rizzi (1978), relies on the Subjacency Condition, which was also proposed in Chomsky (1973) but not applied there to *wh*-island phenomena.

Here we will discuss the latter proposal, which has turned out to be preferable.

If S is viewed as a *bounding node*, the Subjacency Condition can be formulated as follows:

(9)

Subjacency Condition

No rule can relate X, Y in the structure

... X ... [$_\alpha$ ... [$_\beta$ ... Y ...   (or: ... Y ...]$_\beta$ ...]$_\alpha$ ... X ...)

where α, β are bounding nodes.

This principle rules out (7), as desired, because step II in its derivation (8) crosses two S-boundaries (two bounding nodes).

The Strict Cycle Condition is crucially involved in this account. Without it there would be an alternative derivation for (7):

(10)

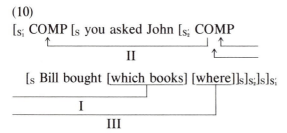

The Strict Cycle Condition rules out step III, because III is only possible after II has emptied the lower COMP. This means that III must take place on the S'_1 cycle, which is not permitted under the Strict Cycle Condition.

Now, is a *wh*-phrase in a COMP position accessible, on the higher cycle, to rules other than *Wh*-Movement? Apparently it is not. Consider (11a–c):

(11)

a. He asked which books to buy

b. Which books did he ask to buy

c. *Which books were asked to buy by him

(11c) has the following derivation:

(12)

COMP [$_{NP}$]$_{NP}$ were asked COMP to buy [which books] by him

     III   II   I

Step II is effected not by *Wh*-Movement but by (the NP-Preposing part of) Passive. Clearly, this must be prohibited. The successive cyclic mode of application for *Wh*-Movement must therefore be tightened in the following manner (discussed in Chomsky (1973:243ff.)):

(13)
COMP-to-COMP Condition
Once a phrase is in COMP, it can only move to a higher COMP.

This may seem like a large amount of machinery to achieve the meager result of deriving Ross's *Wh*-Island Constraint. But in fact it achieves much more. First, these principles contribute to a richer, more restrictive theory of Universal Grammar. Second, several of these principles (such as the Strict Cycle Condition and the COMP-to-COMP Condition) have since been shown to follow (as theorems) from other principles of Universal Grammar. Third, the Subjacency Condition is not merely a reformulation of the *Wh*-Island Constraint; it has much wider scope in that it also accounts for the phenomena subsumed under the Complex NP Constraint and the Sentential Subject Constraint (section 4.3) and has interesting consequences for a wide range of phenomena in other languages. Fourth, the Subjacency Condition, in combination with the Specified Subject Condition and the Tensed-S Condition discussed in chapter 7, permits a unified definition of the domain of transformational rules.

To see this, consider again the domain of application of transformations as conceived of in Ross (1967). As noted in chapter 2, Ross assumed that there were three types of transformations: monocyclic, bicyclic, and unbounded:

(14)
a. Monocyclic or "clause-mate" transformations: transformations that operate within one clause (S-domain), such as Passive and Reflexivization
b. Bicyclic transformations: transformations that operate across one S-boundary (that is, they are restricted to applying to adjacent clauses) such as Equi-NP-Deletion and Raising-to-Object
c. Unbounded transformations: transformations that operate across arbitrarily many clause boundaries, such as *Wh*-Movement

The Subjacency Condition says, in effect, that all transformations are bicyclic (where *bicyclic* means that a rule may apply either monocyclically or (at most) bicyclically). What then becomes of monocyclic and unbounded transformations? Given successive cyclic *Wh*-Movement, rules of the unbounded type can be reduced to bicyclic application. As for monocyclic rules, note that rules purportedly belonging to this category sometimes seem to apply in a bicyclic fashion:

(15)
a. We believe [John to be a good friend]
b. John is believed [to be a good friend] by us
c. John believes [himself to be a good friend]

Assuming these rules to be in fact bicyclic accounts straightforwardly for cases like (15a–c). The remaining cases in which these rules operate in a clause-bound way constitute a problem that has been solved by the introduction of the Specified Subject Condition and the Tensed-S Condition, two general conditions that further restrict the domain of application of transformational rules. As a result, Subjacency uniformly applies to all transformations, making it unnecessary to stipulate for every transformation whether it is monocyclic, bicyclic, or unbounded. This is a further significant restriction on the class of available grammars.

4.2 More Properties of *Wh*-Movement

Before we investigate the full range of phenomena covered by the Subjacency Condition, let us examine briefly some other properties of the rule of *Wh*-Movement, which plays a crucial role in most of these cases. The formulation of *Wh*-Movement that we have assumed so far is close to trivial. In essence, it says "Move a *wh*-phrase to COMP." Further trivialization will be the object of later chapters. What properties are attributed to this rule?

(16)
a. It is optional.
b. It is cyclic.

Both properties have been disputed. Ross's rules of Question Formation and Relative Clause Formation were obligatory. Under the approach outlined here, the *effect* of *Wh*-Movement may sometimes be obligatory, but whenever this is the case the obligatoriness is the result of independent but interacting principles of subcategorization and interpretation. For example, the apparent obligatoriness of *Wh*-Movement in relative clauses follows from the implementation, partly specific to English, of the principle requiring that the relative clause contain a pronominal element coreferential with the head of the relative clause.

Questions offer direct evidence for the optionality of *Wh*-Movement:

(17)
a. John ate what
b. I wonder when John ate what
c. I wonder for which pairs x and y, x a time and y an object, John ate y at time x

Failure to move *what* in (17a) results in an echo-question interpretation (A: *John ate anchovies and pickled onions for breakfast.* B: *John ate what?*) In (17b) it results in the typically paired interpretation of multiple *wh*-questions shown in (17c). Furthermore, in many languages the rule corresponding to *Wh*-Movement is truly optional in the sense that failure to move still results in normal *wh*-question interpretation. Thus, (18a) and (18b) are equivalent in French:

(18)
a. Tu as vu qui
   you have seen who
b. Qui as-tu vu
   who have you seen
   'Who have you seen'

Closely related is the problem of making the *wh*-phrase move to the right COMP when it is moved successive cyclically. Consider (19a–c):

(19)
a. I wonder COMP you claimed COMP I should read which book
b. *I wonder that/whether you claimed which book I should read
c. I wonder which book you claimed that I should read

The important difference between (19b) and (19c) is that *claim* does not subcategorize for questions, but *wonder* does. Some verbs like *ask* and *tell,* however, subcategorize both for questions and for *that*-complements. Hence, (20a) and (20b) are both possible but differ in meaning in the relevant respect (cf. (24)):

(20)
a. I asked which books he told me that I should read
b. I asked that he tell me which books I should read

Essentially following Bresnan (1970, 1972) and Baker (1970), let us modify rule (2c) in the following way:

(21)

COMP → X^{max} ±WH

The feature +WH introduces direct and indirect questions, and −WH stands for the other complement clauses and relatives. Thus, +WH can be realized as *whether*, and −WH as *that* or *for*. Subcategorization is now straightforward:

(22)

a. *claim*, [+_____−WH]
b. *ask*, [+_____±WH]
c. *wonder*, [+_____+WH]

With this notation two principles of interpretation for normal and multiple *wh*-questions can be formulated. The interpretation principle for normal *wh*-questions is as follows (cf. Chomsky (1973, (248))):

(23)

The phrase $[_\alpha[_{COMP}[wh\text{-phrase}]_i + WH] \ldots [e]_i \ldots]_\alpha$ is interpreted with $[e]_i$ a variable bound by the node $[wh\text{-phrase}]_i$ and . . . the semantic interpretation determined by the derivation of α.

(The notation $[e]_i$ or e_i has been devised to mark the *gap*, that is, the site from which some phrase has been moved. The moved phrase itself has the same subscript as the gap in order to keep track of which phrase was moved from where. For this reason e_i is called a *trace*. (23) will assign the interpretations in (24) to (20a–b), for instance:

(24)

a. I asked [[which books]$_i$ +WH] he told me [−WH that] I should read $[e]_i$
b. I asked [−WH that] he tell me [[which books]$_i$ +WH] I should read $[e]_i$

Multiple *wh*-questions will be assigned an interpretation by (25) (cf. Chomsky (1973, (249))):

(25)

Assign a *wh*-phrase not in COMP to a higher structure $[_{COMP} \ldots +WH]_{COMP}$ and interpret as in (23).

Thus, multiple *wh*-questions can be derived as follows:

(26)
a. I wonder who should read what
b. I wonder for which x, x a person, x should read what (by (23))
c. I wonder for which x, x a person, for which y, y a thing, x should read y (by (25))

These principles also give the desired result in more complicated cases. Consider (27a–b):

(27)
a. I wonder who John told what to read
b. I wonder who John told to read what

Only (27b) has the multiple *wh*-question reading, as (25) correctly predicts:

(28)
a. I wonder for which x, x a person, John told x for which y, y a thing, to read y
b. I wonder for which x, x a person, for which y, y a thing, John told x to read y

(25) also predicts correctly that examples like (29) will be ambiguous:

(29)
Who remembers when I should read what

(30)
a. For which x, x a person, x remembers for which y, y a thing, for which z, z a time, I should read y at z
b. For which x, x a person, for which y, y a thing, x remembers for which z, z a time, I should read y at z

This prediction is made because (25) allows an unmoved *wh*-phrase to be assigned to any higher COMP.

Most of the problems deriving from the optional and cyclic properties of *Wh*-Movement have thus been accounted for in a revealing way. One problem remains, however. As Ross (1967) recognized, one characteristic of *Wh*-Movement is optional pied piping:

(31)
a. In which book did you find that quote
b. Which book did you find that quote in

Postal (1972) points out that this fact argues against successive cyclic *Wh*-Movement, on the basis of examples like (32):

(32)
a. *In which book* did you say that you found that quote
b. **Which book* did you say *in* that you found that quote

Postal's argument is straightforward. If *Wh*-Movement on the lov'er cycle takes the option of pied piping the preposition, there is no way to prevent it from taking the option of not pied piping on the next cycle, thus stranding the preposition in the intermediate COMP. The result is, in Postal's words, a dangling preposition, and consequently an ungrammatical sentence. On the basis of this observation Postal argues that *Wh*-Movement cannot be a (successive) cyclic transformation but must operate in "one fell swoop," crossing all S-boundaries in a single application.

Postal's argument rests on one possible, but not logically necessary, assumption: that optional pied piping is an inherent property of the rule of *Wh*-Movement and that, consequently, the decision whether to pied pipe or not is made at the point of application of the rule. If that assumption is correct, then Postal's argument is correct. However, at the present stage of inquiry pied piping is by and large an ill-understood phenomenon. Sometimes it is obligatory, sometimes optional, sometimes blocked. Moreover, it is highly language-specific. Hence, it seems undesirable to attribute this property to the rule of *Wh*-Movement, which has a fair chance of being universal. Suppose instead that the decision whether a given *wh*-phrase will pied pipe or not is made at D-Structure, in such a way that the distinction becomes a property of the *wh*-phrase (rather than a property of the rule itself, as before). Then the *wh*-phrase will behave uniformly under *Wh*-Movement throughout a complete derivation, and no prepositions will be stranded midway through a derivation. Alternatively, interpretive principles such as (23) and (25) might be refined and interpreted in such a way that sentences containing dangling prepositions are not assigned a well-formed interpretation.

4.3 The Scope of Subjacency

We have seen that Ross's *Wh*-Island Constraint can be deduced from the Subjacency Condition (9) under the assumption that S is a cyclic node. Now, can other island phenomena be accounted for by adding to the inventory of cyclic nodes? This is still a controversial issue, but there is very little doubt that NP also counts for Subjacency. This assumption in effect allows the Complex NP Constraint (CNPC) to be deduced from the Subjacency Condition as well.

So far the terms *cyclic node* and *bounding node* have seemed interchangeable since we have been talking about S, which is in fact an example of both. As the following discussion will show, however, the two sets of nodes are not identical. Therefore, we will from now on adhere to current terminology and call nodes that count for Subjacency bounding nodes.

Consider such violations of the CNPC as the following:

(33)
a. *What did Bill reject the evidence that John did
b. *Which book did Susan visit the store that had in stock

In (33a–b) the second step of *Wh*-Movement must cross both an NP- and an S-boundary:

(34)
a. COMP [$_S$ Bill reject [$_{NP}$ the evidence [$_{S'}$ COMP [$_S$ John did <u>what</u>]$_S$]$_{S'}$]$_{NP}$]$_S$

      α β

b. COMP [$_S$ Susan visit [$_{NP}$ the store [$_{S'}$ COMP [$_S$ that had <u>which book</u>

      α β

in stock]$_S$]$_{S'}$]$_{NP}$]$_S$

Thus, if NP is added to the set of bounding nodes, then the CNPC can be seen to follow from the Subjacency Condition; consequently, the CNPC and the *Wh*-Island Constraint can be unified, a result of major importance. This way of looking at the CNPC has drastic consequences, however. In particular, it implies that no part of an NP can be extracted from that NP directly to COMP, since doing so would always involve crossing both an NP- and an S-boundary. This appears to be generally correct, as observed by Bach and Horn (1976), whose NP-Constraint directly prohibited such extraction:

(35)
a. *Who did [$_{NP}$ your interest in]$_{NP}$ surprise Bill
b. *Whose account did the president stop [$_{NP}$ the treasury's interest in]$_{NP}$

In both of these sentences the movement of the *wh*-phrase to COMP crosses an NP-boundary and an S-boundary, violating the Subjacency Condition. Note that (35a) represents a generalization of Ross's Sentential Subject Constraint to all subject NPs. Thus, this condition is now also subsumed under Subjacency.

Cases like (35b) are, however, somewhat problematic in view of examples like (36a–b):

(36)
a. Who did you see a picture of
b. Which war is John writing a book about

Here it appears that the *wh*-phrase can be extracted from an NP. However, it may be argued that, at the relevant stage of the derivation, such examples have the structure (37):

(37)
COMP NP [$_{VP}$ V NP [$_{PP}$ P *wh*-phrase]$_{PP}$]$_{VP}$

Nothing will block *Wh*-Movement in (37). Such structures may either be base-generated and used as such by the lexical insertion rules directly in the sense that verbs like *see* and *write* are (optionally) subcategorized for them, as proposed in Bach and Horn (1976), or they may arise through a rule of "readjustment" extraposing the PP out of the NP prior to *Wh*-Movement, as suggested in Chomsky (1977a). We will not pursue this matter further but will simply assume that either of these solutions is correct.

The cases discussed so far in which Subjacency is involved have the following structure:

(38)
a. ... X ... [$_S$ ... [$_S$ ... Y ...   (*Wh*-Island Constraint)
b. ... X ... [$_S$ ... [$_{NP}$ ... Y ...   (CNPC, NP-Constraint, (Sentential) Subject Constraint)

Logically, we should also inquire into the two remaining cases:

(38)
c. ... X ... [$_{NP}$ ... [$_S$ ... Y ...
d. ... X ... [$_{NP}$ ... [$_{NP}$ ... Y ...

It turns out that for *Wh*-Movement these reduce to (38a–b), because the *wh*-element, which moves into COMP, must always cross an S-boundary last. Whether there are other rules against which to check these predictions is a tricky question. Rather than pursue it at length, we will give one suggestive example, involving the behavior of the clitic *en* 'of it' in French, that seems to imply that the Subjacency Condition does indeed block movements to positions other than COMP. *En* can be extracted from an NP in simplex cases:

(39)
a. J'ai lu (la préface en)   (*)
b. J'en   ai   lu   la   préface
   I of-it have read the preface
   'I have read the preface of it'

However, extraction across two NP-boundaries, as in (38d), appears to be excluded:

(40)
*J'en   ai   lu   la   critique de la   préface
 I of-it have read the critique of the preface
 'I have read the critique of the preface of it'

4.4 More Bounding Nodes

The Subjacency Condition is an extremely powerful explanatory principle accounting for a wide variety of phenomena that were previously analyzed in terms of a disparate set of conditions such as the CNPC and the Sentential Subject Constraint. In recent years it has become clear that this principle can be extended to seemingly conflicting and very different material in other languages. These extensions, two of which we will outline here, generally involve adding to, or varying, the set of bounding nodes for Subjacency.

Rizzi (1978) has argued that Italian systematically violates the *Wh-*Island Constraint, and hence Subjacency. Thus, for example, it is possible to relativize into an indirect question:

(41)
Tuo fratello, a cui   mi   domando che   storie abbiano
your brother to whom myself I-ask   which stories they-have
raccontato, era   molto preoccupato
told   was very   worried
'Your brother, to whom I wonder which stories they have told, was very worried'

This may mean either that *Wh*-Movement in Italian is simply not subject to Subjacency, or that Subjacency is operative but some other factor makes it inapplicable in (41). That the latter must be the case is shown by the fact that *Wh*-Movement in Italian does obey the CNPC:

(42)
*Tuo fratello, a cui   temo la   possibilità che abbiano
your brother to whom I-fear the possibility that they-have
raccontato tutto, . . .
told   everything

Given the structure shown in (43), how can (41) be derived?

(43)

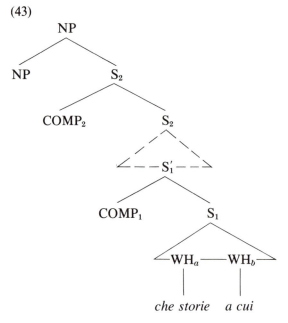

In other words, how can WH_a (*che storie*) end up in $COMP_1$ and WH_b (*a cui*) in $COMP_2$?

Rizzi first discusses, and rejects, a solution that involves violating the Strict Cycle Condition. According to this solution, WH_b first moves to $COMP_1$, then vacates it to move to $COMP_2$. WH_a then moves into $COMP_1$, violating the Strict Cycle Condition. However, eliminating the Strict Cycle Condition would in effect destroy the foundation upon which the Subjacency Condition is built. Hence, this solution is clearly not viable.

Two other solutions appear to exist:

(44)

a. A COMP may be "doubly filled" at the end of a cycle as long as it is not doubly filled at S-Structure.

b. Not S (as in English) but S' is the bounding node for the Subjacency Condition in Italian.

According to (44a), both WH_a and WH_b may move into $COMP_1$ on the lower cycle. On the higher cycle WH_b moves on to $COMP_2$ without violating Subjacency. According to (44b), on the other hand, WH_b can move directly into $COMP_2$ without violating Subjacency, because only one S'-boundary is crossed.

There is in fact empirical evidence on which to choose between the two alternatives. Hypothesis (44b) makes it possible for the pronoun to skip one COMP that contains a *wh*-phrase, but never more than one, since then two S'-nodes would be crossed. Hypothesis (44a), on the other hand, does not discriminate in such cases because the COMPs can be doubly filled on every cycle. Consequently, d-structures of the following type provide the crucial test:

(45)

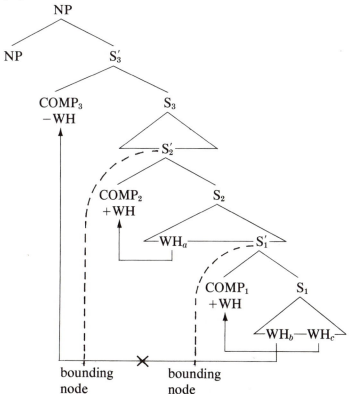

Under hypothesis (44a) it should be possible to extract both WH_b and WH_c, so long as in S-Structure they occupy different COMPs—say, $COMP_2$ and $COMP_3$.

It turns out that sentences of this type are systematically ungrammatical:

(46)

a. Non immagino quanta   gente sappia dove   hanno
   not I-imagine how-many people know where they-have
   mandato Francesco
   sent   Francesco
   'I cannot imagine how many people know where they have sent Francesco'

b. *Francesco, che non immagino quanta   gente sappia
   Francesco who not I-imagine how-many people know
   dove   hanno   mandato, . . .
   where they-have sent

(46b) has exactly the structure (45) as its d-structure, with *che* as WH_b and *dove* as WH_c. (46b) can be derived from that d-structure under Subjacency only by assuming as in (44a) that COMPs can be doubly filled in intermediate stages of the derivation. The fact that (46b) is ungrammatical means that (44a) should be rejected. Hence, the only way to derive (46b) would be to move WH_b (*che*) directly into $COMP_3$, thereby crossing two S'-nodes. If S' is assumed to be a bounding node for Subjacency in Italian, as in (44b), then (46b) violates this principle and is therefore correctly ruled out.

Two central conclusions follow from Rizzi's analysis. First, these complex constructions in Italian, instead of falsifying Subjacency, provide support of the strongest kind for it. Second, the set of bounding nodes for Subjacency appears not to be constant for all languages, but instead may vary somewhat. Minimally, it has been assumed that Universal Grammar includes a binary parameter such that a given language has either S or S' as its bounding node. In the process of language acquisition, the child would fix the parameter in one way or the other on the basis of linguistic evidence.

A second extension involves independent support for Subjacency from a rule other than *Wh*-Movement and an argument for adding PP to the set of bounding nodes for Subjacency, at least for some languages. The argument, which is discussed in more detail in Van Riemsdijk (1978a,b), comes from the rule of *r*-Movement in Dutch. Dutch has a morphological class of pronominal elements that includes *er* and *waar*. These elements have a dual function: either they occur independently and have a locative meaning ('there' and 'where'), or they replace the inanimate pronominal object of a preposition ('it' and 'what'). In the latter case they invert with the preposition just as in English *thereon* or *herewith*, except that in Dutch the process is still fully productive. The independent *er* and *waar* behave like locative PPs, whereas the other *er* and *waar*, which originate as objects of prepositions, are presumably NPs. Both the locative and the prepositional *waar*, being *wh*-pronouns, move to COMP. Both types of *er* undergo a rule (*r*-Movement) that moves *er* into a clitic-like position (R), which is immediately to the right of the subject, except that the verb, which moves into the second position in declarative root clauses, may separate them. This position is considered "clitic-like" because it is the position where unstressed pronouns (clitics) in Dutch tend to occur. Thus, Dutch exhibits the following paradigms:

(47)

a. *Zij heeft vaak [$_{PP}$ waar over]$_{PP}$ gesproken
   she has   often   what about   spoken

b. Waar heeft zij vaak over gesproken
   'What has she often spoken about'

(48)

a. Zij heeft vaak [$_{PP}$ er over]$_{PP}$ gesproken
   she has   often   it about   spoken

b. Zij heeft er vaak over gesproken
   'She has often spoken about it'

(49)

a. *Zij heeft vaak [$_{PP}$ waar]$_{PP}$ [$_{PP}$ over   de   oorlog]$_{PP}$ gesproken
   she has   often   where   about the war   spoken

b. Waar heeft zij vaak over de oorlog gesproken
   'Where has she often spoken about the war'

(50)

a. *Zij heeft vaak [$_{PP}$ er]$_{PP}$ [$_{PP}$ over   de   oorlog]$_{PP}$ gesproken
   she has   often   there   about the war   spoken

b. Zij heeft er vaak over de oorlog gesproken
   'She has often spoken about the war there'

Substituting the prepositional *r*-pronouns of (47) and (48) for the NP *de oorlog* in (49) and (50) results in examples like (51):

(51)
Waar heeft zij er vaak over gesproken

This could be the result of substituting [$_{PP}$ waar over]$_{PP}$ in (47b) for [over de oorlog] in (50b), giving the meaning (52a), or it could be the result of substituting [$_{PP}$ er over]$_{PP}$ in (48b) for [over de oorlog] in (49b), giving the meaning (52b):

(52)
a. Waar$_i$ heeft zij er$_j$ vaak [$_{PP}$ *e*]$_{PP_j}$ [$_{PP}$ *e$_i$* over]$_{PP}$ gesproken
'What has she often spoken about there'

b. Waar$_i$ heeft zij er$_j$ vaak [$_{PP}$ *e*]$_{PP_i}$ [$_{PP}$ *e$_j$* over]$_{PP}$ gesproken
'Where has she often spoken about it'

In fact, however, (51) is unambiguous: it can have only the meaning (52b). This fact rests on the following assumption:

(53)
The bounding nodes for Dutch include PP and S (in addition to NP).

Given (53), it follows that a prepositional *r*-pronoun cannot move directly from inside the PP to COMP but must undergo *r*-Movement to the R-position first:

(54)
a. COMP [$_S$ NP R ... [$_{PP}$ waar+P]$_{PP}$ ... V]$_S$

b. COMP [$_S$ NP R ... [$_{PP}$ waar+P]$_{PP}$ ... V]$_S$

Now consider the two potential derivations of (51):

(55)
a. COMP zij heeft R vaak er [waar over] gesproken (= (52a))

b. COMP zij heeft R vaak waar [er over] gesproken (= (52b))

The crucial element in the analysis is that the locative *er* fills the R-position, making it impossible for *waar* to use this position as an "escape hatch" to evade the Subjacency requirement on its way to COMP.

Derivation (54) requires that *r*-Movement precede *Wh*-Movement. This ordering will also ensure that the R-position is filled in (55a) at the point when *Wh*-Movement applies to *waar*. Again, a version of the Strict Cycle Condition is crucially involved in order to prevent a derivation in which *waar* moves via R to COMP, with *er* subsequently moving into R.

This analysis of "*r*-island" phenomena in Dutch also predicts that if both *er* and *waar* originate in a PP, there is no grammatical output. This is correct:

(56)

a. *Dit is het boek waar$_i$ ik er$_j$ gisteren [e$_i$ voor]
 this is the book which I there yesterday for
 [e$_j$ naartoe] gegaan ben
 to gone have
 'This is the book which I went to it for yesterday'

b. *Dit is de bibliotheek waar$_i$ ik er$_j$ gisteren [e$_j$ voor]
 this is the library which I there yesterday for
 [e$_i$ naartoe] gegaan ben
 to gone have
 'This is the library which I went to for it yesterday'

Since both *r*-pronouns originate in a PP, neither can move into COMP without moving to R first. But once R is filled by *er,* there is no way that *waar* can reach the COMP.

4.5 Summary

In this chapter we have described a first very general and abstract principle of Universal Grammar, the Subjacency Condition, and we have tried to convey some of its explanatory appeal. We will frequently return to this condition, in particular in chapters 6, 8, 9, and 14.

4.6 Bibliographical Comments

The precursors of the Subjacency Condition, essentially the A-over-A Principle and Ross's constraints, were discussed in chapter 2 (see references in section 2.9). The Subjacency Condition was first proposed in Chomsky's "Conditions on Transformations." Though this paper was circulated in manuscript form in 1970, it first appeared in print as Chomsky (1973) and was later reprinted in Chomsky (1977b).

Among the basic ingredients for the Subjacency Condition are the following:

a. The internal structure of COMP (see Bresnan (1970, 1972))
b. The principles for *wh*-interpretation (in addition to Chomsky (1973), see Baker (1970) and, for a diverging view, Grimshaw 1979))
c. The COMP-to-COMP Condition, which various linguists have attempted to derive from other principles of the grammar (see Jenkins (1976), May (1979))
d. The Strict Cycle Condition, which has found interesting application in phonology (see Kean (1974)) and which has also turned out to be derivable from other principles (see Freidin (1978))

The principle of the cycle itself partially governs the ordering of transformational rules, a topic we will not pursue here in detail. See Williams (1974) for a proposal to extend the principle of cyclic rule application so as to predict the ordering of rules.

The possibility that the inventory of bounding nodes for Subjacency may vary from language to language was first discussed in Chomsky (1977a). The classical article exploiting this possibility is Rizzi (1978), reprinted in Rizzi (1982). For proposals involving the addition of new bounding nodes, see Van Riemsdijk (1978a,b) and Sportiche (1981).

No other theoretical principle has given rise to such intense and heated debate as the Subjacency Condition. This debate, which lasted for several years during the late 1970s, is instructive in itself, and we therefore recommend examining at least some of the references just to get a feel for the concentrated argumentation it engendered. A good source is *Linguistic Inquiry* 9.4 (1978), which contains papers from the 1977 Generative Linguists of the Old World (GLOW) conference that was entirely devoted to this debate.

A first attack on successive cyclicity, and thereby on the Subjacency Condition, is Postal (1972), the article in which the dangling preposition argument (section 4.2) appeared. This article was strictly speaking a precursor of the debate itself, which centered around the claim that unbounded deletion rules exist (transformations, in other words, that do not obey Subjacency). This claim was defended in Allen (1977, 1980), Bresnan (1973, 1976b), and Grimshaw (1975). These arguments were countered in Chomsky and Lasnik (1977) and Vat (1978). Evidence from a great variety of languages and constructions was also adduced in support of Subjacency by Den Besten (1978), Kayne and Pollock (1978), Milner (1978), Taraldsen (1978a), and Torrego (1984), among others. On the other hand, alternative conditions intended to replace Subjacency have been proposed, in particular the NP-Constraint of Bach and Horn (1976) and the Bounding Condition of Koster (1978a).

The debate was largely resolved when the proponents of the unbounded deletion approach agreed that even on their analysis a successive cyclic chain of coindexed intermediate complementizers, governed by Subjacency, had to be assumed. This was proposed in Bresnan and Grimshaw (1978); also see McCloskey (1979). Similar proposals have been advanced in a new theoretical setting in Cinque (1983) and Rizzi (1983). A proposal to subsume Subjacency under a more general constraint was advanced in Kayne (1981b) but criticized in Aoun (1981b).

Chapter 5
The Place of Semantics
in the Grammar

5.1 The D-Structure Hypothesis vs. the S-Structure Hypothesis

Syntax is a *constructive* system, in that it defines a set of structures. Grammar as a whole also includes the *interpretive* systems of semantics and phonology. Semantics is especially important in the context of this book because of the interactions between syntactic form and structural aspects of meaning.

The question of how the meaning of a sentence is related to its syntactic form was not treated systematically in *Syntactic Structures* and received only passing attention in *Aspects*. The hypothesis put forward in the latter work—that Deep Structure (D-Structure) determined meaning (the "Standard Theory")—was quickly overturned, though its intuitive appeal was so strong that it flourished in a number of guises and has persisted as a background assumption to the present day. For many, unfortunately, it had the status of a self-evident truth. In fact, almost none of the progress made in syntax since 1970 would have been possible had the D-Structure Hypothesis prevailed.

Though we will not trace the history of the D-Structure Hypothesis in detail, we will review the earliest arguments against it, since they are not only of interest in themselves but also underscore the empirical nature of the question of how meaning relates to form. Furthermore, the role of the semantic component as a filter on overgeneration by the syntactic component, and the consequent simplification of the syntactic component, depend crucially on the details of how semantics and syntax are related.

Here we will consider whether it is D-Structure, Surface Structure (S-Structure), or both, that determines the meaning of a sentence. In chapters 11 through 13 we will discuss a hypothesized level of linguistic representation, Logical Form, that is related to S-Structure in a certain way and represents some aspects of meaning. For present purposes, however, we can ignore questions both about the existence of such a level and about how meaning is to be represented. Given that meaning is related to form in some manner, and given that the syntactic form of a sentence is quite rich (including its d-structure, its s-structure, all intermediate structures, and the history of the application of the transformations), we would of course like to be as specific as possible about how syntactic form is related to meaning. From this perspective, the D-Structure Hypothesis is a quite specific and informative partial answer to this question, for it says that only one part of the complete syntactic form of a sentence is relevant to meaning. From the same perspective, though, an S-Structure Hypothesis would be equally specific and informative, if true. Hence, there is no a priori reason to prefer the D-Structure Hypothesis to an S-Structure Hypothesis.

In this chapter we will look at empirical considerations that favor both hypotheses, in an effort to set preliminary limits on the answer to the question of how form is related to meaning. We will also show how the S-Structure Hypothesis, as opposed to the D-Structure Hypothesis, permits a simplification of the rules of syntax, a simplification that leads to a more insightful, tighter, and more coherent theory of syntax.

The most obvious sense in which D-Structure determines meaning is in its representation of grammatical relations such as "subject of" and "object of." To the extent that these fix the semantic roles of NPs in a sentence, it appears that transformations of D-Structure do not alter these roles. For example:

(1)
a. John ate meat
b. Meat was eaten by John

(2)
a. John talked to Mary
b. Who did John talk to

(3)
a. It seems that John feels sick
b. John seems to feel sick

(4)
a. It is easy to please John
b. John is easy to please

(5)

a. That John is here surprises me

b. It surprises me that John is here

In the above pairs, the (a)-sentences, although not technically the d-structures of the (b)-sentences, are nevertheless closer to the d-structures of the (b)-sentences than the surface forms of the (b)-sentences themselves. In an intuitive and traditional sense, the roles of identical NPs in these pairs are the same, despite the differences in surface form of the sentences in which they appear. For example, *meat* is the thing eaten in both (1a) and (1b), and *John* is the eater in both; whether this relation between *meat* and *eat* is called "theme of," "patient of," or "logical object of" does not matter, so long as the grammar recognizes that there is a relation between the two, and so long as that relation is constant between the (a) and (b) examples in (1) through (5). These relations are known as *thematic relations* or (more currently) *θ-roles* (*theta-roles*).

In each of the pairs (1) through (5), (b) is thought to be derived from a d-structure similar to (a) by some transformation. If these are representative transformations, and representative instances of these transformations, then it appears that transformations do not alter $θ$-role assignment; that is, the $θ$-role assignments in the "more basic" (a)-sentences are exactly the same as the $θ$-role assignments in the transformed (b)-sentences.

Of course, it was partly the perception of identical relations in such pairs that led to positing transformational relationships in the first place. Nevertheless, it is of some empirical interest to see whether the constancy of $θ$-roles holds across all transformations, since it is anything but necessary that it should do so.

If the $θ$-roles of sentences are determined by their d-structures, then sentences having the same d-structure but different s-structures (via transformations) will have the same $θ$-role assignments. It thus follows that transformations do not alter $θ$-roles. This specification of the level of syntactic structure at which $θ$-roles are determined is a part of our general idea of the relation between syntactic and semantic structure. The constancy of $θ$-roles under transformations, rather than having the status of an observation or law, follows from the organization of the theory.

A simple generalization of this notion leads to the full D-Structure Hypothesis: all features of meaning, not just $θ$-roles, are determined at

D-Structure. The preliminary evidence for the D-Structure Hypothesis, as in (1) through (5), is substantial and interesting; however, linguists have found little to support it beyond that first, intriguing fact, the constancy of θ-roles.

Some of the data relevant to rejecting the full D-Structure Hypothesis appeared in *Syntactic Structures*, though their full relevance was not explored until Jackendoff's important work of the late 1960s (published in Jackendoff (1972)). The examples Chomsky discusses are (6a–b):

(6)
a. Everyone in this room knows two languages
b. Two languages are known by everyone in this room

These sentences appear to differ in meaning, in the following way: the first seems to say that everyone is bilingual, without specifying whether any languages are known in common; the second seems to say that everyone knows the same two languages. This difference in meaning can be represented in a sort of predicate calculus as a difference in the scope of the two quantifiers *everyone* and *two:*

(7)
a. [for every x, x a person
   [there are two languages y [x knows y]]]
b. [there are two languages y
   [for every x, x a person [x knows y]]]

If (7a–b) represent the meanings of (6a–b), respectively, then it appears that D-Structure is not determining this aspect of meaning (namely, the order in which quantifiers are interpreted), since (6a–b) have identical d-structures, differing only in whether Passive applies. (Note that in our rendering of the passive construction in chapter 3, the d-structure of (7b) will not be identical to (7a); but it is the same as (7a) in the respects important for this discussion.)

We may quickly conclude that the D-Structure Hypothesis is false, though this would perhaps be premature, since several points about (6a–b) deserve mention. First, the hypothesis as it applies to θ-roles is untouched by these examples: the relation of *languages* to *know* in the two sentences is the same, since *languages* corresponds to the "thing known" in both. Thus, the D-Structure Hypothesis makes valid predictions about even this troublesome case, and to the extent that we want to preserve such predictions we cannot cavalierly dismiss it.

Second, it is probably the case that each of the examples in (6) can have each of the meanings in (7), although there is some preference for the meanings in which the order of interpretation of the quantifiers corresponds to their surface order in the sentence. This makes it difficult to draw firm conclusions from (6a–b); it is possible, for example, to say that D-Structure determines the order of interpretation of quantifiers, and that extragrammatical stylistic or rhetorical components of the language faculty are responsible for determining such things as "preferred interpretations." This was the reaction of Katz (1972) to such examples.

Third, ignoring the difficulty of interpreting the data in (6), the D-Structure Hypothesis might be preserved in the following way: one might continue to affirm that meaning, including the order of interpretation of quantifiers, is determined at D-Structure, and then devise some means of guaranteeing that if the order in (7a) is assigned, then Passive is blocked from applying, and if the order in (7b) is assigned, then Passive applies obligatorily. This may be achieved by specifying that the order of quantifiers in the representation of meaning (7) must correspond to their order in S-Structure (6). This solution was adopted by the proponents of Generative Semantics, a popular linguistic theory in the late 1960s and early 1970s.

The Generative Semantics solution faces three problems. First, the nature of the rules that enforce such correspondences between meaning and S-Structure must be specified. Second, it is not clear how this ultimately saves the D-Structure Hypothesis, since S-Structure is really determining the aspect of meaning having to do with the order of quantifier interpretation. Third, such a theory must still draw the distinction between θ-roles and quantification, because the former is still determined purely by D-Structure, whereas the latter is determined at least in part by S-Structure.

Another aspect of sentence meaning that can be shown to be determined by S-Structure is the possibility of coreference between a pronoun and an NP, as in (8):

(8)
A picture of John upset him

Here, coreference is possible between *John* and *him;* that is, the sentence may be used to mean 'A picture of John upset John'. This possibility disappears in the passive:

(9)

He was upset by a picture of John

(9) is perfectly grammatical, but it cannot mean 'John was upset by a picture of John'. Certainly, determination of the coreference possibilities between pairs of NPs is part of the meaning of a sentence; one could not, for example, say whether (8) was true of a given state of affairs without first deciding whether or not *John* and *he* referred to the same person.

Coreference is barred under a number of conditions (to be considered in greater detail in chapter 12 and subsequent chapters). A pronoun cannot be coreferential with an NP that follows it, except under certain conditions. *Wh*-Movement, like Passive, alters coreference possibilities, though in this case the transformed structure has more of them rather than fewer:

(10)

a. He likes [which picture of John]

b. He likes [that picture of John]

c. [Which picture of John] does he like

In (10a–b) coreference is not allowed between *John* and *he;* but in (10c), the transform of (10a), it is allowed. Again, the restriction seems to be that the pronoun cannot precede the NP if it is to be coreferential with it. Clearly, though, such a restriction must be imposed on s-structures, not d-structures, since the d-structures of (10a) and (10c) are identical.

Similar examples can be constructed with reflexive pronouns. Essentially, a reflexive pronoun, unlike *he, she,* and *it,* must have an antecedent; the antecedent must not follow the reflexive, except under certain conditions; and the antecedent must be the closest subject, roughly speaking (see chapter 12 for a more precise statement). These observations readily account for the following cases:

(11)

a.   John saw himself

b. *Himself was seen by John

Now consider (12a–b), which involve both *Wh*-Movement and reflexives:

(12)

a. *John knows that Mary likes the picture of himself

b. John knows [which picture of himself] Mary likes

(12a) is ungrammatical because the intended antecedent of *himself* is not the closest subject: the subject *Mary* intervenes between *John* and the reflexive. But (12b), derived from (12a) by *Wh*-Movement, is grammatical, apparently because after *Wh*-Movement the subject no longer intervenes. Thus, the requirement on the relation between a reflexive and its antecedent appears to hold at S-Structure, and the fact that it might not hold at D-Structure is irrelevant.

It thus appears that certain aspects of meaning—for example, the part involving the semantic roles that NPs bear to verbs—are determined at D-Structure and are therefore "unaltered" by transformation; other aspects of meaning—for example, the parts involving the relative scopes of quantifiers and coreference between pronouns—are apparently determined by S-Structure. The model of the organization of the grammar that this suggests can be outlined schematically as follows:

(13)

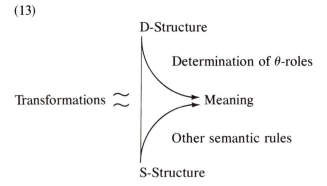

D-Structure

Determination of θ-roles

Transformations ≈   Meaning

Other semantic rules

S-Structure

This model is called the "Extended Standard Theory." As far as it goes, it is a specific hypothesis about the relation of meaning to syntactic form, as specific, if not as elegant, as the D-Structure Hypothesis or the S-Structure Hypothesis:

(14)

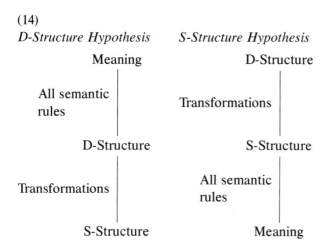

D-Structure Hypothesis	S-Structure Hypothesis
D-Structure Hypothesis	*S-Structure Hypothesis*
Meaning	D-Structure
All semantic rules	Transformations
D-Structure	S-Structure
Transformations	All semantic rules
S-Structure	Meaning

(These diagrams will be discussed in more detail in chapter 10.)

Note that under the conception of transformations discussed so far, it is nearly impossible to adopt the S-Structure Hypothesis, because of θ-role assignment. In (15), for example, the phrase *which meat* is distantly removed from the verb that assigns it a θ-role (*eat*):

(15)
[Which meat]$_i$ did John think that George wanted Fred to eat [e]$_i$ before it rotted

Clearly, the assignment of this θ-role to this phrase is connected to the fact that in D-Structure the phrase is adjacent to the verb assigning the role, occupying the position marked by e_i. As we will see in chapter 9, however, a means has been found to assign θ-roles to s-structures even where the assignee and the assigner have been separated by movement.

5.2 Bibliographical Comments

The D-Structure Hypothesis as discussed here originated with Katz and Postal (1964) and was incorporated into the so-called Standard Theory of *Aspects*. The dominant conception in the mid-1960s of what semantics was supposed to deal with was largely determined by Katz and Fodor (1963). Katz has continued to pursue this basic approach, as illustrated in Katz (1972).

The close link between D-Structure and semantics that is embodied in the D-Structure Hypothesis contributed to the initial promise of Generative Semantics, which in fact identified D-Structure with semantic representation. Generative Semantics was ultimately unsuccessful, however, because of a failure to distinguish between syntactic and non-syntactic properties of sentence structure and an unwillingness to subject the D-Structure Hypothesis to empirical scrutiny. We have not included a discussion of Generative Semantics in this book since its main historical role has been to serve as a catalyst in developing the current conception of semantics. But it engendered a vast literature, and many of these publications, though perhaps no longer pertinent theoretically, contain interesting and worthwhile observations, analyses, and generalizations. As a guide, we recommend Newmeyer (1980), which offers a historical account of the rise and fall of Generative Semantics and numerous references to its literature. It also examines the other influential current in thinking about semantics in the late 1960s and early 1970s, the theory of Case Grammar as developed in Fillmore (1968).

As Generative Semantics flourished, opposition rallied against it and numerous arguments in favor of the S-Structure Hypothesis appeared. Many of these are discussed, summarized, or at least mentioned in Chomsky (1972). The other important study of semantics around this time, which also incorporated many ideas about semantic roles from Fillmore's work, is Jackendoff (1972).

More recent work on the role of semantics in grammar will be discussed beginning in part III.

Part II

TOWARD A THEORY
OF PRINCIPLES

Chapter 6
Toward "Move *Wh*"

In this chapter we will examine further steps that linguists have taken in dismantling the rich descriptive language provided by the theory of transformations that was developed in the 1950s and assumed in the Standard Theory stage of *Aspects*. This theory provides a general formalism for transformations, which allows the writer to specify complex descriptions, the kind of adjunction the rule carries out, whether the rule is obligatory or optional, and where the rule is ordered with respect to others. The rich possibilities of description allowed by this formalism naturally lead to the writing of different rules for different constructions. If a construction involves a long-distance movement rule and also has several idiosyncratic properties, it is quite simple to write the idiosyncratic properties into the movement rule. For example, consider the *cleft construction* illustrated in (1b), derived from (1a):

(1)
a. Bill saw John
b. It was John that Bill saw

Construction (1b) involves a long-distance movement rule (the "unbounded transformations" discussed in section 2.8). It also has the following peculiarities: *it* in subject position, a copula, and *that* as complementizer of the embedded clause. It is easy to write these peculiarities into the movement rule itself:

(2)

$$X - \begin{bmatrix} NP \\ PP \end{bmatrix} - Y$$

SD: 1   2   3   →
SC: *it be* 2 *that* 1 3

This rule accounts for the observed peculiarities. As further peculiarities are discovered, the rule can be amended to reflect them. Why the attested peculiarities and not others? It is left up to the evaluation measure to rate highly what is "natural" about this rule, and poorly what is not.

The theory of transformations allows an entire construction—and every detail of that construction—to be described in a single rule. Consequently, this theory, or rather the transformational formalism, is useful for describing constructions in detail, but the ease with which details can be recorded does not make the explanation of various features of a construction a pressing problem. Suppose we abandoned the general theory of transformations, or at least the theory of transformations that allows arbitrary, complex structural descriptions. We might do this in various ways—perhaps the most radical way would be to eliminate structural descriptions altogether. Instead of an infinite number of possible construction-specific movement rules, then, of which (2) would be one, we would have the general movement rule "Move something somewhere." The rule itself would be incapable of saying what was moved, where it was moved to, whether the movement was obligatory, whether various contextual features were relevant to the movement, etc. In other words, the movement rule would be incapable of describing the details of particular constructions.

This is precisely the approach that generative linguists began to take. In doing so, they had to address the following questions:

a. Can other parts of linguistic theory be elaborated to compensate for the loss of descriptive detail in the specification of movement, without reintroducing the combinatorial explosion of descriptive possibilities inherent in the general descriptive language that is being abandoned?

b. If the specificity of the movement rule is reduced, is the range of constructions in whose analysis it takes part correspondingly widened?

We will begin by considering the second question, showing that an abstract rule "Move *wh* somewhere" does indeed play a role in a number of constructions. The first question will receive a partial answer in this chapter, an answer that will be improved upon in subsequent chapters.

6.1 *Wh*-Relatives

Relative Clause Formation is a well-studied rule in English. Linguists have discovered many of its properties, which we will list below. Various theories have sorted out in various ways which of these properties are features of the structural description (SD) and structural change (SC) of the transformation itself, and which can be attributed to general laws governing transformations, transformational derivations, or levels of representation. Anyone wishing to dismantle the formalism for writing transformations will obviously take an extreme position on this question: *none* of the properties of *Wh*-Movement are features of the SD or SC of a transformation.

What are these properties? They can be approached by considering in turn the properties of relative clauses in which there is a *wh*-word on the surface:

a. This construction has a *wh*-word on the surface in the COMP position of an S'.

b. It has a gap in the S dominated by that S':

(3)
a.   the man [$_{S'}$ who$_i$ [$_S$ Bill saw e_i]$_S$]$_{S'}$
b. *the man [$_{S'}$ who$_i$ [$_S$ Bill saw him$_i$]$_S$]$_{S'}$

c. The relation between the *wh*-word and the gap is governed by Subjacency, as shown in chapter 4. From this it follows, for example, that that relation must obey the Complex NP Constraint:

(4)
*the man who I repeated the suggestion that Bill saw

d. Nevertheless, the relation between the *wh*-word and the gap can span arbitrarily many cycles (that is, it is unbounded), so long as Subjacency is maintained, again as outlined in chapter 4.

e. Prepositions can be "stranded," at least in English (see section 9.2.1).

f. Only NPs and PPs can be moved.

g. The gap left by the rule blocks contraction (see section 9.2.2):

(5)
a.   the man who$_i$ I want e_i to be there
b. *the man who I wanna be there

Relative clauses also have other properties not directly connected with the movement rule. For example, they are introduced into NP by the base rule (h):

h. NP → NP S'

They also have property (i):

i. The head NP of the relative clause is related to the gap, presumably via the *wh*-word and its relation to the gap.

Chomsky (1977a) refers to properties (a) through (d) as the *wh-diagnostics;* they are automatic properties of any rule that moves *wh*-phrases into COMP. Given the strategy of formulating rules as abstractly as possible, we may say: they are automatic properties of *the* rule that moves *wh*-phrases into COMP:

(6)
"Move Wh"
Move a *wh*-phrase into COMP.

Since it is a movement rule, "Move *wh*" (or *Wh*-Movement; the terms are interchangeable) yields a *wh*-phrase in COMP (property (a)), leaves a gap (property (b)), and is subject to Subjacency (property (c)); since it moves an element to COMP, it will be able to iterate, no matter whether the language chooses S or S' as the bounding node for Subjacency (property (d)). Hence, of the properties (a) through (i) of the relative clause construction, (a) through (d) can be accounted for by specifying that "Move *wh*" applies in the derivation of this construction.

Now, how can the other properties be accounted for? Clearly, not by complicating the SD of some movement rule, since only the SD-less rule "Move *wh*" is available for movements to COMP. Consider property (f): only NPs and PPs can be moved in the relative clause construction. This certainly does not follow from the rule "Move *wh*," which is capable of participating in the derivation of such relatives as (7), where it has moved the adverbial phrase *how fast:*

(7)
*the man how fast we ran

This is a clear case of "overgeneration" or "misgeneration"—the rule "Move *wh*" (in combination with the base rules, of course) is inherently incapable of discriminating the grammatical relatives from the ungrammatical—specifically, (3a) from (7).

There are two possibilities here. One is to abandon "Move *wh*" and instead write a rule (particular to relatives) that is capable of moving only NP and PP. For example (from Bresnan (1976a, 35)):

(8)

$$\text{NP} - [_{\bar{\text{s}}} \text{ COMP} - W_1 - (P) - [_{\underset{[-V]}{\bar{\bar{\text{x}}}}} W_2 - rel - W_3] - W_4]$$

SD: 1   2   3   4   5   6   7   8   →
SC: 1   5 6 7   3   4   ∅   8

(Recall that the feature [−V] picks out NP and PP, thereby stipulating the property in question. Note also that term 4 of the SD of this transformation is included specifically to permit the stranding of prepositions, property (e).) On the other hand, if some other explanation could be devised for the ungrammaticality of (7), then it would be possible to preserve the rather strong assumption that transformations moving items to COMP do not have language- (or construction-) particular SDs.

Pursuing the second possibility, linguists have in fact constructed an explanation for (7) that is independent of the SD of a movement rule. Briefly: Suppose that relative clauses are interpreted as one-place predicates (or simple modifiers) that restrict the reference of the NP of which they are a part, just as an AP in an NP would. Now suppose that the rule that effects this interpretation can operate only when COMP contains an NP—an NP that is moreover a *wh*-phrase (that is, contains a *wh*-word). The NP in COMP will correspond to the *free position* that will make the sentence into a one-place predicate. The requirement that the fronted phrase contain an NP will permit the fronting of NPs and PPs, for example, and exclude the fronting of adverbial phrases. (Certain problems do arise. This analysis will permit relatives like *the man proud of whom we certainly are . . .* , which is grammatical as a nonrestrictive relative (pronounced with a "comma" between *man* and *proud*) but ungrammatical as a restrictive relative.)

Of course, to make a real comparison between the two alternatives—a rule of *Wh*-Movement with an SD or the rule "Move *wh*" plus the interpretive rule just mentioned—it would be necessary to work out many details, as well as examine other *wh*-constructions, the full variety of relative clauses, etc. But short of that, the following considerations may still be brought to bear. First, even under the *Wh*-Movement analysis, a rule will undoubtedly be needed to interpret relative clauses as one-place predicates, and it will still be an open question whether the explanation of (7) should lie in the SD of the movement rule or in the rule of interpretation. Second, the interpretive rule explains phenomena other than those it was developed to explain. For example, it has the effect of making the rule "Move *wh*" obligatory in the relative clause: only if the *wh*-phrase is in COMP can the relative be properly interpreted. Since "Move *wh*" is not obligatory in other sentence types (for example, echo questions), obligatoriness cannot be associated with the rule of movement. Instead, it must be associated with the construction itself, which the rule of interpretation does. In the theory with a transformation of Relative Clause Formation, this rule must be made obligatory, and consequently the theory of transformations must be enriched to include the distinction between obligatory and optional rules. But in fact, as noted in *Aspects,* even making the rule obligatory is not sufficient. Suppose the base rules generate a relative clause with no *wh*-word in it? Then, obligatory or not, the rule will not apply. Of course, there are no such relatives (**the man that Bill saw Mary*), but how are they blocked in the two theories? In the "Move *wh*" theory with the interpretive rule, they are blocked because the relative, lacking a *wh*-phrase in COMP, cannot be assigned an interpretation, just like relatives with unmoved *wh*-words. In the *Wh*-Movement theory, some further elaboration of the rule, or some further condition governing the structure, must be given.

These considerations indicate that the proposed interpretive rule is not so ad hoc as it might first appear. Not only does it account for the obligatoriness of *Wh*-Movement in relatives; it also accounts for the fact that a *wh* must be generated in the relative clause in the first place. This, coupled with the fact that no matter how complicated the SD for Relative Clause Formation becomes, a rule for interpreting relatives will still be needed, at least leads one to suspect that the complications in the rule, and concomitant enrichments of the theory of transformations, are unnecessary.

6.2 Extending the Rule's Coverage

6.2.1 *That*-Relatives
The *that*-relative in English shares nearly all of the properties of the *wh*-relative: it occupies the same position in NP; it has a gap; it obeys Subjacency; it involves an unbounded relation between the gap and the COMP of the relative; the gap blocks contraction; and the relative must contain no unmoved *wh*-words.

Given that this construction involves an unbounded relation governed by Subjacency, it follows that movement must be involved, since only through movement is it possible to chain together several subjacent relations into one (apparently) nonsubjacent relation. Furthermore, the existence of a gap suggests that movement is involved. But movement of what? There is no *wh*-word, or anything else, on the surface that could have been moved.

Perhaps *that* at the beginning of the relative is the moved element. But Bresnan (1972) gives strong reasons for considering *that* not as a relative pronoun but as the complementizer *that*. For one thing, it does not pied pipe:

(9)

the man $\begin{Bmatrix} \text{*to that I was talking} \\ \text{that I was talking to} \end{Bmatrix}$

So *that* is not a plausible candidate for the moved item. Perhaps instead the moved item has been deleted. Since the proposed movement rule moves *wh*-items, let us suppose that the item deleted is a *wh*-word, say *who* in this example. The following derivation would result:

(10)
the man COMP I was talking to who
the man who   I was talking to
the man   I was talking to

(Note that for this account to be consistent with the previous discussion of the interpretation of relative clauses, the deletion rule must apply after the interpretive rule.) Next a rule is needed that inserts *that* in an unfilled COMP, to derive the *that*-relative:

(11)
the man that I was talking to

Thus, given a rule deleting *wh*-words from COMP and a rule inserting *that* into an empty COMP, we can account for the fact that *that*-relatives obey Subjacency. This pair of rules will allow the derivation of *that*-relatives via the already existing movement rule, "Move *wh*," and no further rules need be posited.

This is a nice result, but of course the proposed deletion and insertion rules must be scrutinized in order to evaluate the analysis as a whole. If, for example, the existence of these rules entailed the full formalism of transformational SDs, the "nice result" would only be a delusion.

Though we will not provide answers to these problems, we will look at some of the considerations that bear on them.

First, consider the rule that deletes *wh*-words from COMP. In fact, it does not delete *wh*-words from COMP; instead, it deletes the entire COMP:

(12)
a. *the man to – I talked
b. the man – I talked to

This deletion process cannot apply everywhere, however:

(13)
a. the man to whom I talked
b. *the man —   I talked

How is this restriction to be accounted for? Building it into the deletion rule would entail invoking the descriptive formalism of transformational SDs again. One way to circumvent this would be to say that the rule freely deletes COMP (that is, deletes it in all contexts), but is subject to a rule condition of *recoverability* that says, among other things, that a lexical item cannot be deleted, except under identity (that is, where it is identical to some other item in the sentence). The proposed general deletion rule would thus apply in (13a), but its output (13b) would be ruled out by the condition on recoverability. The deletion of *to whom* by the rule in question is not recoverable, because of the deletion of *to* (*whom* would not count).

There is some evidence independent of relatives for the deletion of COMP. For example, a rule deleting *for* is needed in the following case:

(14)
 I arranged for Bill to leave
*I arranged for   to leave
 I arranged —   to leave

Also needed is a rule deleting *that* in sentences like (15):

(15)
I know (that) he is here

We will explore further details of this construction, and of the rule deleting COMP, in chapter 10. For the moment, these remarks should at least establish the plausibility of the movement plus COMP-deletion analysis.

6.2.2 *Wh*-Questions

The question construction also shares the following properties with the relative construction: it involves a *wh*-word in COMP (property (a)) and a gap (property (b)):

(16)
Who did you see —

The relation between COMP and the gap involves Subjacency (property (c)),

(17)
*Who do you know when Bill saw —

but it appears to be unbounded (property (d)):

(18)
Who do you think Bill said Mary expected to see —

All of these properties follow if "Move *wh*" is assumed to be involved in question formation.

Questions also share with relatives the properties that prepositions can be stranded (property (e)), as in (19), and that contraction is blocked (property (g)), as in (20):

(19)
Who are you talking about —

(20)
a.   Who do you want — to leave
b.   *Who do you wanna leave (with same meaning as (20a))

But the question construction also differs from the relative in a number of respects. In order to preserve the generality of "Move *wh*," we will briefly examine the possibility that these differences have nothing to do with this rule, and in each case we will seek another account. First, questions can contain more than one *wh*-word (see (23k) below):

(21)
Who saw who

Presumably, there are interpretive rules that will assign this an interpretation, and there is no analogous rule for relatives.

Second, there are questions that do not involve movement:

(22)

I wonder whether Bill left

Suppose there is a complementizer *whether* and a rule that assigns an S on the surface to the category "question" if its COMP contains a *wh*-word. Then there will be two cases: Ss with a *whether*-complementizer in COMP, and Ss in which a *wh*-word has been moved into COMP. The rule will interpret both cases as questions.

Third, questions involve the full range of *wh*-expressions, whereas relatives involve only *wh*-NPs and *wh*-PPs (property (f)). This follows from the fact that relatives modify nouns and questions do not.

Though these points certainly do not exhaust the differences between relatives and questions, they at least emphasize the research strategy based on the rule "Move *wh*." In each case the difference between the constructions could be accounted for either by writing differing structural descriptions for two different rules (or three, if *that*-relatives are included) or by devising general conditions on the application of two different rules.

6.2.3 Summary of "Move *Wh*" Constructions

To summarize the properties of the three constructions:

(23)

	wh-relative	*that*-relative	question
a. COMP is involved	+	+	+
b. A gap is involved	+	+	+
c. Relation is subjacent, but	+	+	+
d. It appears to be unbounded	+	+	+
e. Prepositions can be stranded	+	+	+
f. Only NP and PP can be moved	+	d.n.a.	−
g. Contraction is blocked	+	+	+
h. NP → NP S'	+	+	−
i. Relation between head and gap	+	+	−
j. *Wh*-word appears on the surface	+	−	+
k. More than one *wh*-phrase allowed per construction	−	−	+
l. *Wh* must be moved when it can	+	+	+

Properties (a) through (d) are inescapable properties of any rule that "moves something to COMP." (d) is a property of such a rule if no constraint is put on it, and of course (c), which is really an abbreviation for a number of facts about movement, although not deducible from the bare idea of movement, is postulated to hold for movement on empirical grounds.

The odd assortment of properties (e) through (l) are not general features of the movement rule "Move *wh*," but are instead properties of particular constructions. To the extent that an explanation is possible, the fact that some constructions have one constellation of these properties and not another is not to be explained in terms of the rule "Move *wh*," which is constant across these constructions, but is instead to be explained independently. Properties (e) and (g), although common to all these constructions, should not be taken to be inherent properties of *Wh*-Movement like (a) through (d), because many languages that have *Wh*-Movement lack these properties (see chapter 9).

6.3 More "Move *Wh*" Constructions: The Cleft Construction, Comparative Deletion, and Topicalization

Thus, to pursue the strategy of eschewing richly descriptive transformational SDs, it has been postulated that "Move *wh*" is part of the description of three constructions (*wh*-relatives, *that*-relatives, and *wh*-questions) and that the differences among these constructions can be attributed to aspects of grammar that are independent of the SD of the movement rule involved in each construction.

A next logical step would be to extend this rule to *all* constructions that involve a relation that exhibits the *wh*-diagnostic properties (a) through (d). In other words, the details of each construction that do not follow from the *wh*-properties themselves must be attributed to factors independent of the movement involved. We will discuss three constructions in this light: the cleft construction, comparative deletion, and topicalization. In each case the proposed research strategy raises considerable empirical problems (that is, problems of description). That the program creates these problems is its main virtue, however, for it forces linguistic analysts to articulate other modules of the theory of grammar in very particular ways. The hope is always that we are building a theory that is so specific that it runs great risk of being false. Below we will exhibit solutions to some, but not all, of the problems that arise from extending "Move *wh*" to all unbounded relations; the rest remain as research topics.

6.3.1 The Cleft Construction

Like the *wh*-relative, the cleft construction can appear both with and without a *wh*-word:

(24)

It was John $\left\{ \begin{array}{l} \text{(who)} \\ \text{(that)} \end{array} \right\}$ we saw *e*

Since the relation between the *who* and the gap obeys Subjacency (as the reader may verify), the cleft construction involves a relation that meets the *wh*-diagnosis. Thus, it involves "Move *wh*." This much is forced on us. It remains (a) to figure out *why* "Move *wh*" is involved in this construction, and (b) to account for those details of the construction that do not follow from the fact that "Move *wh*" is involved.

Let us suppose that there is a semantic rule specifying that in structure (25) the S′ is to be interpreted as a property predicated of the NP that precedes it:

(25)
it be NP S′

If our theory of semantics is sufficient to guarantee that an S′ can be interpreted as a property only if it has undergone "Move *wh*" (a similar approach was outlined for relatives earlier), then the first question is answered.

The details of the construction that do not follow from the fact that "Move *wh*" is involved are these:

a. Either a *wh*-phrase or *that* can appear.
b. If a PP appears in the focus position (the position following *it* and the copula), then *that* must appear in COMP:

(26)
a. *It was to John to whom I spoke
b. It was to John that I spoke

c. *It* appears in the subject position.

Adopting the convention that complementizers can delete if they are "recoverable" will account for (a). (b) has two parts: Why is it possible for the PP to delete, as in (26b)? and Why must it delete? Again, recoverability might answer the first question. In this case, the PP in COMP is recoverable because it is nondistinct from the PP in focus position. The principle for recoverability that would allow this deletion remains to be given, but it is plausible to assume that such a principle would distinguish free deletion from deletion under identity (or "nondistinctness") and allow a greater range of deletions in the latter case. As for why the PP must delete, we have no answer, but we can point out that it would be inappropriate to seek a universal principle for this, since in the analogous sentences in Spanish, deletion is apparently not required.

We will defer discussion of the appearance of *it* in subject position (property (c)) until chapter 15. At least one other construction has this property:

(27)
It seems that John will leave

In both constructions fully "referential" NPs are excluded from subject position:

(28)
a. *The man was to John that I spoke
b. *The man seems that John will leave

The theory to be developed in chapter 15 will essentially account for the fact that referential NPs cannot appear in certain syntactic configurations.

6.3.2 Comparative Deletion

Comparative deletion provides a good example of a construction where a strong and general hypothesis generates descriptive problems. The hypothesis is that all unbounded island-sensitive relations involve applications of "Move *wh*." We take the comparative construction to be structurally identical to the relative clause construction, except that it can also be headed by AP: $[_{AP} \text{ AP S}']_{AP}$. The comparative construction, unlike the cleft, relative, pseudocleft, and question constructions, never has an overt *wh*-word. Nevertheless, it exhibits the *wh*-diagnostics:

(29)
John is $[_{AP}$ bigger $[_{S'}$ than we thought you said $[_{S'}$ ... Bill believed $[_{S'}$ Paul was $e]_{S'}]_{S'}]_{S'}]_{AP}$ (property (d))

(30)
*John is [$_{AP}$ bigger [$_{S'}$ than we recalled [$_{NP}$ the idea [$_{S'}$ that ... Bill believed Paul was e]$_{S'}$]$_{NP}$]$_{S'}$]$_{AP}$ (property (c))

Are the *wh*-diagnostics sufficient evidence that "Move *wh*" is involved in this construction, even though it contains no *wh*-words? Yes, if the hypothesis is correct. If "Move *wh*" is involved, then some mechanism is needed to delete *wh*-words. Assuming that *than* is a complementizer, representations like (31) must be ruled out:

(31)
*John is bigger what than I thought Bill was

Since there is already a rule that deletes *wh*-words from complementizer position, it is necessary only to ensure that the rule must apply. A filter excluding double filling of the COMP position would accomplish this (a *filter* being a rule that declares as ungrammatical any string that meets its structural description):

(32)
Doubly Filled COMP Filter
*[$_{COMP}$ X^{max} complementizer]$_{COMP}$

Such a filter applies generally in English. We will discuss this filter in more detail in chapter 10.

A second descriptive problem posed by the hypothesis that movement is involved in the formation of the comparative construction, a problem explored by Bresnan (1977), is that in some cases the deletion site in the comparative clause does not correspond to anything that could have been moved:

(33)
John has more horses than Bill has e cows

Here, what has been deleted is the specifier of the NP *cows*. Ordinarily, though, specifiers cannot be moved:

(34)
*[How many]$_i$ does Bill have [e]$_i$ cows

Bresnan calls these cases of *subdeletion* and cites them as evidence that movement cannot be involved in at least some cases of the comparative construction.

Such a conclusion has far-reaching implications. If there are some kinds of comparatives in which movement cannot be involved and that nevertheless exhibit the *wh*-diagnostics, then we are in a quandary. If movement is not involved, then deletion must be; but the deletion must be long-distance deletion that obeys island constraints, if it exhibits the *wh*-diagnostics. But any such rule nullifies the Subjacency Condition, since there is no analogue of successive cyclic movement in the case of deletion. Another way to look at it is this: for the rule of "Subdeletion" there must be a rule (Subdeletion itself) that is not governed by Subjacency, and the island conditions must hold for it, but not in such a way that they can be derived from Subjacency. The enrichment of the theory that would be required to do this would render Subjacency redundant. Such a conclusion would thus refute the principle altogether.

Chomsky discusses this descriptive problem at length in "On *Wh*-Movement" (1977a). Basically, he entertains two possibilities. First, he suggests that Subdeletion does not really exhibit the *wh*-diagnostics— that it is not an unbounded rule. This depends on judgments of grammaticality of such sentences as (35):

(35)
John has more cows than Bill believes he has *e* horses

If Subdeletion does not exhibit the *wh*-diagnostics, but is rather a purely local rule (obeying Subjacency in appearance as well as in fact), then it does not threaten the Subjacency Condition. The second possibility involves the fact that movement in general cannot remove left branches; but since this solution would take us too far afield here, we simply refer the reader to Chomsky (1977a) for discussion.

6.3.3 Topicalization
Topicalization is another construction that exhibits the *wh*-diagnostics even though overt *wh*-words never appear:

(36)
a.　John$_i$ I believe Sally said Bill believed Sue saw e_i
b.　*John$_i$ I interrupted the proof of the proposition that Bill saw e_i

If we accept the *wh*-diagnostics as evidence that "Move *wh*" is involved, we must account for the fact that *wh*-words never appear on the surface.

If "Move *wh*" is involved, then the topicalized constituent must be base-generated. Chomsky (1977a) proposes a structure like (37), generated by the phrase structure rules S″ → TOP S′ and S′ → COMP S:

(37)

[$_{S''}$ TOP [$_{S'}$ COMP [$_S$ ...]$_S$]$_{S'}$]$_{S''}$

In such a structure, "Move *wh*" must take place, presumably so that interpretive rules will be able to interpret the S as a property applied to the NP topic. Furthermore, the rule deleting *wh* from COMP can apply to delete the *wh*-word. That it *must* apply cannot be explained, but can be described by positing a filter that rules ungrammatical all such structures in which the *wh*-word has not been first moved and then deleted.

We might approach this problem in a different way. "Move *wh*" has two essential features: it moves a *wh*-phrase, and it moves it to COMP. Suppose that the latter is the characterizing property. Then "Move *wh*" can be stated even more generally:

(38)

"Move wh"

Move (something) to COMP.

Then the fact that in many applications the movement affects a *wh*-phrase becomes an incidental fact about certain constructions.

With this new version of "Move *wh*" we can say that the topicalization construction arises from the movement of an NP (or PP) to COMP. Since the movement can be iterated (from COMP to COMP) and since each movement is subject to the Subjacency Condition, the construction displays the *wh*-diagnostics, exactly like a construction with an overt *wh*-word.

One problem is that this analysis requires admitting doubly filled COMPs, when topicalization takes place in embedded sentences:

(39)

They believe *that John* Bill saw

Furthermore, the phrase structure rule for COMP given in chapter 4 (COMP → X^{max} complementizers) would predict the order **John that* rather than *that John*. We will not resolve these problems here.

The *wh*-diagnostics force us to choose one of these proposals, either of which will render topicalization consistent with the general hypothesis that all unbounded island-sensitive rules are instances of "Move *wh*," though in each case certain descriptive problems arise. Whichever we choose (and for expository reasons we choose the analysis in which the topic itself is moved), they both contend that topicalization involves a movement to COMP that is governed by Subjacency. From this, an intriguing prediction follows immediately: not only is topicalization island-sensitive, it is island-creating:

(40)

a. You think that these records I gave — to Bill

b. *Who$_j$ do you think that these records$_i$, I gave e_i to e_j

Here the extraction of *who* is ungrammatical, but in the related case where Topicalization has not taken place, it is fine:

(41)
Who$_i$ do you think that I gave these records to e_i

We may explain (40b) by appealing to the COMP-filling property of Topicalization: at the end of the embedded cycle the *wh*-word *who* must have been in the COMP of the lower S; otherwise, extracting it from the lower S would violate Subjacency. However, that COMP must also be occupied by the phrase *these records,* which has been moved there by Topicalization (which, according to the Strict Cycle Condition, must have applied by the end of the embedded cycle, if it is to apply at all). But the COMP cannot be occupied by both *who* and *these records* at the same time, since under this analysis the COMP has only one fillable position. Thus, (40b) cannot be derived. The correctness of the prediction thus confirms the hypothesis from which it follows, namely that all unbounded island-sensitive relations involve "Move *wh*."

6.4 Conclusion

In this chapter we have shown how the general hypothesis has been examined in the light of various constructions. In every case the hypothesis has created descriptive problems that would not have existed without it. In some cases the solutions to these problems are simple. For example, the variation in the form of relatives and clefts can be accounted for by postulating a COMP-deletion rule, and the fact that *wh*-words do not appear in the comparative construction can be accounted for by postulating a COMP filter. Some cases, notably the island-creating effects of Topicalization, offer a descriptive bonus, in that they accurately predict the behavior of other constructions. And in other cases, notably comparative deletion, certain descriptive problems remain unsolved. Thus, the results are mixed. This might be expected, given that the fundamental hypothesis bears on such a wide range of facts. But the mixed result has been sufficiently encouraging for linguists to take the further research directives seriously: to construct the subtheories of interpretive rules, filters (such as the Doubly Filled COMP Filter), and deletion rules (such as the COMP-deletion rule) that are required to support the hypothesis. The goal in constructing each of these subtheories has been to reduce the descriptive possibilities to a bare minimum. The direction in which this strategy has taken linguistic theory is again distinctly modular: the general theory can be decomposed into a number of distinct subtheories that interact to explain complex phenomena. In subsequent chapters we will explore the first steps that have been taken toward defining these subtheories.

6.5 Bibliographical Comments

The program that was to lead to a general theory of "Move *wh*" was initiated by Chomsky (1973). But the main steps in carrying it out were taken in "On *Wh*-Movement" (Chomsky (1977a)). The diagnostic method employed there and discussed in this chapter has since been recognized as an important tool in syntactic research. For an early example, see Van Riemsdijk (1978a).

Among the main properties of "Move *wh*," boundedness (Subjacency) has already been discussed in chapter 4; see the references given there.

Some of the construction-bound properties discussed in this chapter will be examined in more detail later: the structure of COMP (after "Move *wh*") in section 10.1 and preposition stranding in section 9.2.1. On these constructions, see the references given in those chapters.

There are many publications dealing with the specific constructions subsumed under "Move *wh*," of which we will give only a limited selection. Much of what is known about these constructions of English comes from two main studies that cover a large domain of English syntax: Ross (1967) and Emonds (1976).

Relative clauses are discussed in great detail in Vergnaud (1974) (updated in Vergnaud (1982)). For a detailed analysis of Italian relative clauses, see Cinque (1982). One particular type of relative clause has given rise to an abundant subliterature. This is the headless or free relative, as in *I will eat whatever is left*. The dispute concerning this construction was triggered by Bresnan and Grimshaw (1978) and followed up by many authors, among them Groos and Van Riemsdijk (1981). On the analysis of *wh*-questions, see Baker (1970) and Bach (1971).

The cleft construction has received relatively little attention, but an excellent discussion of the closely related pseudocleft construction (sentences like *What John ate was a herring*) can be found in Higgins (1973). Work on comparatives and subdeletion is closely connected with the boundedness debate; see Bresnan (1973, 1975, 1977) and the references given in chapter 4. More recent articles contrasting topicalization with left dislocation (a construction like topicalization except that it has a personal pronoun instead of a gap, as in *John I don't like him*) are Van Haaften, Smits, and Vat (1983) and Cinque (1983).

Chapter 7
Toward "Move NP"

In several chapters we have considered general properties of certain transformations that generative linguists have examined, in particular the properties that can be factored out from the rule itself and stated in terms of general principles or constraints. For example, the formulation of the rule of *Wh*-Movement (or "Move *wh*") can be drastically simplified, many of its surprising properties being predicted by the Subjacency Condition and a small number of other principles. At the same time this simplification broadens the empirical coverage of the rule to include a large number of constructions formerly handled by separate rules. The main import of this strategy is that it brings closer a solution to the language acquisition problem: the expressive possibilities of transformational rules are drastically reduced, thereby reducing the options from which the language learner (the child) must choose in the process of grammar construction. The general principles, which take over the burden of regulating when and how the rules apply, are assumed to be part of Universal Grammar and hence constitute linguists' first crude attempt at characterizing the biological endowment with which the child can face this overwhelming task. This strategy, then, is of crucial importance to progress in linguistic theorizing.

In section 2.4 and chapter 6 we showed how linguists have applied this strategy to the rule of *Wh*-Movement. In chapter 3 we likewise showed the first step that has been taken toward reducing the expressive power of the Passive transformation. In particular, we showed that Passive has been divided into two very general subrules: NP-Preposing and NP-Postposing. In this chapter we will pursue the research that has been devoted to these subrules. In particular, we will address three questions:

a. Are the general principles formulated in connection with *Wh*-Movement also relevant for NP-Preposing and NP-Postposing? In particular, are these rules subject to the Subjacency Condition?
b. Aren't NP-Preposing and NP-Postposing so general that they will yield wrong results in many cases? That is, how can these rules be prevented from generating many ungrammatical sentences—in other words, from overgenerating?
c. Do NP-Preposing and NP-Postposing show up in other constructions as well? Can the empirical coverage of these rules be broadened?

We will tackle these questions in reverse order. Linguists have concluded that there is every reason to postulate the existence of an optimally simple rule that underlies several constructions including the passive, a rule that, in accordance with the findings discussed in chapter 6, has been called *"Move NP"* (or *NP-Movement;* as with *"Move wh"/Wh-Movement,* we will use the two terms interchangeably).

7.1 The Empirical Range of "Move NP"

The original Passive transformation really consisted of two movement operations: NP-Preposing and NP-Postposing. These rules were already formulated in such a general way that they could potentially apply in many cases having nothing to do with the canonical passive construction. In fact, in accordance with the principle of structure preservation, they jointly had the effect that any NP could move to any other NP position. This, in brief, is what postulating the even more general rule "Move NP" would imply. Is there any empirical justification for such a drastic move?

First of all, *passive* is actually a cover term for many separate cases. Informally speaking, the passive construction is often described as one in which the direct object appears as the surface subject. Although this is the case in (1), it is not in (2) through (5):

(1)
The city was destroyed (by the enemy)

(2)
Mary was given a book (by John)

(3)
This solution is argued for (by many linguists)

(4)

a. John was taken advantage of (by his boss)

b. Advantage was taken of John (by his boss)

(5)

Reuteman is expected to come in third (by the press)

In (2) it is the indirect object, not the direct object, that appears in subject position. In (3) it is the NP of a prepositional object, in (4a) the object of an idiomatic expression, and in (4b) an NP-like chunk of the idiom itself. Finally, in (5) the subject of an infinitival complement clause has been moved to the subject position. Still, these sentences share certain properties:

(6)

a. Passive morphology (auxiliary *be* plus passive participle)

b. An optional *by*-NP agent phrase

c. A subject that derives some of its essential properties from an NP position somewhere to the right of the passive verb

In striving to broaden the empirical scope of the Passive rule, it would seem wise to regard properties (6a) and (6b) as construction-bound, especially since the former is not relevant for passive derived nominals (chapter 3). But (6c) is the property that provided the motivation for postulating a Passive rule in the first place, and it might be expected to show up in other constructions as well.

With this in mind, consider (7a–b):

(7)

a. Few linguistics books read easily

b. Cognitive science sells well

Neither (6a) nor (6b) is met. The verb has active morphology, and agent phrases are impossible:

(8)

a. *Few linguistics books read easily by philosophers

b. *Cognitive science sells well by clever linguists

But the third property, (6c), is clearly met: the subject NPs of (7a–b) are interpreted in an obvious way as the direct objects of the verbs *read* and *sells*, respectively. The verbs are interpreted as transitive, yet they appear to lack a direct object. Though they normally take an agent phrase as subject, their surface subjects in (7) are not possible agent

NPs but rather seem to be taken from the set of NPs that would normally appear as their direct objects. Hence, it appears reasonable to assume that "Move NP" is at work in this construction (usually called the *middle voice* construction). In light of (6), we would expect this construction to have a number of construction-bound peculiarities as well. For example, middle voice sentences must normally be interpreted as generic, and they preferably contain a manner adverb (such as *easily* and *well* in (7)). Idiosyncratic properties such as these are not surprising and, although they must eventually be accounted for in some way, they should not deter us from recognizing the presence of the diagnostic property (6c) in this construction. However, there are more fundamental discrepancies between the two construction types. In the middle voice construction only true direct objects may be moved to subject position. In other words, the pattern of (2) through (5) cannot be reproduced:

(9)
*Women give poetry books more commonly than men
 (with *women* interpreted as the indirect object, not as the agent)

(10)
*Ad hoc solutions argue for quite frequently in linguistics

(11)
a. *Graduate students don't take advantage of very often in this country
b. *Advantage doesn't take of graduate students very often in this country

(12)
*Female students generally expect to do better at written examinations
 (in the sense of 'Female students are generally expected to do better at written examinations')

Any account of the middle voice construction in terms of "Move NP" will have to account for this discrepancy. Unless an independent explanation can be found, it may be necessary to conclude that this construction does not really constitute a case of "Move NP" at all, but that it accidentally shares property (6c) with the passive construction to a certain extent. We leave the matter open here, but we may conclude that care is needed in applying the diagnostic criterion (6c) to other constructions.

Before we turn to another construction where "Move NP" might be involved, consider again an important implication of (6c). If a subject derives its essential properties of selection and subcategorization from some other NP-position, this must mean that the subject position itself does not fulfill this selectional role in the cases where (6c) applies. Thus, consider the active-passive pair (13a–b):

(13)
a. John read a book
b. The book was read

In (13a) the verb assigns the subject position the role of agent. This role cannot plausibly be derived from any other position. In (13b), however, the verb does not assign this role to the subject, and this, we may conjecture, makes it possible for this subject position to receive another NP that brings its own selectional and subcategorizational role with it.

In light of this interpretation of (6c), are there other verbs (or predicates) that do not assign a role to their subject position? Good candidates would be predicates that take the semantically empty expletive *it* as their subject. For example:

(14)
a. It seems that John has left
b. It appears that there has been an earthquake
c. It is likely that Bill was murdered

In all these cases an NP can appear in the matrix subject position, which has property (6c):

(15)
a. John seems to have left
b. There appears to have been an earthquake
c. Bill is likely to have been murdered

We would expect any NP that can occur as the subject of the complement clause in (14) to appear in the matrix subject position of (15). This is because the matrix subject position does not fulfill any semantic rule of its own with respect to the matrix verb (in contrast to cases like *John wants to leave,* where *John* is both the wanter and the leaver). (14b) and (15b) illustrate this for the "dummy" subject *there,* for example. Note that *there* normally requires the presence of *be.* But *appears* in (15b) is not accompanied by *be.* Hence, it must be the *be* of the complement clause that licenses the presence of *there* in the matrix subject position.

Verbs like *want*, which do assign roles to their subject position, cannot take dummy *there* as subject (*There wants to be an earthquake*). A movement analysis will immediately account for this fact. (14c) and (15c) show that derived subjects also behave according to this pattern. Finally, idiomatic subjects—whether derived (as in (16)) or not (as in (17))—have the same property:

(16)
a. It seems that advantage has been taken of John
b. Advantage seems to have been taken of John

(17)
a. It appears that the shit has hit the fan
b. The shit appears to have hit the fan

We may therefore conclude that "Move NP" is involved in this construction, which is usually referred to as *raising* or *raising-to-subject* (as opposed to raising-to-object; sections 2.8 and 7.3).

Although its application to raising constructions is the most important extension of the scope of "Move NP," there are other constructions in which the rule might be involved. These include the constructions of *there*-insertion (*There was someone there*), heavy-NP-shift (*John gave to Mary all that he had*), and the subject inversion of the Romance languages (see chapter 18). However, since it is far from obvious that the diagnostic criterion (6c) applies to these, we will not pursue this issue here. The properties of these constructions will become more readily explicable as we go along, in terms of later developments of the theory.

Since Raising has the effect of moving an NP from the complement subject position to the matrix position, we expect Raising and Passive to interact. We have already seen such cases, where the derived subject of a passive clause has undergone Raising: (15c) and (16b). Similarly, we expect the output of Raising to be the input of Raising or Passive. Both cases occur:

(18)
a. John seems to be certain to leave
b. Bill is expected to be likely to win the race

Consequently, as with "Move *wh*," multiple successive cyclic applications of "Move NP" are possible within one complex sentence:

(19)
This solution is expected to be likely to appear to have been discovered by a genius

In (19) "Move NP" has applied four times. The NP *this solution* has been moved from the bottom to the top via Passive, Raising, Raising, and Passive. Criterion (6c) applies to every individual application. Thus, these processes have created a chain of four links along which the property of "being the object of *discover*" has been transmitted to the surface subject of (19).

Criterion (6c) has been kept deliberately vague here. The notion of "essential properties," which we have so far characterized roughly in terms of subcategorization and selection, will become more precise in later chapters, particularly in chapter 15.

7.2 Blocking Overgeneration of "Move NP": The Specified Subject Condition and the Tensed-S Condition

To this point there has been a discrepancy in our treatment of "Move NP." The rule is formulated as in (20), but we have characterized its effect more like (21):

(20)
Move any NP to any other (NP-)position.

(21)
Move any NP to a subject position that does not receive an independent selectional or subcategorizational role.

We must now address this discrepancy; that is, we must address question (b) from the beginning of this chapter. This question breaks down into two parts:

(22)
a. Why is movement always to a subject position that lacks an independent role?
b. Is it true that *any* NP may be moved there?

Briefly, the previous section has already implicitly answered (22a). If movement must be to an NP-position that lacks an independent role, then perhaps subject positions are the only positions that can have this property. This is in fact roughly the view that has been adopted (see chapters 8, 14, 15). Suffice it to say here that this line of reasoning will account for problems of the type mentioned in section 3.4, such as the absence of any constructions that involve movement from, say, prepositional object position to direct object position or vice versa.

Clearly, the answer to (22b) must be no. Many NPs cannot undergo Passive or Raising. Examples (1) through (4) show that within a clause many NP-positions are accessible to "Move NP." However, many others are not:

(23)
a. Mary was given a book
b. *A book was given Mary

(24)
a. This solution is argued for by many linguists (= (3))
b. *Many hours were argued with Bill for by Harry

Across clause boundaries, indiscriminate application of "Move NP" generates many more ungrammatical sentences:

(25)
a. Bill is expected to beat Harry
b. *Harry is expected Bill to beat

(26)
a. It is likely that John will leave early
b. John is likely to leave early
c. *John is likely that will leave early

(27)
a. John believes Bill to expect Harry to leave early
b. Bill is believed to expect Harry to leave early
c. John believes Harry to be expected to leave early
d. *Harry is believed Bill to expect to leave early

Linguistic theory has had little to say about cases like (23) and (24). The application of "Move NP" across clause boundaries, however, has given rise to a fruitful line of research that will be an important recurring theme in subsequent chapters.

Examples like (23) and (24) involve the Passive subcase of "Move NP," since Raising operates across clause boundaries by definition. The impossibility of (23b) and (24b) may therefore very well be linked to a construction-specific property of passive sentences, just like (6a) and (6b). In fact, it appears that the NP that undergoes movement in a passive structure must originate immediately to the right of what has been called a *natural predicate*. Thus, *argue for* in (24a) can be regarded as a natural predicate, since it could easily be replaced by a single word like *advocate*. On the other hand, *argue with Bill for* in (24b) is an arbitrary chunk of the sentence rather than a natural predicate; it would be very surprising to find a language in which a single word had the meaning of *argue with Bill for*. Unfortunately, although in many cases it is intuitively straightforward to determine what is and what is not a natural predicate, so far no one has been able to make this notion precise. Clearly, the explication of this notion remains an unsolved problem. However, we will let it rest here, returning to it briefly in chapter 9 in connection with preposition stranding. For the moment we will tentatively assume that intraclausal cases of overgeneration by "Move NP" such as (23) and (24) can be accounted for in terms of this principle, which has been termed the *Natural Predicate Condition*.

As for interclausal overgeneration by "Move NP," observationally speaking, it appears that no NP in a tensed clause is accessible to "Move NP," and that even in an infinitival clause only the subject position is accessible. These two observations have been couched in two general constraints on the application of grammatical rules whose implications go far beyond the simple case of "Move NP" (Chomsky (1973)):

(28)
Tensed-S Condition (TSC)
No rule may relate X and Y in the structure
... X ... $[_\alpha$ ... Y ...$]_\alpha$ ...   (or: ... $[_\alpha$ ... Y ...$]_\alpha$ ... X ...)
where α is a tensed clause.

(29)
Specified Subject Condition (SSC)
No rule may relate X and Y in the structure
... X ... $[_\alpha$ ... Z ... W_1 Y W_2 ...$]_\alpha$ ...
(or: ... $[_\alpha$ ... Z ... W_1 Y W_2 ...$]_\alpha$ ... X ...)
where Z is the subject of W_1 Y W_2.

Several of the notions employed in these conditions are intuitively clear and others will be further explicated below. X and Y are NP-positions; Y is the position from which the NP moves and X the position it is moved to. Hence, the notion "relate" includes movement, as in the case of Subjacency (section 6.1). The domain α is a clausal domain; in other words, $\alpha = S'$. As illustration, consider how these conditions apply in (25) through (27). (For expository reasons we will again use the notation $[_{NP} e]_{NP_i}$ to identify the empty position from which an NP has been moved.)

(26)

c'. $[_{NP} \underline{John}]_{NP_i}$ is likely $[_{S'}$ that $[_{NP} \underline{e}]_{NP_i}$ will leave early$]_{S'}$

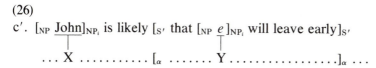

... X .... $[_\alpha$ .... Y ....$]_\alpha$ ...

Since the S'-complement to *likely* in (26c') is a tensed clause, the TSC applies, identifying the relation between X and Y as illicit. In (25b) and (27d) the SSC applies, ruling out both:

(25)

b'. $[_{NP} \underline{Harry}]_{NP_i}$ is expected $[_{S'} \underline{Bill}\ \underline{to\ beat}\ [_{NP} \underline{e}]_{NP_i}\ ]_{S'}$

... X .... $[_\alpha$ Z W_1 Y $W_2]_\alpha$ ...

(27)

d'. $[_{NP} \underline{Harry}]_{NP_i}$ is believed $[_{S'} \underline{Bill}\ \underline{to\ expect}\ [_{S'} [_{NP} \underline{e}]_{NP_i}\ \underline{to\ leave\ early}]_{S'}]_{S'}$

... X .... $[_\alpha$ Z W_1 Y W_2 $]_\alpha$ ...

One might wonder whether these examples could be ruled out by the Natural Predicate Condition. However, similar examples involving Raising instead of Passive show exactly the same pattern:

(30)

*Harry is certain (for) Bill to beat

(31)

*Harry is certain (for) Bill to expect to leave early

Thus, the Natural Predicate Condition cannot be at work here, and these examples must be excluded by the SSC. (27d) and (31) are instructive because they show that being a subject is a necessary but not a sufficient condition for escaping the effect of the SSC. Observe also that nonsubjects of tensed clauses cannot undergo "Move NP" by virtue of both conditions:

(32)

*John is likely that Bill will beat

(32′)

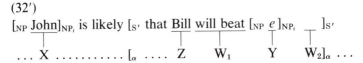

$[_{NP}$ John$]_{NP_i}$ is likely $[_{S'}$ that Bill will beat $[_{NP}$ e $]_{NP_i}$ $]_{S'}$

... X .... $[_α$ .... Z   W$_1$ Y   W$_2]_α$ ...

Thus, the effects of the two conditions overlap in some cases. We will return to this issue in chapter 12.

Despite their highly general formulation, the SSC and TSC as presented so far are straightforward extrapolations from the facts of (25) through (27). In that sense they provide an ad hoc account of these facts; that is, they are generalizations over the facts rather than explanatory principles. Indeed, if that were all there is to these conditions, there would be little interest in studying them further. But the general formulation was chosen for a good reason: the SSC and TSC are much more widely applicable than just to "Move NP." Many other rule-governed "relations between X and Y" are subject to these conditions (although *Wh*-Movement may seem to present a problem since successive cyclic movement appears to be excluded by both of them; see section 7.3). Thus, they may justifiably be regarded as truly explanatory principles. We will briefly look at some of the evidence here; more will be discussed in later chapters.

Consider first the behavior of reflexive pronouns. The most salient property of reflexives is that they must have an antecedent. It turns out that the relationship between antecedent and reflexive is governed by the SSC and TSC. In other words, if we take the antecedent to be X and the reflexive to be Y in (28) and (29), the "distance" (in effect, lack of distance) between reflexive and antecedent is correctly predicted:

(33)

a.   John believes himself to be a genius
b. *John believes that himself is a genius
c. *John believes Mary to like himself

Application of the conditions is straightforward:

(33)

b′. $[_{NP}$ John$]_{NP_i}$ believes $[_{S'}$ that $[_{NP}$ himself$]_{NP_i}$ is a genius$]_{S'}$

... X .... $[_α$ .... Y ....$]_α$ ...

c'. $[_{NP}$ John$]_{NP_i}$ believes $[_{S'}$ Mary to like $[_{NP}$ himself$]_{NP_i}$ ___ $]_{S'}$

... X .... $[_{\alpha}$ Z W_1 Y $W_2]_{\alpha}$ ...

Reciprocals, which also require an antecedent, behave identically:

(34)
a. The boys believe each other to be geniuses
b. *The boys believe that each other are geniuses
c. *The boys believe Mary to like each other

Finally, consider disjoint reference. Unlike reflexives and reciprocals, personal pronouns do not require an antecedent, though they may have one. A pronoun that does have an antecedent must be a certain distance from it. In this respect pronouns are virtually in complementary distribution with reflexives and reciprocals. The expected pattern is therefore the mirror image of (33) and (34), and this is exactly what we find:

(35)
a. *John$_i$ believes him$_i$ to be a genius
b. John$_i$ believes that he$_i$ is a genius
c. John$_i$ believes Mary to like him$_i$

(Stipulated coreference is indicated by identical subscripts.) This pattern can be easily accounted for by assuming a rule that specifies under which conditions a given NP *cannot* be the antecedent of a given pronoun. The existence of the SSC and TSC now allows this rule to be formulated in the most general way:

(36)
Disjoint Reference
*... NP$_i$ ... pronoun$_i$ ...
(antecedent)

If X is the antecedent and Y the pronoun, the desired result follows: rule (36) will apply, preventing the pronoun from taking the NP as its antecedent, unless the SSC or the TSC applies to prevent rule (36) itself from operating. When either of these conditions does apply, the pronoun is free to take the NP as its antecedent:

(35)

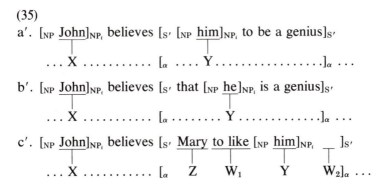

a'. [$_{NP}$ John]$_{NP_i}$ believes [$_{S'}$ [$_{NP}$ him]$_{NP_i}$ to be a genius]$_{S'}$

...X .... [$_\alpha$ .... Y..................]$_\alpha$ ...

b'. [$_{NP}$ John]$_{NP_i}$ believes [$_{S'}$ that [$_{NP}$ he]$_{NP_i}$ is a genius]$_{S'}$

...X .... [$_\alpha$ .... Y.............]$_\alpha$ ...

c'. [$_{NP}$ John]$_{NP_i}$ believes [$_{S'}$ Mary to like [$_{NP}$ him]$_{NP_i}$ __]$_{S'}$

...X .... [$_\alpha$ Z W_1 Y W_2]$_\alpha$ ...

In (35a') neither condition applies to block (36). Consequently, (36) applies to exclude the antecedent-pronoun relation. In (35b') and (35c') the TSC and the SSC respectively apply to block rule (36), with the result that the antecedent-pronoun relation is licit.

Clearly, then, these principles account straightforwardly for a wide range of seemingly disparate phenomena. Before we turn to yet another interesting empirical extension of the SSC and TSC, though, let us reconsider the question of establishing a typology of transformations in terms of their domain of application (sections 2.8, 4.1). Recall that

a. Earlier work had assumed that there were three types of transformations: monocyclic (such as Passive and Reflexivization), bicyclic (such as Equi-NP-Deletion and Raising), and unbounded (such as Wh-Movement).

b. Wh-Movement is really a bicyclic transformation, given the principle of the cycle and the Subjacency Condition.

c. There are counterexamples to the monocyclic nature of such rules as Passive and Reflexivization, counterexamples that so far could only be accounted for by introducing the ad hoc rule of Raising-to-Object (although nothing in our theory about "Move NP" excludes the possibility of subject NPs being raised to the object position of a matrix clause (see chapter 15)).

But observe now that the SSC and the TSC jointly explain the very nature of the counterexamples in (c). These conditions, say, essentially, that whenever a rule operates bicyclically (i.e., across a cyclic boundary), the lower of the two positions related by that rule must be the subject of an infinitival clause. This is exactly correct for the "exceptional" bicyclic application of such allegedly monocyclic rules as Passive and Reflexivization. But it is equally true of those rules that were assumed to be bicyclic all along, namely, Equi-NP-Deletion and Raising: all of these involve the subject of an infinitival clause. Thus, three highly general universal principles—the Subjacency Condition, the SSC, and the TSC—make it possible to eliminate all domain restrictions from the formulation of individual rules, thereby again drastically reducing the expressive power of transformational rules. A transformation can only be formulated as an unbounded rule. However, its functioning is limited to adjacent cyclic domains by the Subjacency Condition and further to the subject of an infinitival clause by the SSC and TSC whenever the application is bicyclic. (One important proviso must be added for the case of *Wh*-Movement; this will be discussed in the next section.) This reduction in the expressive power of transformations is another important step toward a theory of grammar that may pretend to explain the child's acquisition of grammar.

To conclude our discussion of the SSC and TSC, consider a further range of facts. We have seen that NPs can have subjects. That is, the position of the possessive NP is, in a sense, the subject position of the NP. Now, does the SSC apply to these subjects as well? In other words, can α in (29) have NP, as well as S', as its value? The answer is yes. We would not expect to be able to show this for "Move NP," because the A-over-A Principle prevents the extraction of an NP from a larger NP in any case, regardless of whether that NP contains a subject or not. But what about reflexives and reciprocals? Here the effect of the SSC is directly detectable:

(37)
a.   John read a story about himself
b. *John read Mary's story about himself

(38)
a.   The boys read stories about each other
b. *The boys read Mary's stories about each other
c.   The boys read each other's stories about Mary

The rule of Disjoint Reference (36) appears to be equally sensitive to the SSC, though for some reason the possessive pronoun does not act like a normal pronoun:

(39)
a. *John$_i$ read a story about him$_i$
b.   John$_i$ read Mary's$_j$ story about him$_i$
c.   John$_i$ read his$_i$ story about Mary

In (39c), as opposed to (39a), the intended coreference is permitted. These extensions of the SSC are by no means as uncontroversial as the above remarks suggest. For details, see the works mentioned at the end of the chapter.

Finally, consider whether α ranges over S' and NP for the TSC as well as for the SSC. One might say that it does but that $\alpha = $ NP is vacuous for the TSC since NPs can never be tensed. But there is more to the issue than that, for this assumption predicts that the effect of the TSC will show up in a language that does distinguish between tensed and nontensed NPs. George and Kornfilt (1981) have argued that Turkish is indeed such a language. They observe that the head noun sometimes agrees with the possessive NP and sometimes does not, and suggest that there is a close parallelism between NPs with agreement and tensed clauses, on the one hand, and NPs without agreement and infinitivals, on the other. Such a parallelism is natural because English, French, Dutch, and many other languages display subject-verb agreement in tensed clauses but not in infinitivals. Whenever agreement is present in a Turkish NP, that NP is an island; that is, not even its subject is accessible for relations with positions outside that NP. On the other hand, NPs without agreement do exhibit the expected accessibility. Consequently, the TSC could have been formulated in terms of presence vs. absence of agreement. George and Kornfilt argue that this option should be chosen because it directly extends to the Turkish case. This constitutes further interesting evidence for the TSC and the extension of α to NP.

7.3 Which Constraints Apply to Which Rules?

We now turn to question (a): Does the Subjacency Condition, which governs the behavior of "Move wh," also apply to "Move NP"? Given the results of the previous section, we should also ask the question the other way around. Do the SSC and TSC, which govern the behavior of "Move NP," also apply to "Move wh"? Both questions are complex, and we cannot do them full justice here. In one form or another they will, however, reappear in later chapters.

Considering the second question first, observe that the theory so far predicts that "Move wh" cannot cross clause boundaries:

(40)
Who do you think that Bill saw

(40′)

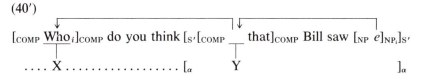

$[_{\text{COMP}} \underline{\text{Who}}_i]_{\text{COMP}}$ do you think $[_{S'}[_{\text{COMP}} \underline{\quad} \text{that}]_{\text{COMP}}$ Bill saw $[_{\text{NP}} e]_{\text{NP}_i}]_{S'}$

.... X .... $[_\alpha$ Y $]_\alpha$

Although the first step of movement into COMP is clearly allowed, the second step is prohibited by the TSC and perhaps the SSC. In the case of the SSC, we might say that the complementizer is not part of the predicate of which *Bill* is the subject. On this assumption we would not expect the SSC to take effect—a desirable result. With the TSC, however, things are different. There is no denying that $\alpha = S'$ is a tensed clause. Nevertheless, extraction is possible. It would thus appear necessary to assume that the TSC (and the SSC) do not apply to "Move *wh*." It will turn out later (see in particular chapter 9) that this solution has much to recommend itself, even though at the moment it seems to be merely the easy way out.

In fact, we have been tacitly assuming a type of null hypothesis with regard to the relationship between rules and constraints, namely, that every constraint applies to every rule. This is simply a consequence of the general scientific endeavor of keeping the theory as simple and elegant as possible. Note that this goal of simplicity and elegance is quite independent of the desire to reduce the expressive power of the theory of grammar. The latter is a crucial element in accounting for the language acquisition problem, whereas the former applies with equal force to Universal Grammar, that part of the grammar which does not have to be learned.

To maintain the null hypothesis, the constraints must be reformulated somewhat. Two possibilities suggest themselves. The first would be to stipulate that $\alpha = S$. This would be in line with the fact that, in English at least, S (not S′) is the bounding node for Subjacency. The assumption that the α of the SSC and TSC is S would straightforwardly predict that the second step of "Move *wh*" in (40′) is possible. On the other hand, this assumption has the disadvantage of creating problems for the first step, since now every movement from within a clause to the COMP of that clause will cross an S-boundary. The first step in (40′), for example, would be ruled out by both the SSC and the TSC. Consequently, this solution would require further modifications that we will not pursue here (see Chomsky (1977a) for discussion).

Another solution is simply to stipulate that the constraints do not apply to elements that are moved from COMP. Under this approach, which is the one advocated in Chomsky (1973), COMP has come to be called an *escape hatch* via which elements can escape from the effect of the SSC and TSC. This escape hatch proposal can be formalized by adding a proviso to the TSC (28) and the SSC (29):

(41)

. . . where Y is not in COMP

This allows a straightforward definition of the conditions that must be fulfilled for any element to escape from a clause: either it must be moved from a COMP by (41), or it must be the subject of an infinitival clause.

As for the converse question, the same null hypothesis leads to the assumption that "Move NP" is also subject to the Subjacency Condition. None of the examples we have studied violates Subjacency. In fact, "Move NP" cannot violate Subjacency without simultaneously violating the SSC, the TSC, or both. This can be seen in example (27d) (repeated here):

(27)

d.   *Harry is believed Bill to expect to leave early

d'. $[_{NP}$ Harry$]_{NP_i}$ is believed $[_S$ Bill to expect $[_S[_{NP}$ $e]_{NP_i}$ to leave early$]_S]_S$

(27d) is ruled out by Subjacency, but as (27d') shows, it is also ruled out by the SSC. This is characteristic. The conclusion must be that "Move NP" never violates Subjacency but that Subjacency does not do any work for "Move NP." In other words, "Move NP" obeys Subjacency vacuously. It is interesting to see whether cases can be constructed that would provide direct evidence on whether or not "Move NP" is subject to Subjacency. But there are no interesting results to report.

Thus, it appears so far that although some problems exist, there are no *immediate* reasons to abandon the null hypothesis that every constraint applies to every type of rule. However, over the years more serious reasons have been found for doing so, which we will discuss in section 9.2.3.

7.4 Concluding Remarks: "Move α"

Linguists have found that the strategy that led to postulating "Move *wh*" is applicable to certain constructions in which an NP moves to another NP position. In particular, the earlier rules constituting Passive and Raising have been reduced to a very general rule of "Move NP." The massive overgeneration that results from this generalization can be effectively neutralized by introducing two extremely general universal constraints, the Specified Subject Condition and the Tensed-S Condition.

The conclusion that both rules of syntax, "Move NP" and "Move *wh*," are subject to the three main constraints of syntax, Subjacency, the SSC, and the TSC, is an important one. It suggests that even greater generalization is possible. And in fact it has been proposed that the two rules be united into one single, optimally general rule schema: "Move α":

(42)

"Move α"

Move any category α anywhere.

(It will be important to keep in mind that although "Move NP" (NP-Movement) and "Move *wh*" (*Wh*-Movement) have been collapsed as two subcases of "Move α," they have been found to have many different properties; hence, for ease of reference, we will continue to refer to these two instances of "Move α" by their individual names.)

Many new problems of overgeneration have arisen, of course. And many of these have so far not been adequately dealt with. Nevertheless, the postulation of "Move α" dramatically illustrates the attempt to reduce the expressive power of transformations and to shift the descriptive burden to highly general universal constraints. It suggests an interesting and appealing hypothesis about the core of the syntactic component of Universal Grammar: that it consists of one universal rule, "Move α," and three universal constraints, Subjacency, the Specified Subject Condition, and the Tensed-S Condition.

7.5 Bibliographical Comments

The theory of "Move NP" described in this chapter is essentially that of Chomsky (1973), the article in which the Specified Subject Condition and the Tensed-S Condition were first proposed. The approach introduced there is extended in Chomsky (1976) and a number of other important articles. Since most of these are written in the framework of so-called trace theory, which we will discuss in chapter 9, more references concerning "Move NP" are given there.

Whether some phenomena that look like cases of "Move NP" should be treated in the lexicon is an important issue, to which our brief discussion should be considered only an introduction. Freidin (1975) argues that passives should not be handled by a transformation, and Wasow (1977) proposes that certain instances of the passive construction should be handled in the lexicon. On the other hand, Keyser and Roeper (1984) suggest that the middle voice construction should be dealt with in the syntax. In the absence of a solid theoretical distinction between lexical rules and syntactic rules, the issue remains complex and unresolved. Hoekstra, Van der Hulst, and Moortgat (1980a) provides a good overview. More recently, Williams (1981b) has developed a framework for dealing with rules that change argument structure (like Passive) in the lexicon within the framework presented here.

A more fundamental change in the theory has been advocated by Joan Bresnan, who argues that all of what is here presented as syntax should be handled in the lexicon. This proposal has been developed as the theory of Lexical Functional Grammar (see references in section 3.8).

As we have barely hinted, the Passive rule interacts in interesting ways with semantics. The relationship between the syntax of passives and their model-theoretic interpretation is discussed in Bach (1980), Hellan (1981), and Keenan (1980).

Finally, George and Kornfilt (1981) is just one of a great many publications discussing passive-like constructions in a great variety of languages.

In the context of developing the rule "Move α," it is interesting to note that the possibility of a universal theory of transformations was envisaged very early by Bach (1965), who recognized that certain transformations such as Passive and Question Formation seem to occur with many of the same fundamental properties in many different languages. This insight led him to propose a conception of Universal Grammar that offered a short list of "major transformations" from which specific languages could select their rules.

Chapter 8
Control

NP-Movement ("Move NP") represents a large empirical generalization, encompassing at least the syntactic relations of passive and raising. Might NP-Movement be generalized further to include such structures as (1) (known as *control structures*), in which a relation holds between the subject of the matrix (here, *John*) and the subject of the embedded infinitive?

(1)
John wants to leave

For instance, such examples might be given a d-structure similar to that of passive sentences—in other words, a d-structure to which NP-Movement could apply:

(2)
a. e wants John to leave → John$_i$ wants e_i to leave
b. e is believed John to have left → John$_i$ is believed e_i to have left

However, there are reasons for not extending NP-Movement to these control structures. In this chapter we will review these reasons and consider the nature of the mechanism by which the relation in (1) is generally thought to be governed, the mechanism of PRO Construal.

8.1 The θ-Criterion

The earliest writing on control structures distinguished them from NP-Movement structures, one of the arguments for this being the "argument from selectional restrictions." In the case of NP-Movement to subject position, as in (2b), the passive verb *believed* imposes no selectional restrictions on the surface subject. Anything that can be an NP can be a subject of the passive verb *believed:*

(3)
a. There was believed to have been a riot
b. It was believed to be clear that John was there

However, the subject *is* sensitive to the choice of the embedded verb:

(4)
a. *There was believed to have left
b. *It was believed to have introspected

This is typical of movement: the moved NP is restricted not by virtue of its surface position, but rather by virtue of its D-Structure position.

The "selectional restrictions" imposed by a verb are restrictions on the types of arguments it can have. If we say that *believe* is a two-place predicate, a relation between a believer and a thing believed, then we might expect the first argument to be a human, or at least something to which it would be sensible to ascribe beliefs, and the second argument to be roughly propositional. In other words, a verb like *believe* assigns the semantic role or θ-*role* (theta-role) of believer to its first argument and the θ-role of belief to its second argument. Though we will not go into the semantic content of such θ-roles, we will use the term to identify the arguments of predicates.

From this, we might conclude that where a verb does not impose selectional restrictions on its subject, the NP in that subject position does not receive a θ-role from that verb. This seems entirely appropriate for the case of *believed,* the passive participle of *believe,* for which we could reasonably say that the surface subject is not an argument, but rather that the subject plus the embedded infinitive form a discontinuous argument:

(5)
John was believed to have left
The argument of *believe* is "John to have left"

John is an argument of *left,* not of *believed.* Thus, the subject position of a sentence whose main verb is *believed* is not a θ-role-receiving position (in short, a non-θ-position or $\bar{\theta}$-*position;* the overbar here means 'non' and should not be confused with the bar in $\overline{X}$-theory). At least, it is not a position in which an argument of the verb *believed* is to be found.

NP-Movement in general is movement to $\bar{\theta}$-positions; or, to state matters more neutrally, movement is a relation between a θ-position and a $\bar{\theta}$-position (of course, iterated movements will involve relations between $\bar{\theta}$-positions and $\bar{\theta}$-positions). This fundamental characteristic of movement was called the *Argument Uniqueness Condition* (Freidin (1978)) and later the *θ-Criterion* (Chomsky (1981c)). We may state the criterion as follows:

(6)

θ-Criterion

A lexical NP must occupy one and only one θ-position.

It is necessary to be precise in interpreting the term *occupy* in (6), particularly in cases where an NP has been moved. Using the notation introduced in chapter 4, such cases have the structure ... NP_i ... e_i ..., where e_i is called the *trace* of the moved NP_i and where (for reasons that will become apparent in chapter 9) NP_i is said to *bind* the trace e_i. Now *occupy* can be defined to mean "occupy in the ordinary sense or bind a trace that occupies." Thus, for example, in the passive sentence (5) *John* occupies a θ-position of *left,* since *John* binds a trace in the subject position of *left* and since that subject position is a θ-position of *left*. Moreover, that is the only θ-position that *John* occupies, because the subject position of *believed* is not a θ-position.

The most striking thing about control constructions is that they do not obey the θ-Criterion, at least if the empty subject of the infinitive involved is taken to be a trace, or trace-like. That is, control structures involve a relation between two θ-positions, one of them null—a relation prohibited for movement by the θ-Criterion, which allows only relations between θ- and $\bar{\theta}$-positions or $\bar{\theta}$- and $\bar{\theta}$-positions. Consider (7), for example:

(7)

John wants to introspect

We can independently vary the main and subordinate verbs, and we see that the subject is sensitive to both of these verb choices, thus implying that the surface subject is an argument of both verbs:

(8)

a. *The argument wants — to be convincing
      (Cf. *The argument was convincing*)
b. *John wants — to be transfinite
      (Cf. *John wants to be patient*)

If the surface subject in such constructions is an argument of both the main and the subordinate verbs, and if such constructions arise via movement, then the θ-Criterion cannot hold. Thus, identifying control structures as a further case of movement would at least make the statement of the θ-Criterion more difficult.

For the remainder of this chapter, we will identify cases of control as the cases where the θ-Criterion fails to hold, that is, as the cases in which an NP and a null position to which it is related are each independent θ-positions.

8.2 The Mechanism of Control

Since the above considerations discourage positing movement in control structures, it remains to define the status of the empty subject position in control structures—if movement is not involved, it cannot be trace. The abbreviation *PRO* has been devised to stand for a phonetically null (i.e., "inaudible") pronoun that occupies the subject position of infinitives in control structures. Thus, example (1) will look like this:

(9)
John wants PRO to leave

The problem of control structures will then come down to the problem of determining (a) the distribution of the item PRO and (b) the rules for fixing the antecedent or controller for this item, like *John* in (9). In the rest of this chapter we will discuss preliminary efforts at resolving these issues.

PRO is not to be identified with trace, even though the two share certain properties. We will discuss the relation of PRO to trace, and to other items, in chapters 9, 12, 16, and 17. For the time being, we will leave matters in the following state: PRO is distinct from trace, at least insofar as the θ-Criterion is concerned. In fact, PRO will count as a "lexical NP" for the θ-Criterion. PRO is generated in D-Structure, whereas traces arise as a consequence of movement in the derivation of S-Structure. We will further assume that PRO is assigned an antecedent at some level of representation, a level known as *Logical Form* or *LF* (see chapters 11 through 13). (*Assigned an antecedent* means "is co-indexed with some NP," just as a reflexive would be.) As before, the current research strategy is to state the rule as generally as possible and then seek to constrain its operation by general principles:

(10)

PRO Construal

... NP ... PRO ... → ... NP$_i$ ... PRO$_i$ ...

In the next two sections we will consider constraints on the PRO-antecedent relation, as well as absolute constraints on the distribution of PRO. First, however, let us consider the semantic status of PRO— that is, the "interpretation" of PRO.

The Standard Theory, in which D-Structure was the full determinant of meaning, held that control relations were to be expressed by a deletion transformation, this transformation being governed by a condition of identity: the subject of an infinitive was deleted if it was identical to some previous NP. However, it was later shown that certain notions of identity were not sufficient. For example, the alleged d-structure (11a) does not have the same meaning as the s-structure (11b); rather, (11b) means something like (11c), and (11a) has the interpretation (11d):

(11)
a. Everyone wants everyone to win
b. Everyone$_i$ wants PRO$_i$ to win
c. For all x, x wants x to win
d. For all x, x wants that for all y, y win

Translating this into the terms provided by the rule of PRO Construal, we might say that a PRO coindexed with a quantified NP acts like an instance of the same variable that the quantified NP binds. Thus, by translating PRO$_i$ in (11b) as the third x in (11c), we say it is an instance of the same variable as the second x in (11c). In this respect, PRO is like reflexives and pronouns:

(12)
a. Everyone likes everyone
b. Everyone$_i$ likes himself$_i$
c. Everyone thinks that everyone is sick
d. Everyone$_i$ thinks that he$_i$ is sick

Here, the ordinary pronoun and the reflexive are also acting like bound variables, variables bound by the quantified phrase they are coindexed with. If we regard coindexing as a means of indicating "instance of the same variable as," then it is reasonable to extend this notation to PRO.

8.3 Structural Conditions on PRO Construal

Since the NP ... PRO relation cannot obtain in every possible configuration, principles must be found that determine the limits of that relation. In this section and in section 8.5 we will consider the relation
between PRO and its antecedent, and in section 8.4 we will consider its
distribution.

Since PRO is coindexed with its antecedent, just like trace (though
by different means) and reflexives, the null hypothesis would predict
that the relation of PRO to its antecedent should be governed by the
SSC, the TSC, and Subjacency. The following example, while showing
that control is not subject to the TSC, at least indicates that it might be
governed by the SSC:

(13)
a. John$_i$ thinks [that [PRO$_i$ to kill himself$_i$] would be a mistake]
b. Susan$_i$ believes [Mary$_j$ thinks that [PRO$_{\left\{{*i \atop j}\right\}}$ to kill herself$_{\left\{{*i \atop j}\right\}}$]

   would be a mistake]

Here the intervention of *Mary* seems to make a control relation between PRO and *Susan* impossible. However, (14) seems to show that
control is in fact not subject to the SSC or Subjacency:

(14)
John$_i$ thinks that [it is impossible [PRO$_i$ to kill himself]]

The net result of these examples is that control is subject to no constraints, and in fact they conflict with regard to the SSC. We will sort
out some of this in section 8.5.

8.4 The Distribution of PRO

One of the most striking facts about the control relation is that PRO is
always the subject of an infinitive, and never occurs in any other position. We will broach this topic here and return to it in chapters 9, 10,
and 14.

One attempt to explain PRO's appearance in subject position simply
denies the existence of PRO altogether, maintaining that what this theory calls an S with a PRO subject is actually a base-generated VP:

(15)
a. John wants [$_S$ PRO to win]$_S$ (S-theory)
b. John wants [$_{VP}$ to win]$_{VP}$ (VP-theory)

In fact, such an assumption has far-reaching consequences. For instance, it entails that Passive cannot be a movement transformation, and that passive VPs must be generated in their surface form, because of examples like (16):

(16)
John wants to be arrested

In fact, the movement component of the description of raising constructions must be eliminated as well. Evaluating these consequences here would take us too far afield, but we will return to this issue in chapter 10.

One problem for the VP-theory is the existence of structures like (17):

(17)
John wondered what PRO to do

It is difficult to escape the conclusion that *what PRO to do* is a sentence. If it is a VP, then a COMP slot must be added to VP:

(18)
VP → COMP VP

But then further otherwise unnecessary restrictions will be needed to prevent this slot from occurring, and from being filled in ordinary tensed sentences:

(19)
*John [$_{COMP}$ who$_i$]$_{COMP}$ saw [e]$_i$

Thus, there must be at least some cases where the nonappearance of a subject NP of an infinitive cannot be attributed to the direct (non-S-dominated) generation of VP. If PRO exists even just for these infinitival *wh*-question constructions, one might still ask why its distribution is limited to subject position. One possible answer will be given in chapters 16 and 17, based on the notions of government and case.

A related question is, What can be the subject of an infinitive besides PRO? In general, infinitives in English do not seem to allow lexical subjects:

(20)
a. *John tried Bill to win
b. *Bill to win would be fun
c. *I don't know who Bill to talk to

The exceptions are when the infinitive contains the complementizer *for*, or when it is the complement of a certain narrow class of verbs:

(21)
a. John is anxious for Bill to leave
b. John Xs Bill to leave   (X = want, expect, believe)

In fact, most languages do not seem to have even these options. It seems, then, that having a PRO subject is the "unmarked" case for infinitives, and having a lexical subject is the "marked" case.

One way to construe the notions "marked" and "unmarked" is in terms of language learning. The marked case must be learned as a language-particular fact, whereas the unmarked case is what the language learner will assume to be the case (because it is determined by the innate language faculty), in the absence of facts to the contrary.

A straightforward way of stating the unmarked situation is by means of a filter blocking infinitival S with a lexical subject:

(22)
*[NP to VP], where NP is lexical

This filter combines with the interpretation of trace and PRO to predict the following pattern:

(23)
a. John wants PRO to leave
b. John expects PRO to leave
c. *John tried Bill to leave
d. *It seems John to be there

The exclusion of lexical NPs from the subject position of infinitivals is part of a broader and more complicated pattern including trace, which we will take up in section 10.1.3.

8.5 Obligatory and Optional Control

Returning now to the relation between PRO and its antecedent, we will introduce a distinction that will be important in later discussion.

One class of control structures, known as cases of *obligatory control,* is characterized by a number of properties:

(24)

a. There must be a controller.
b. The controller must be the subject or object of the immediately dominating clause.
c. Lexical NP cannot be substituted for PRO.

Typically, but not always, these cases occur in the complements to certain verbs. One such verb is *try:*

(25)

a. *It was tried [PRO to leave]
b. *It was tried by John [PRO to leave]
c. *John tried (for) Bill to leave

In (25a) there is no possible controller; in (25b) the controller is not in subject or object position; and in (25c) a lexical NP has been substituted for PRO.

A fourth property, which is actually subsumed under (24b), is that the control relation for obligatory control is subject to the SSC:

(26)

*John$_i$ wants Mary to try [PRO$_i$ to shave himself]

There are also many control structures that do not exhibit properties (24a–c), known as cases of *optional* or *nonobligatory control.* Typical instances are infinitives in subject position and infinitival indirect questions. These constructions need not have a controller at all, and if they have one, it need not be the subject or object of the higher S:

(27)

a. It is unknown (to us) [what PRO to do]
b. [PRO to leave] would be nice (for us)

In the subject infinitive, a lexical NP can be substituted for PRO:

(28)

For Bill to leave would be nice

(This is not true for the infinitival indirect question, but for reasons not pertinent here.) Finally, nonobligatory control cases seem not to be subject to the SSC, as noted earlier in example (14).

When PRO does not have an antecedent, as in (27a–b) with the parenthesized phrases omitted, it receives an "arbitrary" or "generic" interpretation; for example, (27a) means "It is unknown what one should do." This interpretation arises only for nonobligatory control PRO, of course, since only this PRO can lack an antecedent.

8.6 Bibliographical Comments

The analysis of control in the Standard Theory alluded to in section 8.2 was due to Rosenbaum (1967). The deletion rule he proposed was called *Identity Erasure,* but it soon became known as *Equi-NP-Deletion* or simply *EQUI.* An extensive examination of the properties of EQUI is found in Postal (1970), where the terms *control* and *controller* were also introduced. The first argument to the effect that control phenomena cannot be handled by deletion under identity was offered in Partee (1971), the paper having been presented originally in the spring of 1969. The ensuing interpretive conception of control was incorporated into the semantic theory of Jackendoff (1972, chap. 5).

The θ-Criterion was formulated under the name "Argument Uniqueness Condition" in Freidin (1978). Further references can be found in chapter 15, where we discuss the role of the θ-Criterion in linguistic theory in greater detail.

The VP-complement analysis of control, which has had a certain appeal in view of attempts to eliminate both transformations and lexically empty positions such as *e* and PRO altogether, has been perhaps most forcefully defended in Brame (1976, 1979). This is also, in essence, the conception of control that is adopted in Generalized Phrase Structure Grammar and Lexical Functional Grammar. Within the latter framework a detailed account of control phenomena is presented in Bresnan (1982a). For a model-theoretic discussion of control, see Bach (1979).

Our discussion of the distribution of PRO in section 8.4 is largely based on Chomsky and Lasnik (1977), to which we return in chapter 10.

The distinction between obligatory control PRO and optional control PRO is explored in detail in Williams (1980). More recent advances in control theory will be presented in part IV. Contributions that presuppose those advances are Bouchard (1984) and Koster (1984).

Chapter 9
Trace Theory

9.1 The Concept of Trace

In several chapters we have used traces as an expository device. In many cases it has been useful to be able to refer to the "extraction site" or "gap" (the position from which some element has been moved). We have variably used devices like □ or e to indicate such an extraction site. Should such "traces" or diacritics for extraction sites be permitted in linguistic theory? The main questions, which we discuss in order, are these:

(1)
a. Does the introduction of traces not unduly increase the expressive power of the theory?
b. Can the use of traces be empirically motivated?

9.1.1 The Status of Traces
A trace is a syntactic category (such as NP) that has been voided of phonological content and internal structure, retaining only an index that is identical to the index of the material that was moved out of the trace position. The index is necessary to keep track of which category the trace is the trace of. This is particularly important if more than one movement has taken place in the same clause. A trace, then, is a co-indexed empty category. The notation in (2a) has been devised to represent the trace and the moved element (though for typographical ease the category labels (which are generally obvious) and the brackets are often omitted, as in (2b)):

(2)

a. [$_{NP}$ Who]$_{NP_i}$ did you see [$_{NP}$ e]$_{NP_i}$

b. Who$_i$ did you see e_i

As in mathematics, e is the identity element, not a terminal. t and sometimes τ are also used for trace.

We have already encountered the concept "empty category." For example, the existence of such categories is necessary in formulating the structure-preserving property of transformations. PRO also shares with trace the property of being phonologically empty.

The only really new property of trace, then, is that it is coindexed with the moved element. Traces make it possible to keep track of any movement that has occurred in the sentence. To what extent does the introduction of a device that keeps track of derivations increase the expressive power of the theory? In a direct sense, not at all. What is being compared is two conceptions of derived structure, with and without traces. Whether to include traces in the theory or not is thus on a par with a host of other questions about derived structure, such as: How does adjunction work? When a rule deletes an element, does it also delete the dominating category or categories? When a grammatical morpheme is inserted, how much structure must be introduced? Where trace is concerned, the question is, What does linguistic theory say about derived structure after movement? Does the extraction site disappear or does the empty category remain? Does *Wh*-Movement produce structures like (3a) or (3b)?

(3)

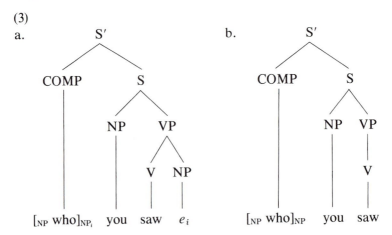

The most important thing to realize is that the choice between (3a) and (3b) is a choice at the level of linguistic theory and not at the level of the grammar. In other words, positing the existence of trace does not create a situation such that for every movement rule the language learner must learn whether or not its output contains a trace. Once it is decided that movements leave traces, then all movements leave traces. Hence, the expressive power of the theory is not directly increased.

Nevertheless, care is needed, because it is possible to make illicit use of traces: if they are permitted in syntactic representations, other rules could be made to refer to them in unwanted ways. For example, it would be possible to formulate rules such as (4):

(4)
a. Delete a *wh*-phrase in COMP if its trace is preceded by V and followed by PP.
b. $Who_i \rightarrow whom_i$ if who_i has been moved three times (i.e., has three traces).
c. Delete a trace if it is in COMP and precedes *that*.

This we might call an indirect increase of the expressive power of the theory—clearly an undesirable effect. But the real problem resides not in the introduction of traces, but rather in the absence of a general and restrictive theory of deletion and substitution rules, among others. Suppose, for example, that we had a theory about deletion saying that deletion rules and substitution rules are always local rules and that the contextual triggers (or, mentioned but unaffected elements) must always be phonologically realized. Then the rules in (4) could not be written. Assuming the pursuit of such a theory of deletion to be the right strategy in the general search for a more restrictive theory about rules of grammar, the introduction of traces will not have any unwanted side effects.

We may conclude, then, that concern about the expressive power of the theory is largely irrelevant to the introduction of traces. The relevant question—to which we now turn—is purely empirical: Does this move increase the explanatory depth of the theory?

9.1.2 The Motivation for Traces: Proper Binding

The principal motivation for traces comes from the parallelism between movement structures and antecedent-anaphor relations. Relevant to this parallelism are two new notions: *anaphor* and *c-command*. Anaphors are NPs that require an antecedent. In particular, reflexives, reciprocals, and obligatory control PRO are anaphors. C-command is an important structural relation among nodes in a tree. Its definition is given in (5a) and illustrated in (5b):

(5)

a. *C-command:* A c-commands B if and only if the first branching node dominating A also dominates B, and A does not itself dominate B.

b.

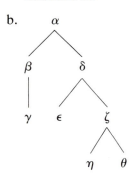

Both β and γ c-command δ and every node dominated by δ. β does not c-command γ. ϵ c-commands ζ, η, and θ, but not β and γ.

The notion of c-command is crucially involved both in movement structures and in anaphoric relations. Essentially, movement must always be to a c-commanding position and an anaphor must always be c-commanded by its antecedent.

In NP-Movement the position to which movement takes place is the subject NP of VP, which therefore c-commands all positions dominated by that VP, including the trace positions (an NP dominated by the VP, or the subject position of an infinitival complement dominated by that VP). In *Wh*-Movement the COMP to which a *wh*-phrase moves will always c-command the S from which that *wh*-phrase was extracted. Similarly, an antecedent must c-command its anaphor. This suggests the following generalization:

(6)
$$\begin{Bmatrix} \text{A moved element} \\ \text{An antecedent} \end{Bmatrix} \text{ must c-command } \begin{Bmatrix} \text{its trace} \\ \text{its anaphor} \end{Bmatrix}.$$

To carry the analogy further, we might say that a trace has anaphor properties and that the moved phrase has antecedent properties. Then the fact that movement must always be to a c-commanding position will automatically follow from the independently necessary principle that an anaphor must be c-commanded by its antecedent. This property is often referred to as *proper binding:*

(7)

Proper binding: An anaphor (including trace) must be properly bound (i.e., coindexed and c-commanded) by its antecedent (including moved phrases).

In the case of NP-Movement the parallelism is quite impressive. As we saw in chapter 7, the Specified Subject Condition (SSC) and the Tensed-S Condition (TSC) apply not only to NP-Movement but also to the antecedent-anaphor relation. The following patterns emerge:

(8)
a. John$_i$ was killed e_i
b. John$_i$ killed himself$_i$

(9)
a. John$_i$ was expected e_i to win
b. John$_i$ expected himself$_i$ to win

(10)
a. *John$_i$ was expected that e_i would win
b. *John$_i$ expected that himself$_i$ would win

(11)
a. *John$_i$ was expected Bill to kill e_i
b. *John$_i$ expected Bill to kill himself$_i$

(10a–b) are ruled out by the TSC and (11a–b) by the SSC, strongly confirming the essential unity of movement patterns and anaphoric patterns. (We will see in section 9.2 that this unity, which is straightforward for NP-Movement, is much less obvious for *Wh*-Movement.)

To what extent do these observations bear on the existence of traces? To answer this question, we must first consider how the relationship between antecedents and anaphors is established. (See chapters 5, 13, and 18 for more details.) In line with the lexicalist approach, it is commonly assumed either that reflexive and reciprocal pronouns are base-generated without an index and that some rule of semantic interpretation assigns them an antecedent, subject to the SSC and TSC, or that they are base-generated with some arbitrary index and the rule establishes whether they have a legitimate antecedent. This may be called the *Anaphor Rule*.

One way of expressing the parallelism, then, is to say that the SSC and TSC apply both to movement and to the Anaphor Rule. This would be a natural assumption in light of the null hypothesis that all constraints apply to all rules. However, the introduction of the concept of trace allows the two cases to be unified in another, ultimately preferable way. If NP-Movement leaves behind a coindexed trace, we can say that the Anaphor Rule must apply to such traces since they have the status of anaphors. In other words, NP-Movement appears to be constrained by the SSC and TSC—in fact, however, it is not, but its output must undergo the Anaphor Rule, which is. Thus, the TSC and SSC can now be viewed as conditions on representations rather than as conditions on rule applications.

The phenomena discussed in section 9.2, along with further developments of the theory to be described later, also provide motivation for trace theory.

9.1.3 The Projection Principle

Recall the statement of the θ-Criterion:

(12)

θ-Criterion

A lexical NP must occupy one and only one θ-position.

The θ-Criterion makes crucial use of the notion "trace" since *occupy* means "lexically occupy or bind a trace that occupies." (These notions will be made more precise in terms of the notion "chain" to be introduced in later chapters.) For example:

(13)

John$_i$ was killed e_i

By virtue of (12), *John* cannot be both the subject argument and the object argument of *kill*. Since *John* binds a trace in the object argument position, it cannot be a subject argument. It then also follows from (12) that the subject position in which *John* stands at S-Structure must be a nonargument position.

The Projection Principle carries the θ-Criterion one step further. It requires, in effect, that (12) hold at all nonphonological levels of representation:

(14)

Projection Principle

The θ-Criterion (12) holds at D-Structure, S-Structure, and LF.

Since information about the argument structure of verbs is represented in the lexicon, (14) says basically that the major properties of the three nonphonological levels of representation of any given derivation can be independently projected from the lexicon—hence the name *Projection Principle*. (We take up consequences of this principle in chapter 15.) Again, this is a principle that could not hold if traces were not available.

9.2 A Preliminary Classification of Empty Elements

This section discusses some of the consequences of "Move α" and trace theory. Chapter 7 ended with the tentative conclusion that there is just one core rule of syntax: "Move α." In other words, even the two highly general rules "Move NP" and "Move *wh*" are completely identified. On the other hand, there are differences, sometimes significant ones, between the constructions in which these rules are crucially involved. If the full generality of the "Move α" hypothesis is to be maintained, any differences must be attributed to the traces occurring in these constructions. To put it more generally, without challenging the "Move α" hypothesis, we may ask whether all traces exhibit the same behavior under rules and principles that apply *after* the transformational component (that is, after "Move α"). Significantly, it will turn out that some of the differences between "Move NP" and "Move *wh*" will now reappear in the guise of differences between what are called *NP-trace* and *wh-trace*. Moreover, it will turn out that these two types of traces have properties that differ in ways that cannot easily be attributed to any properties of the rules that give rise to them. Finally, we will see that it is fruitful to broaden the discussion to include the third type of empty element, PRO.

In itself, the discovery that there is a typology of empty elements is extremely significant. Empty elements are by their very nature unobservable entities. It is inconceivable that their existence could be discovered by direct observation in language acquisition. Even more inconceivable is the notion that the distinctive properties of such elements could be discovered through direct, or even indirect, observation. Therefore, the study of the typology of empty elements provides a particularly important tool in the quest for new insights into the structure of Universal Grammar.

This section is organized as follows. Section 9.2.1 deals with the phenomenon of preposition stranding. This phenomenon is central to the question at hand because it illustrates both striking similarities and striking differences between NP-trace and *wh*-trace. Section 9.2.2 takes up contraction, which behaves quite differently in the two cases. Contraction will also offer preliminary clues about the status of PRO. Finally, section 9.2.3 returns to Rizzi's proposal concerning the role of Subjacency in Italian, which appears to be incompatible with the theory of "Move α" described here. The resolution of the difficulty will again reveal a quite fundamental difference among empty elements. In conclusion, section 9.2.4 discusses consequences of this new typology of empty elements.

9.2.1 Preposition Stranding

In English, "Move α" can have the effect of removing the object of a preposition, leaving the preposition "stranded" behind:

(15)
John was counted *on* by everybody

(16)
Who did everybody count *on*

This is a remarkable fact about English, because many languages do not allow such prepositional stranding. In French, for example, the equivalents of (15) and (16) are ungrammatical:

(17)
*Jean a   été   compté sur par tout le monde
Jean has been counted on by everybody

(18)
*Qui est-ce que tout le monde a   compté sur
who is it   that everybody   has counted on

In constructional terms this means that a language like French lacks the possibility of forming passives of prepositional verbs such as *compter sur* (so-called pseudopassives) and that pied piping is obligatory when the object of a prepositional verb undergoes *Wh*-Movement:

(19)
Sur qui est-ce que tout le monde a compté

It appears that, among the languages that have been studied in some detail, preposition stranding is limited to a subset of the Germanic languages. Thus, preposition stranding may be considered a "special property" of these languages.

The phenomenon is remarkable in another respect as well. As (15) and (16) demonstrate, the special property is apparently one that affects "Move NP" and "Move *wh*" alike. Thus, preposition stranding seems to provide a straightforward argument in favor of the "Move α" hypothesis. However, things are not quite that simple. Closer investigation reveals that stranding is much freer with *Wh*-Movement than with NP-Movement:

(20)
a. What did you talk to Bill about
b. *This problem was talked to Bill about by no one

(21)
a. How many hours did you argue for
b. *Many hours were argued for

(22)
a. Which president did you read a book about
b. *President de Gaulle was read a book about

We have already examined a solution, albeit a very imprecise one, to the problem posed by the (b)-sentences: the Natural Predicate Condition, invoked in chapter 7 to account for certain limitations in the passive construction. This condition is not met in the (b)-sentences: *talk to Bill about*, *argue for* (temporal), and *read a book about* cannot reasonably be interpreted as natural predicates.

At this point two theories could be adopted:

Theory 1
Preposition stranding is an essentially unitary phenomenon.
It is not an accident that it shows up with both "Move NP" and
"Move *wh*." Hence, there must be a single "special property,"
corresponding to a single grammatical device, that must be
present in the grammar of a given language to permit preposition
stranding. The asymmetry between pseudopassives and stranding by *Wh*-Movement is peripheral and must be attributed to
a construction-specific property of passives (the Natural
Predicate Condition).

Theory 2
Preposition stranding is not a unitary phenomenon. It is an accident that it occurs with both "Move NP" and "Move *wh*" in English. The asymmetry between pseudopassives and stranding by *Wh*-Movement indicates a more fundamental difference between the mechanisms permitting stranding in the two cases.

In practice, of course, the two theories are not quite as distinct as these descriptions suggest (for example, both make crucial use of the Natural Predicate Condition), and the decision between them is far from settled. Rather than argue for or against one or the other, then, we will simply examine some of the proposals that most researchers agree on.

One important notion in the discussion is *reanalysis*. This notion was first introduced to account for idiom passives like (23b):

(23)
a. Bill took advantage of John
b. John was taken advantage of by Bill

John is moved across the sequence V–N–P, a sequence that normally does not permit passivization:

(24)
a. Bill drinks brandy after dinner
b. *Dinner is drunk brandy after by Bill

Assuming (24) to be the normal case, even though it is not fully clear what condition prohibits "Move NP" in (24b), a special principle must be invoked to account for the grammaticality of (23b). Chomsky's idea (1974) is that *take-advantage-of* is reanalyzed as a single verb by a rule of *Reanalysis*. This rule, which is essentially a formalization of the Natural Predicate Condition, introduces an extra pair of V-brackets around verbal constructions that meet that condition. Thus, (25a) is reanalyzed as (25b):

(25)
a. Bill [$_V$ took]$_V$ [$_{NP}$ advantage]$_{NP}$ [$_{PP}$[$_P$ of]$_P$ [$_{NP}$ John]$_{NP}$]$_{PP}$
b. Bill [$_V$[$_V$ took]$_V$ [$_{NP}$ advantage]$_{NP}$ [$_{PP}$[$_P$ of]$_P$]$_V$ [$_{NP}$ John]$_{NP}$]$_{PP}$

We may take Reanalysis to be part of the lexical insertion rule for idiomatic expressions. It is natural to extend this rule to prepositional verbs, thus accounting straightforwardly for pseudopassives.

So far, most analysts agree. However, adherents of Theory 1 have argued that Reanalysis is also the mechanism that licenses stranding by *Wh*-Movement. It immediately follows that Reanalysis is not in itself a formalization of the Natural Predicate Condition, and consequently that it is not part of the lexicon but rather an independent rule of syntax. The Natural Predicate Condition must then be implemented in a different way, for example as a semantic condition that applies to the passive subset of the set of structures to which Reanalysis has applied. Under Theory 2 Reanalysis is limited to pseudopassives, and a quite different mechanism is required to account for stranding by *Wh*-Movement.

Note that we still have no account for the impossibility of stranding in the normal case (that is, in languages like French and in those structures in languages like English in which none of the special mechanisms that license stranding have applied). One way of accounting for this impossibility is to invoke Subjacency, though the execution of that idea is far from simple. Another is to invoke another constraint. Particularly important is the Empty Category Principle (ECP) (see chapter 18). For the time being we will simply assume that there is some constraint that has the effect of making prepositional phrases islands for movement.

Returning now to the main theme of this chapter, what is the relevance of preposition stranding to the typology of empty nodes? The first part of the answer is quite straightforward. The asymmetry between pseudopassives and stranding by *Wh*-Movement cannot follow from properties of the rules, given the "Move α" ("Move *wh*" and "Move NP") hypothesis. The principles causing the asymmetry might operate either before or after "Move α." Theory 2 suggests that, at least in the case of pseudopassives, the principle (namely, Reanalysis) applies first, since it is most naturally taken to be part of lexical insertion and hence to operate at D-Structure. Under Theory 1, however, the generalized rule of Reanalysis does not distinguish the two cases, regardless of where in the grammar it operates. Consequently, the asymmetry must probably be accounted for at a level subsequent to "Move α." Hence, the principle distinguishing the two cases, presumably the Natural Predicate Condition (now applying at or after S-Structure), must be able to refer to NP-traces as opposed to *wh*-traces.

9.2.2 Contraction

If there are systematic differences between NP-trace and *wh*-trace, then we must embrace the notion that there are different types of empty elements, each with its own distinctive properties. Therefore, we should consider the third type of empty element: PRO. The much-studied phenomenon of *wanna*-contraction in fact draws a very clear distinction between *wh*-trace on the one hand and PRO and NP-trace on the other hand.

Among the various forms of contraction that affect auxiliaries and other verbs, we are interested in the contraction of *want* and *to* to *wanna*. Consider the following contrast:

(26)
a. Which wine do you want to drink
b. Which wine do you wanna drink

(27)
a. Who do you want to get the wine
b. *Who do you wanna get the wine

This contrast can be related to the presence of a *wh*-trace between *want* and *to* in (27) but not in (26), and to the fact that PRO, which intervenes between *want* and *to* in (26), apparently does not block contraction.

(26)
c. [Which wine]$_i$ do you$_j$ want [$_S$ PRO$_j$ to drink [e]$_i$]$_S$

(27)
c. [Who]$_i$ do you want [$_S$[e]$_i$ to get the wine]$_S$

The next question is whether NP-trace patterns with PRO or with *wh*-trace. Unfortunately, the answer is not easily found, since *want* is not a raising verb. But there are two plausible arguments that NP-trace does not block contraction. The first comes from a use of *want* that could be argued to involve raising, since no θ-role is assigned to the subject. This use is illustrated in (28):

(28)
a. These papers want to be finished by tomorrow
b. These papers wanna be finished by tomorrow

If raising is involved, (28) has the following structure:

(28)
c. [These papers]$_i$ want [$_S$[e]$_i$ to be finished [e]$_i$ by tomorrow]$_S$

Here the trace between *want* and *to* would be an NP-trace, and, as the grammaticality of (28b) attests, it does not block contraction.

Next, consider the contraction of *supposed to* to *sposta:*

(29)

a. John is supposed to leave before noon

b. John is sposta leave before noon

c. [John]$_i$ is supposed [$_S$[e]$_i$ to leave before noon]$_S$

If this is an instance of contraction like *wanna,* then (29a–c) offer a second argument that NP-trace patterns with PRO in not blocking contraction.

Note now that there is a fourth type of empty element as well— namely, the trace left by a *wh*-phrase in an intermediate COMP under successive cyclic *Wh*-Movement. (26c) and (27c) were simplified in this respect. More exactly, they would have the following structure:

(26)

d. [Which wine]$_i$ do you$_j$ want [$_{S'}$ [$_{COMP}$ [e]$_i$]$_{COMP}$ [$_S$ PRO$_j$ to drink [e]$_i$]$_S$]$_{S'}$

(27)

d. [Who]$_i$ do you want [$_{S'}$[$_{COMP}$ [e]$_i$]$_{COMP}$ [$_S$ [e]$_i$ to get the wine]$_S$]$_{S'}$

These observations suggest a tentative rule of (*Wanna-*) Contraction:

(30)

Wanna-Contraction

Want to may contract to *wanna* unless a *wh*-trace in subject position intervenes. Other empty elements do not block the rule.

Note that lexical NPs also block contraction, since they physically intervene between *want* and *to:*

(31)

a. I want John to drink this wine

b. *I wanna John drink this wine

c. *I John wanna drink this wine

Apparently, then, a *wh*-trace in a subject position patterns with lexical NPs, whereas other empty elements behave as if they weren't there.

This, then, is the second element in the typology of empty categories: *wh*-trace has a property that distinguishes it from the others. Recall the importance of studying empty elements as a guide to Universal Grammar. In this instance it is highly unlikely that children will hear any negative evidence bearing on the inadmissibility of contraction in cases like (27b). Yet every speaker of English knows that (27b) is ungrammatical. Surely this is a powerful indication that deep and fundamental properties of Universal Grammar are at work here. Ideally, we would wish to say that all the child has to learn is that *want* and *to* can contract to *wanna*. Any other properties of the process should be derivable from other principles. And the typology of empty elements will be an important link in such an account.

9.2.3 *Wh*-Trace and the Opacity Condition

Now let us consider how empty elements behave under the TSC and the SSC. Since these two constraints behave alike with respect to the phenomena discussed here, they are often jointly referred to as the *Opacity Condition* (or the *opacity conditions*). We saw in section 9.1 that this condition can be interpreted as a constraint on representations rather than a constraint on rule application. This was a way to capture the insight that the relation between a trace and the corresponding displaced element is of the same nature as the relation between a lexical anaphor and its antecedent. If empty elements are to be subject to the Opacity Condition, then they must be "visible" to it. However, in light of the preceding discussion it would be prudent to ask whether *all* empty elements are visible to the Opacity Condition.

This is the same type of question as the one raised in section 7.3— namely, whether all constraints apply to all rules. There we tentatively concluded that there was no reason to abandon the null hypothesis that indeed every rule is subject to every constraint. Let us now transpose this question to the new situation involving conditions on representations: Are all empty elements subject to all constraints? In light of the preceding sections we would not be surprised to find it necessary to abandon the null hypothesis in this case; since there are a number of fundamental distinctions to be drawn among empty elements, we had best investigate carefully whether all empty elements are really subject to the Opacity Condition.

Starting with PRO, we have already seen in section 8.5 that obligatory control PRO is subject to the Opacity Condition. About optional control PRO there is nothing to add to the properties discussed earlier.

The same argument can be constructed for NP-trace. Whenever "Move NP" (i.e., Passive or Raising) operates across a clause boundary, it can only affect the subject position of an infinitival clause. Movement from all other embedded positions is blocked by the SSC and TSC. Hence, to preserve this result, it must be assumed that NP-trace is also subject to the Opacity Condition.

But what about *wh*-trace? We have already seen that to maintain the null hypothesis for *wh*-trace that all constraints apply to all rules, it is necessary to add the proviso that COMP is an escape hatch for *Wh*-Movement. But this proviso raises two concerns. First, we might wonder whether the two positions that are singled out as transparent (or accessible to rule) by the definitions given in chapter 7 (namely, subject of infinitival and COMP) form a natural class. Second, the Opacity Condition does not help to explain any particular properties of *Wh*-Movement. All the crucial properties, such as the *Wh*-Island Constraint and the Complex NP Constraint, are apparently accounted for by the Subjacency Condition. If the escape hatch proviso is assumed, then *Wh*-Movement does not appear to violate Opacity, but that does not really buy us anything we did not have already.

In fact, we already have the ingredients for an argument that *wh*-trace *cannot* be subject to Opacity. This argument follows directly from Rizzi's solution to the violations of the *Wh*-Island Constraint in Italian (section 4.4). The crucial case of grammatical double *wh*-extraction has the following general structure:

(32)

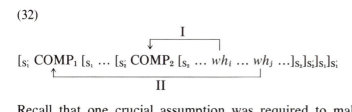

Recall that one crucial assumption was required to make the long *Wh*-Movement (II) possible—namely, that S', not S, is the bounding node for Subjacency. But what about the Opacity Condition? Clearly, operation II can violate both the SSC and the TSC, since wh_j need not be a subject and S_2' can be a tensed clause. The important fact about these examples is that the COMP escape hatch proviso will not work, simply because wh_j does not move through $COMP_2$, the latter position being filled by wh_i. This fact, which we suppressed in section 7.3, demonstrates conclusively that *wh*-traces should not be taken to be subject to the Opacity Condition.

In view of this conclusion we must now abandon the null hypothesis proposed in section 7.3. It simply cannot be maintained that all rules are subject to all constraints.

9.2.4 Concluding Remarks

The above remarks about the properties of empty elements can be summarized in the preliminary typology shown in table 9.1. This typology has suggested two major lines of research. First, it has suggested another way of looking at grammatical phenomena. Instead of trying to discover properties of rules, generative syntacticians have begun to single out classes of elements—types of categories—and to ask how they behave under the constraints on representation that are being developed. Thus, the typology has been extended to include different types of lexical elements as well, such as full lexical NPs, personal pronouns, and lexical anaphors (reflexives and reciprocals). Second, such a typology is not really an explanation of anything, but rather a curious fact about grammars that itself requires explanation. In other words, linguists would like to know *why* these empty elements have the properties they have. The theory as described so far says little about these cases. For example, no principle we have discussed will explain *why* PRO can never occur as the object of a preposition. However, in subsequent chapters we will see various ways in which the present theory of empty elements, and of classes of categories in general, can be improved and simplified. Why the typology looks as it does has been a significant guiding principle in establishing the modular organization of the theory of grammar, which we will elaborate in part IV.

9.3 Bibliographical Comments

The idea that syntactic representations can sometimes contain lexically empty (phonetically unrealized) categories had been current before these categories assumed their specific status within trace theory. Before trace theory they were used for various purposes: to formalize the

Table 9.1
Preliminary typology of empty categories

	PRO	NP-trace	*Wh*-trace
Preposition stranding	Never (i.e., PRO can never be the object of a preposition)	Only subject to the Natural Predicate Condition	Fairly free (at least in English)
Wanna-contraction	Does not block contraction	Does not block contraction	Blocks contraction
Opacity Condition	Subject to Opacity (at least for obligatory control PRO)	Subject to Opacity	Not subject to Opacity

notion "structure-preserving transformation," as in Emonds (1970, 1976), to avoid certain ordering problems in the formulation of the constraints, as in Chomsky (1973), and to justify a specific conception of phonological representations, as in Selkirk (1972). Trace theory as described here took shape in Wasow (1972) (later published as Wasow (1979)), Fiengo (1974) (summarized in Fiengo (1977)), and Chomsky (1976).

The notion of c-command, which plays a central role in the theory of proper binding, has had a long history. It originated as the relation "in construction with" (Klima (1964, 297)), which is really the converse of c-command. The definition given here is due to Reinhart (1976). In recent years various modifications of the definition have been proposed. We will return to some of these in later chapters, since c-command plays an important role in the notion of government, which in turn is central in the theory to be developed in part IV.

After Ross (1967) preposition stranding did not attract much attention until the appearance of Van Riemsdijk (1978b), where the nonunitary nature of preposition stranding was defended. The notion of reanalysis, which Van Riemsdijk extends to the analysis of pseudo-passives, is due to Chomsky's (1974) Amherst lectures, which were never published. It is the subject of a number of later publications, in particular Hornstein and Weinberg (1981) and Kayne (1981c). The problem of preposition stranding is taken up again in chapter 18.

Contraction is another "classical" topic about which there is a vast and still growing subliterature. The main fact about *wanna,* first discussed in Lakoff (1970), was quickly seen to support some notion of trace (see in particular Selkirk (1972)). As far as we know, the first to notice that there is a difference between NP-trace and *wh*-trace under contraction was Emonds (1977), in his reply to Lightfoot (1977), who argued that there is no difference. A critical survey of these and subsequent publications is presented in Postal and Pullum (1982).

The main argument that *wh*-trace is exempt from the Opacity Condition is from Rizzi (1978); it has been extended in Freidin and Lasnik (1981). The issue is still debated, however, and will be taken up briefly again in chapter 19.

Besides the dependencies between moved NP and NP-trace and moved *wh*-phrase and *wh*-trace there is a third type of dependency, which we will not take up here. This is the dependency between unstressed pronouns (*clitics*), which can be moved (*cliticized*) to some special clitic position, and their traces. Among the main questions concerning the syntax of clitics is whether their traces pattern with NP-trace, *wh*-trace, or neither. An early major discussion is found in Kayne (1975). An extensive discussion within the framework to be developed in part IV is found in Borer (1984).

\

Chapter 10
The Organization of the Model of Grammar

In a research program designed to strip rules of grammar of most of their expressive power by extracting highly general and (one would hope) universal principles from the formulation of specific rules, the most persistent problem is overgeneration. The highly trivialized transformational component—essentially, "Move α"—will generate nearly anything. To compensate for this overgeneration, linguists have developed a system of constraining principles. Some of these principles, like the Subjacency Condition, can be thought of as conditions on the application of the rule "Move α." Others, like the Specified Subject Condition, can be stated in terms of the configuration created by an antecedent and some anaphor (like a reflexive pronoun or an NP-trace). Consequently, the SSC is a principle that operates on a syntactic representation reached after the application of "Move α." As far as its effect on "Move α" is concerned, we may say that part of the overgeneration problem is solved by a set of *filtering devices.*

The introduction of filtering devices into the model of grammar has sometimes drawn misconceived criticism. In particular, some have felt that it is a priori wrong to first generate a wide range of structures only to filter out most of them later. But the appeal of this view is inspired by a procedural interpretation of the model. If the model were a production model (a model of how speakers actually generate sentences), excessive reliance on filtering devices could (indeed, should) be frowned upon. However, since the model linguists are developing is a competence model (a model of what speakers of a language know about it), no such considerations apply. The only valid criteria for evaluating filters, like any other component of grammar, are the degree to which they correctly characterize and explain grammatical phenomena and the degree to which they add to the overall elegance of the theory of grammar.

Not all problems of overgeneration are solved by optimally simple and general principles like Subjacency or the SSC. In section 10.1 we examine various problems that can be solved by the introduction of filters. Most of these filters provide solutions that it is hard to feel happy about. Thus, they constitute a new research program, in that they reformulate certain problems of overgeneration in a new and insightful way and are responsible for many extremely interesting attempts to explain them away, some of which we will discuss in later chapters.

In section 10.2 we dwell on questions concerning changes in the model brought about by the theoretical modifications argued for in preceding chapters.

10.1 Filters

In a seminal article Chomsky and Lasnik (1977) propose to (re)introduce a class of surface filters in order to solve certain problems of overgeneration and thereby improve the prospects for restricting the descriptive options for transformations. Surface filters were first systematically discussed by Perlmutter (1971), to some of whose proposals we return below. For the moment we will focus on certain salient proposals in Chomsky and Lasnik's article.

10.1.1 Doubly Filled Complementizers

In section 4.1 we assumed that COMP consists of two positions: an empty slot for wh-phrases to move into, and a position in which the lexical complementizer word (*that, for, whether*) is realized. In other words, COMP has the following structure after Wh-Movement:

(1)

$$[_{COMP} [wh\text{-phrase}] - [\begin{Bmatrix} that \\ for \\ whether \end{Bmatrix}]]_{COMP}$$

Note now that the process of Wh-Movement that puts a wh-phrase into the leftmost COMP slot is an epiphenomenon resulting from the application of "Move α." Hence, Wh-Movement cannot by hypothesis be sensitive to the presence or absence of a lexical complementizer element. Consider, for example, a simple relative clause structure:

(2)

a. I saw the man [*to whom* ∅] you talked
b. *I saw the man [*to whom that*] you talked

How is the ungrammaticality of (2b) to be accounted for? The "Move α" hypothesis precludes formulating *Wh*-Movement so as to avoid generating (2b), though the earlier descriptive apparatus would have made such a "solution" easily available:

(3)

$$X - [_{COMP} \; e \; - \; \emptyset]_{COMP} - Y - \textit{wh}\text{-phrase} - Z$$

SD: 1   2   3   4   5   6 →
SC: 1   5   3   4   *e*   6

(3) avoids the problem arising from (2) by requiring that the complementizer slot (term 3) be empty.

Since (3) is excluded, however, other solutions must be found. Several options suggest themselves. For example, we might exploit the fact that a rule of *that*-deletion is independently required for cases like (4) (cf. chapter 6):

(4)

John claims $\left\{ \begin{array}{c} \textit{that} \\ \emptyset \end{array} \right\}$ he is sick

Unfortunately, the formulation of this rule would be far from trivial. First, it would have to be optional for complement clauses like (4) but obligatory in relative clauses containing a *wh*-phrase. Second, *that* is not always absent in relative clauses. Consider the following paradigm:

(5)

a. *I saw the man [*who that*] you talked to
b. I saw the man [*who* ∅   ] you talked to
c. I saw the man [∅   *that*] you talked to
d. I saw the man [∅   ∅   ] you talked to

Thus, apparently (a) a second deletion is required to delete the *wh*-phrase under certain conditions, and (b) *that*-deletion in relative clauses must be assumed to be optional, unless the *wh*-phrase is not deleted—truly an undesirable rule.

Another way of looking at the problem is to observe that what is actually impossible is for COMP to contain more than one element. To account for this, a much simpler deletion rule has been proposed:

(6)
Delete freely an element in COMP.

To avoid "doubly filled COMPs," it has been assumed in addition that the output of (6) is filtered by (7) (see chapter 6):

(7)
Doubly Filled COMP Filter (DFC)
*[$_{COMP}$ X^{max} complementizer]$_{COMP}$
(where X^{max} and complementizer are both filled)

The grammar consisting of free deletion (6) and the DFC (7) is obviously the simplest solution. One problem arises, however:

(8)
a. *I saw the man [*to whom that*] you talked
b. I saw the man [*to whom* ∅　　] you talked
c. *I saw the man [∅　　　　*that*] you talked
d. *I saw the man [∅　　　　∅　] you talked

(8a) is excluded by the DFC, but why are (8c–d) ruled out? Intuitively, the answer appears to be that the preposition (*to*) may not be deleted since it is not recoverable. Why, then, can the *wh*-word be deleted in (5)? The answer must be that the *wh*-word is recoverable since it is related to the head of the relative clause in some way, perhaps through coindexing. If this is correct, then free relatives (relative clauses that lack a head) and questions must also display the pattern in (8). This is indeed the case:

(9)
a. *I saw [*whoever that*] you talked to
b. I saw [*whoever* ∅　　] you talked to
c. *I saw [∅　　　*that*] you talked to
d. *I saw [∅　　　∅　] you talked to

(10)
a. *I wonder [*who that/whether*] you talked to
b. I wonder [*who* ∅　　　　　　] you talked to
c. *I wonder [∅　　*that/whether*] you talked to
d. *I wonder [∅　　∅　　　　　　] you talked to

It appears, then, that even though the concept of recoverability is not very precise, it is intuitively quite clear and useful. Accordingly, (6) must be reformulated as follows:

(6')
Delete an element in COMP freely up to recoverability.

The revised but still extremely simple grammar consisting of (6') and the DFC thus succeeds in accounting for a wide variety of facts. In fact, it accounts for more than we have described here; see section 10.1.3.

Now, what is the status of the DFC? It is probably not a universal principle of grammar. For example, it is violated in certain constructions in Dutch:

(11)
a. Ik vroeg hem [*wie of*] hij had gezien
   I asked him who whether he had seen

b. Ik vroeg hem [*wie* ∅] hij had gezien

Similarly, Old English had many doubly filled COMP structures. But if filters like the DFC can be language-particular, how is such a filter to be learned during language acquisition? In particular, what kind of evidence could lead the child to hypothesize such a filter? It would appear that the only evidence having this effect would be negative evidence, in particular explicit correction by the speech community when the child produces DFC violations. But the systematic availability of negative evidence is highly implausible, and furthermore there appears to be no evidence of frequent DFC violations in the speech of young children learning English. How then can the DFC be learned? A much more plausible hypothesis is the following. Let us assume that the DFC is universally available, and that its presence in the grammar of a particular language is the unmarked option. This means that children learning English will automatically assume that the DFC is operative in the grammar they are learning. In the case of children learning Dutch, positive evidence in the form of sentences like (11a) is readily available, dictating the choice of the marked option—that is, that the DFC does not apply to Dutch. (Note that this markedness assumption is an entirely empirical issue: it can in principle be tested. For example, though presumably more subtle tests could also be devised, one could raise children learning Dutch so that they never hear a violation of the DFC and then investigate their behavior with respect to the relevant sentences.)

10.1.2 The *That*-Trace Filter
Gaps in the subject position adjacent to a COMP also have interesting properties that depend on the structure of that COMP. The relevant contrast is shown in (12) and (13):

(12)

a. Who do you think saw Bill
b. Who do you think Bill saw

(13)

a. *Who do you think that saw Bill
b. Who do you think that Bill saw

It appears that extraction of a *wh*-phrase from the subject position next to a lexically filled COMP is excluded. Extraction from the object position is not so constrained, however, as the (b)-sentences show. Moreover, only "long" *wh*-movement (movement across at least one clause boundary) is subject to this effect; cases of "short" movement, on the other hand, are well-formed:

(14)

a. Who saw Bill
b. the man that saw Bill

(14a) suggests that *that* is the element that crucially triggers the effect. (14b) seems to imply that if the *that* of a relative clause is adjacent to the head of that relative clause, it is exempt from the relevant principle.

What do we know about this principle? For one thing, it cannot be a property of the rule of *Wh*-Movement. It cannot be part of its structural description by virtue of the "Move α" hypothesis, but it cannot be a general condition on the application of *Wh*-Movement either. This is so for two reasons. First, the principle applies to cases of long *Wh*-Movement only. But recall that we have argued in chapter 4 that *Wh*-Movement operates successive cyclically. If the principle were to apply to the first, local application, there would be no way of knowing whether the *wh*-phrase in question would be moved again on the second cycle. And if the principle were to apply to the second application, it would have to be made sensitive to the origin of the *wh*-phrase in question. Second, and more important, the principle must be sensitive to whether or not *that* has been deleted. The discussion in the preceding section implies the following order of rules and principles:

(15)

Wh-Movement (i.e., "Move α")
Free deletion in COMP (6')
Doubly Filled COMP Filter (7)

Since the principle follows free deletion in COMP, it cannot be a property of *Wh*-Movement. Furthermore, (15) suggests that the principle might be a filter. This is indeed the conclusion reached by Chomsky and Lasnik (1977). They propose the following formulation:

(16)
That-Trace Filter
$*[_{S'} \text{ that } [_{NP} e]_{NP} ...]_{S_i}$,
unless S_i (or its trace) is in the context $[_{NP} \text{ NP } \underline{\qquad} ...]_{NP}$.

The formulation "or its trace" is required because the effect of the unless-condition is preserved under extraposition of the relative clause:

(17)
a. Three bottles that fetched more than $100 each were sold
b. Three bottles were sold that fetched more than $100 each

This is on the assumption that extraposition, being a movement process, is an instance of "Move α" and therefore precedes the *That*-Trace Filter.

Another important property of the *that*-trace effect—namely, its nonuniversality—was discovered by Perlmutter (1971) and is often referred to as *Perlmutter's conjecture*. Perlmutter observed that the effect is systematically absent in languages such as Spanish and Italian (among many others) in which subject pronouns may freely be absent. (Such languages are often referred to as *null-subject languages* or *pro-drop languages*.) In Italian, for example, it is possible to say (18a) or (18b):

(18)
a. Io vengo
   I   come
   'I come'
b. Vengo
   come (1st person sg.)
   'I come'

And, corresponding to Perlmutter's conjecture, it is possible to violate the *That*-Trace Filter in Italian:

(19)

Chi credi   che verrà
who you-believe that will-come
'Who do you believe will come'

An initial suggestion might be that the rule that deletes subject pronouns in null-subject languages deletes subject traces as well; thus, sentences like (19) could escape from the *That*-Trace Filter, which could
then be assumed to be a universal principle. There is much more to be
said, however, about the interaction between *that*-trace phenomena
and null-subject phenomena. We defer this discussion to chapter 18.

Clearly, the *That*-Trace Filter, as formulated in (16), is a messy principle. Historically, it has led to an interesting account of some phenomena of English, and it has provided a rationale for Perlmutter's
conjecture. But its main contribution has been to provoke many questions: Why should the *that*-trace effect exist at all? Why does it interact
with null-subject phenomena? Why does it apply after deletion? To
what extent is it universal? And so on. Thus, it has prompted a great
deal of research, some of the major results of which we will examine in
chapter 18.

10.1.3 The NP-*to*-VP Filter

One way to characterize the *That*-Trace Filter is to say that it determines the (non)occurrence of certain NP-types in subject position. We
have already encountered a similar principle in connection with the
problem of determining the distribution of PRO. Recall that in the unmarked case the subject of an infinitival clause must be PRO. This is
true of the class of pure control verbs, such as *try:*

(20)

a.   We try PRO to win
b.   *We try John to win
c.   *We try for John to win

This principle apparently has exceptions of two types. First, certain
preposition-like complementizers, such as *for* in English, can license a
lexical subject in an infinitival clause. Second, certain exceptional
verbs can license a lexical subject in the infinitival complement they
subcategorize:

(21)
a. We would prefer PRO to win
b. *We would prefer John to win
c. We would prefer for John to win

(22)
a. *We believe PRO to have won
b. We believe John to have won
c. *We believe for John to have won

Prefer is not one of the exceptional verbs; hence, either it must take PRO or, if it is to be construed with a lexical subject, it must be combined with the complementizer *for* in order to license that lexical subject. *Believe,* on the other hand, is one of the exceptional verbs and accordingly produces the opposite pattern. These two properties can be combined. A verb like *want,* for example, has both:

(23)
a. We want PRO to win
b. We want John to win
c. We want very much for John to win

Given two properties, then, and the possibility of having or not having either one of them, four types of verbs can be distinguished: *try* (neither property), *prefer* (the first property but not the second), *believe* (the second property but not the first), and *want* (both properties).

Verbs also vary according to a third property: namely, the property of being (or not being) a control verb. But here there is an important subregularity: all verbs that take *for* can also take a control complement. A verb like *try* must be a control verb, of course, since it cannot avail itself of any of the other options. However, alongside *believe,* which does not have the control option, we find *expect,* which does:

(24)
a. We expect PRO to win
b. We expect John to win
c. *We expect for John to win

Taken together, the three properties characterize eight types of verbs taking infinitival complements, five of which are attested in English (see table 10.1). Why *for*-verbs are always control verbs is still an interesting, unsolved question in linguistic research. Recall, however, that

Table 10.1
Typology of verbs taking infinitival complements

Verb type		Can exceptionally license lexical subject in infinitival complement	Can take *for*	Can be a control verb	Example
I	want	+	+	+	(23)
		+	+	−	does not exist
II	expect	+	−	+	(24)
III	believe	+	−	−	(22)
IV	prefer	−	+	+	(21)
		−	+	−	does not exist
V	try	−	−	+	(20)
		−	−	−	does not exist

control structure types I and IV have properties very different from those of type V. We will not pursue these differences here, however.

The NP-*to*-VP Filter has the status of the "unmarked" or normal state of affairs in Universal Grammar, and the exceptional licensing factors of taking a *for* complement and taking a complement with a lexical subject will have the status of special exceptions to this unmarked state of affairs. All languages that have infinitival complements have verbs of type V, but not all of them have any or all of the other types. Dutch, for example, lacks an infinitival complementizer like *for* that licenses lexical subjects. Other languages, such as Swahili and Vata, appear to have no verbs of the exceptional type. This observation, in conjunction with the general problem of learnability and filters discussed earlier, leads to the following universal formulation of the filter:

(25)
NP-to-*VP Filter*
*[NP *to* VP]

$$\text{except in the context} \begin{Bmatrix} \text{V} \underline{\quad} \text{ (i.e., exceptional verbs)} \\ \text{P} \underline{\quad} \text{ (i.e., } for) \end{Bmatrix}$$

Again, this formulation leaves much to be desired, and it has in fact been significantly improved, as we will see in chapter 14. Here, however, we will simply explore the considerable array of facts that can be adequately described by the NP-*to*-VP Filter in combination with the other filters.

First, the NP-*to*-VP Filter predicts that lexical NPs must always occur *immediately* after the licensing verb or preposition. This correctly accounts for the following contrasts:

(26)
a.   We want John to win (= (23b))
b.   *We want very much John to win
c.   We want very much for John to win (= (23c))

The filter also predicts (via the context "V ____") that adjectives and nouns taking infinitival complements can never be of the exceptional type and (via the context "P ____") that the only way they can take lexical complement subjects is by being subcategorized for *for:*

(27)
a.   *It is illegal John to win
b.   It is illegal for John to win

(28)
a.   *Our plan John to win fell through
b.   Our plan for John to win fell through

Consider now the properties of infinitival questions. By virtue of the Recoverability Condition, the COMP of the infinitival question must contain some *wh*-phrase. By virtue of the DFC, that COMP cannot in addition contain *for*. And by virtue of the adjacency requirement imposed by the NP-*to*-VP Filter, a verb taking an infinitival question complement can never be of the exceptional type since the *wh*-phrase will always intervene between it and the subject position. This is so because we have been assuming throughout this discussion that *NP* in the formulation of the NP-*to*-VP Filter always uniquely refers to the subject NP. The prediction is entirely accurate:

(29)
I wonder what PRO to do

(30)
a.   *I wonder what John to do   (* by the NP-*to*-VP Filter)
b.   *I wonder what for John to do   (* by the DFC)
c.   *I wonder for John to do   (* by Recoverability)

Finally, these considerations correctly derive a similarly complex set of facts about infinitival relatives. (31) illustrates the structure of these relatives, and (32) the grammaticality predictions for the various permutations made by the three principles. (+ indicates that a principle rules out a given construction; − that it does not.)

(31)

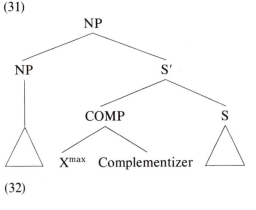

(32)

	NP-*to*-VP	DFC	Rec.
a. *I found a problem on which for John to work	−	+	−
b. I found a problem on which ∅ PRO to work	−	−	−
c. *I found a problem ∅ ∅ for John to work	−	−	+
d. *I found a problem ∅ ∅ ∅ PRO to work	−	−	+
e. *I found a problem on which ∅ John to work	+	−	−
f. *I found a problem ∅ ∅ ∅ John to work	+	−	+
g. *I found a problem which for John to work on	−	+	−
h. *I found a problem which ∅ PRO to work on	−	−	−
i. I found a problem ∅ for John to work on	−	−	−
j. I found a problem ∅ ∅ PRO to work on	−	−	−
k. *I found a problem which ∅ John to work on	+	−	−
l. *I found a problem ∅ ∅ John to work on	+	−	−

This array of facts is correctly described with the exception of (32h), which is ruled out by none of the principles established thus far but which is nonetheless ungrammatical. (Several possibilities (none very attractive) exist to account for this fact; we will briefly return to one of them in the next section.) Despite this problem, we see that three simple and arguably universal principles succeed in accounting for an apparently disparate clustering of facts, a remarkable result.

10.1.4 Visibility

A particularly significant question with respect to identity filters is whether filters are sensitive to traces and other empty elements. First, note that the *That*-Trace Filter explicitly refers to the trace in subject position. Second, we have so far tacitly assumed that the DFC applies to lexical elements in COMP only (that is, that it is not sensitive to trace). In other words, there appeared to be no reason to rule out structures of the following type:

(33)
... *wh*-phrase$_i$ ... [$_{COMP}$ e_i − that]$_{COMP}$ ... e_i ...

On the other hand, were the DFC formulated to apply to lexical NP and trace alike, then an obvious solution would present itself: free deletion in COMP could apply to the trace in COMP. In this case, then, (33) would be ungrammatical, but (34), derived by deletion of the trace, would be all right:

(34)
... *wh*-phrase$_i$ ... [$_{COMP}$ $\emptyset$ − that]$_{COMP}$ ... e_i ...

In the first case, where the DFC is insensitive to the presence of trace, trace is said to be *invisible* to it; in the second, where the DFC is sensitive to it, it is said to be *visible*. Nothing much appears to hinge on the choice here, but the issue turns out to have interesting ramifications, to which we return in chapter 18.

Next, consider the NP in the NP-*to*-VP Filter. Again, we have been tacitly assuming that this filter applies to lexical NPs only. This assumption appears to make sense, since the filter obviously cannot refer to PRO. If it did, the unmarked type of infinitival complement in (35) would be excluded:

(35)
John tried [[$_{NP}$ PRO]$_{NP}$ to win]

But given the distinct properties of PRO and *wh*-trace, the filter might still be sensitive to *wh*-trace. And indeed this seems to be the case. Consider the following pairs:

(36)
a. *We try John to win   (= (20b))
b. *Who$_i$ do we try e_i to win

(37)
a. *It is illegal John to win   (= (27a))
b. *Who$_i$ is it illegal e_i to win

The NP-*to*-VP Filter can rule out the (b)-sentences only if it can analyze the *wh*-trace (that is, only if the *wh*-trace is visible to it). This assumption has a number of interesting consequences. For example, consider the following case (which we had until now omitted from the discussion):

(38)
a. *I wonder [$_{S'}$ who$_i$ [$_S$ e_i to leave]$_S$]$_{S'}$
b. *I found a man [$_{S'}$ who$_i$ [$_S$ e_i to do the job]$_S$]$_{S'}$

So far we have not specified the bracket labels in the NP-*to*-VP Filter, although we did note that *NP* always uniquely refers to the subject position. If we drop this assumption, then α in the statement of the filter can be either S or S':

(25')
*[$_\alpha$ NP *to* VP]$_\alpha$
except . . .

If α = S, then (38a–b) can only be ruled out if the trace is analyzable (visible); if α = S', then the trace must be invisible. Also relevant in this context are (39) and (32h):

(39)
It is unclear [$_{S'}$ what [$_S$ PRO to do]$_S$]$_{S'}$

(32)
h. *I found a problem [$_{S'}$ which [$_S$ PRO to work on]$_S$]$_{S'}$

If α = S', then (39) is incorrectly ruled out, but the problem posed by (32h), which so far defied the analysis, is solved. On the other hand, if α = S, then (39) is correctly ruled in, but (32h) continues to be problematic.

Most of these cases seem to suggest—and we will continue to hold— that α = S and consequently that *wh*-trace is visible. But (32h) remains recalcitrant.

10.2 The Model of Grammar

10.2.1 The T-Model
This book began with a brief discussion of the so-called Standard Theory of generative grammar and its history. Since then we have considered numerous modifications. These modifications suggest that, rather than a rapid succession of radically different models, there has been one model of grammar that is continually subject to critical assessments

as new questions can fruitfully be asked, to enrichments as new empirical domains become accessible, and to modifications as new insights emerge. It is for this reason that we have endeavored to play down the significance of such often cited terms as *Standard Theory* (ST), *Extended Standard Theory* (EST), *Revised Extended Standard Theory* (REST), and *Government-Binding Theory* (GB-theory). These terms can be useful in that they refer to periods in the recent history of generative grammar. But each of these was simply the best approximation to the theory of grammar at its time.

Nevertheless, it may be useful to take stock of how the overall structure of the model has changed since the mid-1960s. Point of departure is the *Aspects* conception of the grammar, often called the *Standard Theory* (fig. 10.1).

The first two modifications were the introduction of the $\overline{X}$-theory of phrase structure and the realization that S-Structure contributes significantly to semantic interpretation. This stage in the development of the model (fig. 10.2) is generally known as the *Extended Standard Theory*.

With the introduction of traces, a new conception of s-structures emerged. S-structures were enriched in such a way as to preserve many of the properties of D-Structure. In particular, it was now possible to apply the rules of thematic structure to S-Structure, thereby simplifying the semantic component. This modification led to the stage known as the *Revised Extended Standard Theory* (fig. 10.3).

Interest in restricting the descriptive power of the transformational mechanism led to the demonstration that the transformational component can be reduced to its absolute minimum—"Move α"—by introducing certain highly general constraints and principles as well as a component of filters. In accordance with these developments, Chomsky and Lasnik (1977) proposed the conception of the model that is often referred to as the *T-model* (fig. 10.4)—so called because it invites a very simple tripartite overall interpretation of the model:

(40)

Syntax	
Phonology	Semantics

Some terminological clarifications are in order here. As used in (40), *phonology* stands for "phonology in the wide sense," because in this use it includes other components besides the phonology in the strict

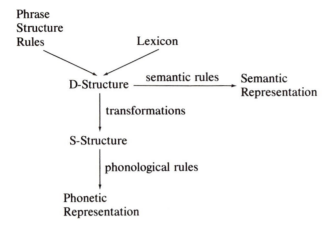

Figure 10.1
Standard Theory model of grammar

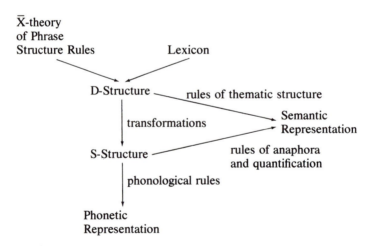

Figure 10.2
Extended Standard Theory model of grammar

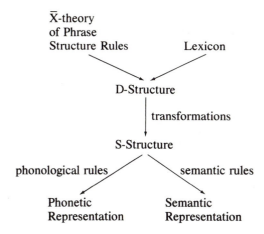

X̄-theory
of Phrase
Structure Rules   Lexicon

D-Structure

transformations

S-Structure

phonological rules   semantic rules

Phonetic   Semantic
Representation   Representation

Figure 10.3
Revised Extended Standard Theory model of grammar

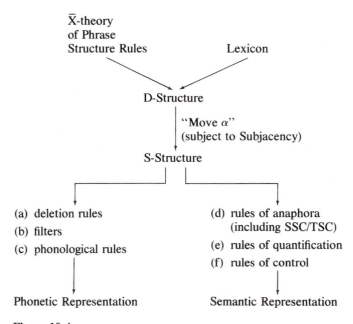

X̄-theory
of Phrase
Structure Rules   Lexicon

D-Structure

"Move α"
(subject to Subjacency)

S-Structure

(a) deletion rules   (d) rules of anaphora
(b) filters   (including SSC/TSC)
(c) phonological rules   (e) rules of quantification
                                     (f) rules of control

Phonetic Representation   Semantic Representation

Figure 10.4
T-model of grammar

sense (component (c) in figure 10.4). Conversely, as used in (40), *syntax* is really "syntax in the strict sense," for both the phonology and the semantics are also concerned with formal properties of s-structures. Hence, they too might be called syntactic, in the wide sense. Finally, *semantics* here is also "semantics in the strict sense," since it is exclusively concerned with structural semantics and by no means with all of meaning; in other words, it refers here to "logical syntax" in the sense in which philosophers use that term (see chapter 11). Consequently, this "semantics in the strict sense" has come to be called *Logical Form* or *LF*. We will explore this component in part III.

The ordering of (a)–(c) and (d)–(f) in figure 10.4 also requires comment. Because the functioning of filters depends heavily on their being ordered after deletion, which is in turn ordered after "Move α," the ordering implied by (a)–(c) is crucial and must be considered a property of the T-model. The same is not true for (d)–(f). As we will see in discussing LF, it is not clear either that the rules of semantics are ordered or, to the extent that they are, what the ordering is. In fact, this is currently a much debated issue.

The T-model conception of grammar invites speculation about the *autonomy hypothesis*—the notion that the grammar as a whole is an autonomous cognitive component that, in interaction with other cognitive components, determines linguistic knowledge and behavior. The T-model suggests an *internal autonomy hypothesis*—that the grammar itself consists of various autonomous subcomponents. According to this hypothesis, the components of the grammar have their own rules and principles, and they interact with each other not freely but only at the interface, in that one component generates an output that provides the input for the next component or components.

It is important to keep in mind that the autonomy hypothesis is an empirical hypothesis: it can be factually proved or disproved. A fortiori, the internal autonomy hypothesis is also an empirical hypothesis. And although it is a very attractive hypothesis to entertain, it is far from obvious that it can be upheld. To mention just one potential problem, there are many intricate connections between intonation and meaning, and it is not at all clear that these connections can be adequately accounted for without assuming that there are direct links between the phonology and the semantics in the T-model.

It is a virtue of the T-model that it raises such questions. In Van Riemsdijk and Williams (1981) we discuss other fundamental problems that arise from this conception of the grammar and propose yet another modification of the model. We will not explore that proposal here, however, since most current work is based on the T-model as depicted in figure 10.4.

10.2.2 Core and Periphery

A major difference between generative grammar and earlier linguistic theories lies in the extent to which the importance of idealization is recognized. This has been one of the most controversial aspects of generative grammar. Nevertheless, the necessity of idealization and abstraction has become increasingly clear since the earliest work in this tradition. From today's perspective most research carried out before the late 1960s appears data-bound, construction-bound, and lacking in appreciation for the existence of highly general principles of linguistic organization.

Has the price for this considerable level of abstraction perhaps become too high? As we have attempted to show throughout this book, the answer must be unequivocally no. If the study of grammar is to provide any satisfactory answers to our questions about the nature and growth of grammatical knowledge, if it is to have any intellectual interest at all, the pursuit of abstraction is absolutely indispensable. Nevertheless, we need to recognize which empirical domains have been sacrificed, or at least relegated to future research, and which theoretical constructs are required solely to compensate for unpleasant side effects of satisfying results achieved in a particular domain of grammar. Filters belong, at least in part, in the latter category. In the former category are phenomena such as gapping, extraposition, and verb movement rules. This is not to say that no progress has been made at all in these domains, but they have been less productive in triggering results.

Will ad hoc mechanisms ever be completely eliminated? Will recalcitrant domains of data ever be fully integrated into the theory with no unpleasant side effects? Such a hope is probably unrealistic. Despite our relative success in discerning general principles of grammar, there is in all likelihood an unassimilable residue of odd facts, exceptions, and quirky constructions. One might say, then, that the grammar consists of a *core* and a *periphery,* where the core determines the general properties of the grammar and the periphery accommodates the exceptional or marked properties.

The T-model, then, is essentially a model of core grammar that will have to be supplemented by a theory about the periphery. The learnability question arises for core and periphery alike; hence, the periphery will have to be structured in such a way as to allow for the learning of peripheral rules. This is largely the task of a theory of markedness. Although versions of such a theory exist for phonology, in syntax the theory of markedness is at present merely a small collection of sketchy ideas.

But the conception that linguists now have of core grammar sheds a new, interesting light on the learnability problem. Solving the learnability problem amounts to showing that only a small number of grammars are available given certain input data. It now appears that the set of core grammars may well be finite. If this result turns out to be correct, it will represent a quantum leap toward solving the learnability problem.

Consider the issue in more detail. There is a finite vocabulary of syntactic categories, made up from a small universal set of syntactic category features. $\overline{X}$-theory determines a universal format for phrase structure rules: only a small number of rules are compatible with the rule schema it imposes. This rule schema is augmented with a very small number of probably binary parameters such as "head-initial" vs. "head-final" (whether the head of each constituent comes at the beginning or the end of the constituent). Hence, the set of possible phrase structure components is arguably finite.

The transformational component is even simpler. It consists of just one rule: "Move α." The operation of "Move α" is constrained by the universal Subjacency Condition. There may be a limited amount of parametric variation with respect to what counts as a bounding node for Subjacency in a given language. However, it seems safe to conclude that the number of possible transformational components can be counted on the fingers of one or two hands.

In the domain of phonology (in the wide sense) the outcome is a little harder to determine. As far as deletion is concerned, it is not unreasonable to assume that the core may contain at most a very small number of very general deletion rules of the type discussed earlier in this chapter. It is not at all clear that the filter component will survive; but if it does, it must undoubtedly consist of a small number of universal filters, the exceptions to which may in part be parametrically fixed and in part belong to the periphery. The phonological component proper presents a significant challenge, but here too suggestive results permit us to expect that there is only a finite set of possible phonological components.

Therefore, it may not be implausible to assume that the phonology (in the wider sense) of core grammar is also a finite domain.

About semantics, too little is known to speak with any assurance. Nevertheless, it would be highly surprising to find a great deal of variation in this domain, given the relative inaccessibility of the relevant data necessary to fix the parameters. Let us assume, then, that the semantics of the grammar is also a finite domain. Therefore, we may tentatively conclude that there is only a finite and not even very large set of possible core grammars.

Needless to say, it would be quite wrong to conclude from this that the learnability problem has been solved. Much more is involved in that task. In particular, it must be shown that the parameters of core grammar can be fixed—in other words, that simple data are easily accessible so that the child may fix them. Furthermore, today's conception of core grammar is much too impoverished to survive long. As solid analyses of new languages become available, as new empirical domains (such as gapping, extraposition, and verb movement) are incorporated, core grammar will be continuously enriched and modified, for it would be methodologically disastrous to relegate everything to the periphery. And every such enrichment or modification constitutes a new challenge to the assumption that the set of core grammars is finite.

10.3 Bibliographical Comments

Though the notion of filtering devices was introduced in Chomsky (1965), the first extensive argumentation in favor of adding filters to the rule types available in grammar was presented in Perlmutter (1971). That work also offered the first analysis of *that*-trace phenomena and established the connection between them and null-subject languages. The presentation of filters in section 10.1 essentially follows the theory elaborated in Chomsky and Lasnik (1977).

We will return to the NP-*to*-VP Filter and the *That*-Trace Filter in chapters 14 and 18, respectively, and will give further references there. For a critical review of the issue of the visibility of empty categories, see Van Riemsdijk and Williams (1981), in which an alternative to Chomsky and Lasnik's T-model, the *L-model,* is proposed.

The notion of core grammar is also introduced in Chomsky and Lasnik (1977). This notion, together with its implied counterpart notion of periphery, is closely related to the concept of markedness. Markedness theory in phonology, originally introduced in Chomsky and Halle

(1968), was further developed in Kean (1975, 1981) and in several other articles in Belletti, Brandi, and Rizzi (1981). On markedness in syntax, see in particular chapter 7 of Van Riemsdijk (1978b), Koster (1978b), Chomsky (1981a), and other relevant articles in Belletti, Brandi, and Rizzi (1981).

Part III

LOGICAL FORM

Chapter 11
Logical Form

In the past several years a rather clear notion has emerged in linguistics of Logical Form (LF) as a level of representation and of LF-representations as representations of sentences determined by principles at that level. Thus, the terms *Logical Form* and *LF-representation* used here are technical terms that receive their specific interpretation within generative grammar. An LF-representation is a partial representation of the meaning of a sentence, representing what might be called its "structural meaning" (abstracting away from such other aspects of meaning as the meaning of lexical items and conditions on "appropriate use" of sentences). It is similar to but certainly not identical with what is traditionally called *logical form* in the philosophical literature. Logical Form is derived from S-Structure by the successive application of the rules of interpretation, applying in a Markovian derivation. It is subject to well-formedness conditions that filter out sentences with improper LF-representations.

In section 11.1 we offer some methodological remarks bearing on the investigation of semantics, remarks that seem to us to represent a consensus view among linguists. Next we outline general properties of Logical Form (section 11.2), along with rules for deriving it and well-formedness conditions it obeys (section 11.3). In section 11.4 we review the development of ideas regarding this level of grammatical representation.

11.1 The Empirical Nature of Logical Form

It is important to emphasize the empirical nature of Logical Form. Like D-Structure and S-Structure, it represents an aspect of sentence structure. Like them, it is postulated as a part of a general theory of sentence

structure, and it is subject to the ordinary canons of scientific confirmation as a part of that theory.

If Logical Form were taken to be the complete explication of the
meaning of a sentence, in the most general sense of meaning, then certain conclusions would follow: Logical Form would have to represent
word meanings, since clearly word meanings partially determine the
meaning of a sentence; it would have to define (or allow for the definition of) the "truth conditions" of a sentence, since, as philosophers
have said, to know the meaning of a sentence is to know, perhaps
among other things, what circumstances the sentence would truly describe; and it would contain, or directly allow for the definition of, the
specification of the roles that a sentence could potentially play in such
larger entities as discourses and logical arguments.

But although these functions must be performed somewhere in the
grammar, they are not the functions of Logical Form. Instead, Logical
Form is postulated as a discrete, coherent *subtheory* of the general theory of meaning. Thus, its existence is a nontrivial empirical issue: is
there a discrete subtheory of meaning that is concerned exclusively
with "structural meaning"? Can "structural meaning" be characterized
independently of other aspects of meaning (where the general theory of
meaning specifies how structural meaning combines with other aspects
of meaning to yield the general notion of meaning)?

The empirical content of the theory of Logical Form can be seen as
having two aspects: one involving the "syntax" of Logical Form and
the relation of Logical Form to the form of sentences, the other involving the role of Logical Form in the explication of the general notion
of meaning.

Any particular proposal concerning Logical Form can correspondingly be disconfirmed in one of two ways: it can be shown to give an
inaccurate account of how Logical Form is related to sentence structure, or it can be shown to fail to support a general theory of meaning.
In practice, it will be far easier to do the former than the latter, given
that the theory of syntax is well understood relative to the general theory of meaning.

However, the fundamental empirical claim of the EST theory of
Logical Form—that there is a discrete, coherent subtheory of meaning
concerned with "structural meaning"—cannot be easily confirmed or
disconfirmed, because of its abstractness. Pending the many years of
research that would be needed to establish its status, then, this tenet

often plays the role of a methodological assumption in the literature. But its essential empirical content must not be dismissed.

These points can perhaps be clarified by comparing the EST theory of Logical Form to alternative points of view. One of these is the view developed by Jerrold Katz. Like proponents of the theory that includes Logical Form, Katz does not consider semantics to exhaust the theory of meaning; like them, he reserves such things as rhetorical force, appropriateness conditions, and reference to the general theory of meaning. However, Katz does not posit a discrete subtheory of semantics that deals with structural meaning alone, as do proponents of LF-theory. Rather, he proposes a semantics that includes both structural meaning and the explanation of such notions as analyticity, entailment, and synonymy. Proponents of LF-theory regard analyticity, entailment, and synonymy as problems for the general theory of meaning, separate from the discrete subtheory of Logical Form that deals with structural meaning, holding that notions like synonymy cannot be explained on the basis of structural meaning alone. (Clearly, the LF-hypothesis and Katz's theory are both empirical in nature, though both are quite abstract and thus both quite removed from the facts.)

Or we might compare LF-theory with the central thesis of model-theoretic semantics. This thesis has two versions, one empirical and the other not; we shall not discuss the latter here. The empirical version is that an interpreted logical language is a discrete, coherent subtheory of the theory of meaning; as such, this claim has exactly the same empirical status as LF-theory and Katz's theory. The reader is referred to Dowty, Wall, and Peters (1981) for an introduction to one line of research in model-theoretic semantics.

LF-theory and model-theoretic semantics are very similar in some respects. Both are concerned with "structural meaning," abstracting away from word meaning and pragmatics, and both postulate a logical language as the representation of the "structural meaning" of sentences. Thus, it could be said that in both theories "Logical Form" is a discrete subtheory of the theory of meaning. Model-theoretic semantics goes one step further, claiming that "Logical Form plus a set-theoretical interpretation of Logical Form is a discrete subtheory of the theory of meaning." Although Cooper and Parsons (1976) have shown that it is in principle possible to give a set-theoretical interpretation of Logical Form, many authors, including Chomsky (1982b), reject this position, and we will not dwell on it here.

We believe that many philosophers and linguists insist that Logical Form be interpreted because otherwise it is merely another language; they feel that in translating English into this other language (the logical forms of English sentences) we can have gotten no closer to meaning. We believe this reasoning is based on a misunderstanding of the empirical nature of Logical Form. To draw the analogy with phonology: phonetic representation is a "language" into which phonological rules translate phonological representations. We do not conclude from this that phonetic representation is "no closer to sound" than phonological representation. Furthermore, though it remains unclear exactly what the correct "interpretation" of phonetic representation is to be— whether an acoustic wave, a pattern of auricular sensations, or a pattern of motor neural commands—phonologists have nevertheless succeeded in discovering a great deal about the nature of phonological and phonetic representations and the mapping between them. This shows that it is not necessary to say in detail how a representation is to be "interpreted"—that is, how it relates to some larger theory—in order to learn about it and its relation to other representations.

11.2 General Features of the Theory of Logical Form

In this section we will sketch some general features of the notions "Logical Form" and "structural meaning." We will introduce a number of theses about the nature of Logical Form and its relation to other syntactic forms that represent a core of shared opinions among linguists working on this subtheory. In subsequent chapters we will examine in detail the role of Logical Form in the explanation of problems concerning sentence meaning and sentence form.

11.2.1 Sentence Grammar
Important to the notion "Logical Form" (LF) is the notion "sentence grammar." "Sentence grammar" is the theory of sentences as objects, not of their uses in larger frameworks such as discourse or logical argument. Of course, sentence grammar must support a general theory of meaning in which such things can be dealt with, but sentence grammar is not about these things. Like LF, the existence of sentence grammar is an empirical issue, and in fact it has been explicitly denied by some linguists. In principle, it could turn out that it is impossible to characterize sentences in and of themselves without reference to their roles in various conversations, situations, etc.

As illustration, let us focus on the English rules of Complement Subject Control and VP Anaphora. One of these, VP Anaphora, is clearly not a rule of sentence grammar. Consider the following sentences:

(1)
John will see Bill. Sam will too.

If *Sam will too* is a sentence, we may conclude that VP Anaphora, the rule that tells us that *Sam will too* in the context of (1) means "Sam will see Bill too," is not a rule of sentence grammar, since this meaning cannot be determined solely with reference to the sentence itself, but must be determined with reference to the conversation of which it is a part.

On the other hand, Complement Subject Control, the rule that tells us that *John promised Bill to go* means (roughly) "John promised Bill that John would go," is a rule of sentence grammar (or at least cannot be so easily disqualified as VP Anaphora), since this meaning can be determined regardless of how the sentence is used in any context—this aspect of meaning is an intrinsic feature of the sentence itself.

This distinction between rule types is quite important empirically. It appears that the rules of sentence grammar are governed by strict, structurally defined conditions that do not apply to the so-called discourse rules. For example, VP Anaphora can "violate" the Complex NP Constraint:

(2)
John *left* because he couldn't find anyone else who wanted to

But this is impossible with rules of sentence grammar such as *Wh*-Movement:

(3)
*What did John find a man who read

These examples suggest a rough criterion for identifying discourse rules. If the rule can apply "across utterance boundaries" or can be shown to apply globally in a discourse, then it is not a rule of sentence grammar, but a discourse rule. Also, if it can be shown to disobey the constraints on the operation of rules of sentence grammar, such as the Complex NP Constraint, then it is a discourse rule. The interest in the distinction between rules of sentence grammar and discourse rules lies in the correlation of these properties: if a rule can apply across utterance boundaries, then it can violate the Complex NP Constraint (and other constraints).

11.2.2 The Revised Extended Standard Theory

In EST both D-Structure and S-Structure were relevant to the determination of meaning: D-Structure in determining those aspects of meaning concerned with grammatical or thematic relations, and S-Structure in determining the scope of quantifiers and operators (see figure 10.2). The introduction of traces, which led to the Revised Extended Standard Theory (REST), had the consequence that at that stage of the model all of semantics was determined from one level, S-Structure. An example will illustrate the role that trace played in making this revision possible. Suppose that the passive of an active sentence is synonymous with the active, at least in some aspects of meaning. Part of that synonymy resides in the fact that the S-Structure subject of the passive is the D-Structure object of the active. In EST, as in the Standard Theory, this correspondence between active and passive is available in D-Structure, where both active and passive have (the same) direct objects; hence, a semantic theory that makes use of the notion "object of" in D-Structure will be able to capture this correspondence.

But if movement rules leave traces coindexed with the constituents that they move, then any aspects of meaning based on "object of" can be determined as easily at S-Structure as at D-Structure. For example, (4) is the derived structure of a passive in trace theory:

(4)
John$_i$ was killed e_i by Bill

It is possible to determine from this s-structure that *John* corresponds to the object of *killed,* because it binds a trace in the object position. This determination can be made without reference to the rule that inserted the trace.

If other cases where D-Structure interpretation is required in EST can be treated in this way, then semantic interpretation could be unified by making it all dependent on S-Structure—though an S-Structure "enriched" with traces, to be sure.

The passive sentence (4) illustrates a problem for REST that cannot be solved with traces: *Bill* corresponds to the deep subject of (4) and to both the deep and the surface subject of the related active sentence. Since *Bill* binds no trace, how is this correspondence determined? One might suppose that *by* in (4) induces an "agent" interpretation parallel to the interpretation that would be given to the subject of the corresponding active. Evidence favoring this view is the agentive use of *by* in nominals like *a sonata by Mozart,* where a rule of subject postposing is implausible.

We cite this example to illustrate that this "revision" in EST was not an extremely deep enterprise. However, it made possible a rather deep hypothesis about the relation of LF to syntax, a hypothesis that can be termed the *Markovian derivation hypothesis.* By this hypothesis, LF is essentially a structure that is derived step by step from S-Structure. That is, rules of interpretation apply in a sequence to S-Structure, transforming it much as D-Structure is transformed into S-Structure by syntactic transformations, and each step depends solely on the previous step. (*Markovian* means simply that the derivation from level X to level Y is a linearly ordered sequence, where each pair of adjacent lines is related by a single rule; see also section 1.3.2.)

There are many alternatives to this hypothesis. In the semantic theories of Jerrold Katz, Ray Jackendoff, and Richard Montague, for example, LF is built up by reference to various levels of syntactic structure, but in those theories it is in no sense a transform of any level of syntactic structure.

Since the rules of interpretation are quite limited, as we shall see, consisting essentially of indexing and scope assignment, LF can be thought of as an "annotated" S-Structure. This means that the vocabulary of LF at least includes the vocabulary of surface syntax, and that such features of S-Structure as the surface constituent structure and the trace binding created by transformation are also relevant features of LF.

Certain rules, such as local deletions of designated lexical items and certain "stylistic" movements, do not seem to affect the LF of sentences they apply to, and furthermore, they often make the definition of LF more difficult; for this reason, it is generally accepted that LF is derived not from "absolute" surface structures, but rather from a "shallow structure" (for example, the level called *S-Structure* in the T-model represented in figure 10.4), a level at which at least the basic rules of NP-Movement and *Wh*-Movement have applied, but at which deletions and stylistic movements have not applied. (An example of a local deletion rule is the deletion of complementizers in certain contexts (*I think (that) Bill will win*); an example of a stylistic movement is the rule of Heavy NP Shift (*I gave to Mary all of the things she requested*).) This organization of the grammar, discussed in chapter 10, has two important empirical consequences—first, that all of the deletions and stylistic movements can be ordered after the transformations, and that the deletions and stylistic movements will not affect the logical form of sentences. We will investigate each of these in some detail in subsequent chapters.

Words are taken as unanalyzed semantic entities (that is, as entities with no internal structure) in LF, as indeed they are in syntax. This is not to claim that problems concerning word meaning are insubstantial, irrelevant, or uninteresting. The theory of LF simply claims that there are aspects of sentence meaning that can be, and should be, characterized in terms of the structure of the sentence above word level, and that the "laws of meaning" that hold above and below word level are significantly different from each other and should therefore be characterized in separate subtheories of the general theory of meaning.

The above remarks characterize a point of view more than a theory. It would be trivial, of course, to incorporate word semantics into an LF-type theory by (for example) assigning every word to a distinct syntactic category; then any discrimination that one might otherwise make on the basis of word meaning could be made on the basis of a syntactic category difference. But this would clearly violate the spirit of the proposal.

From the above discussion, we might conclude that LF has essentially a "predicate calculus" structure. Words correspond to the atomic letters in predicate calculus. The aspects of meaning that are modeled in LF are essentially those modeled in predicate calculus: the scope of operators and quantifiers, sameness and distinctness of variables, and predicate-argument structure (which is essentially given in surface syntax).

11.3 Rules of Logical Form

This section offers a preliminary account of the rules of LF, mostly by way of example: first the rules deriving LF, and then certain well-formedness conditions on LF.

11.3.1 Rules Deriving Logical Form

The rules deriving LF are essentially indexing rules. Some of these, the *construal rules,* are rules that relate syntactic argument positions to other syntactic argument positions. Subject Complement Control, Reflexive Interpretation, and Bound Pronoun Anaphora are three such rules. These rules coindex two NPs under appropriate conditions, structural or otherwise, thus indicating the "sameness" and "distinctness" of variables. (One can regard these rules as assigning coreference, although we feel this is likely to introduce unintended associations; the intent of the rules is to capture something like the "sameness" and "distinctness" of variables in predicate calculus.)

For example, in line with the preliminary notation adopted in chapter 7, the rule for reflexive interpretation might be as follows:

(5)
Reflexive Interpretation
NP ... Reflexive $\rightarrow$ NP$_i$ ... Reflexive$_i$

If the first of these, the NP, is interpreted in LF as a variable bound by some quantifier, then this coindexing means that the reflexive must be understood as an instance of the same variable.

Various restrictions known to hold on the relation between a reflexive and its antecedent are not reflected in this rule—for example, that the antecedent must c-command the reflexive and that no subject may intervene between the reflexive and its antecedent. This is because these restrictions follow from general well-formedness principles that hold of LF.

Since Reflexive Interpretation says so little, it is conceivable that it could be eliminated altogether—for example, it could be replaced by rule (6a) or even by rule (6b):

(6)
a. "Freely coindex NPs"
b. "Freely index NPs"

Well-formedness conditions on LF would then rule out all of the ill-formed cases. We will explore this possibility in later chapters, but for the time being note that if "Freely coindex NPs" replaces Reflexive Interpretation, then it can also replace Subject Complement Control and Bound Pronoun Anaphora. The success of this move of course depends on discovering the right well-formedness conditions on LF. Be that as it may, we will continue to refer to the individual rules that are subsumed under "Freely coindex NPs" for concreteness.

Recall that the EST/REST rule of NP-Movement leaves a trace co-indexed with the moved NP. Although this coindexing is derived in the syntactic component, it is indistinguishable at LF from indexing derived by the rules of interpretation. For this reason, NP-Movement coindexing is subject to the same LF constraints as coindexing introduced by the interpretation rules. That NP-Movement resembles Bound Anaphora in the way this theory predicts is a principal insight of trace theory. It is this insight that has led to generalizing various instances of moved NPs (Passive, Raising, etc.) to "Move NP," just as Reflexive Interpretation can be generalized to "Freely coindex NPs."

The second kind of rule that derives LF is the rule of quantifier scope assignment known as *Quantifier Interpretation*. Since the scope of a quantifier will be some LF subconstituent, one way to indicate scope is to Chomsky-adjoin the quantified NP to some S, that S then being interpreted as the scope of that quantified NP. (See (10) for an example.) Since the quantifier is always interpreted as binding a variable in the position in which the quantifier occurs in S-Structure, the rule should also put a variable in that position.

This variable is rather like a trace, and the quantified NP is rather like a moved NP, so Quantifier Interpretation is rather like a syntactic movement rule, except that this movement takes place in the derivation of LF rather than S-Structure. Still, one might search for a theory of "movement" that pertained to both cases.

Again there is the question of how much to write into the rule of Quantifier Interpretation and how much to leave to LF well-formedness conditions. Although this is a strictly empirical question, we might guess that the same situation holds here as with NP-Movement: that the rule itself is absolutely trivial ("Move quantified phrase") and that most of the work of describing quantifier scope is to be done by well-formedness conditions.

11.3.2 Well-formedness Conditions on Logical Form

What, then, are the well-formedness conditions on LF? This question is currently under intense study, with many incompatible proposals being voiced at the same time. In this section and in this book, though, we will try to indicate the points on which many researchers do agree.

Some of the well-formedness conditions are familiar from constraints in logic. For example, any variable in LF must be *bound* by a quantifier; that is, it must fall within the scope, as defined above, of some NP with which it is coindexed.

Other conditions are specific to natural language and have no counterpart in standard predicate calculus theory. One of these is the Specified Subject Condition (SSC). We have traced the development of this condition from a condition on rule application to a well-formedness condition on representations (sections 9.1 and 9.2.3); now we will see that it can be interpreted specifically as a well-formedness condition on indexing at LF. Assuming that NP-traces, reflexives, reciprocals, and PRO are anaphors, and defining *bound, free,* and *domain of* as in (7),

(7)
Bound: X is bound if it is coindexed with a c-commanding NP
Free: Not bound
Domain of: X is in the domain of Y if $X \neq Y$ and Y c-commands X

then the SSC (still referred to under this formulation, along with the TSC, as the "Opacity Condition") can be stated as follows:

(8)
Specified Subject Condition
An anaphor in the domain of a subject must not be free in the smallest S containing that subject (i.e., the S immediately dominating that subject).

This law unites the following kinds of examples:

(9)
a. *$John_i$ was believed [$_S$ Mary to have seen e_i]$_S$
b. *$John_i$ believes [$_S$ Mary to have seen $himself_i$]$_S$

The bindings in these examples violate the SSC, because in each case the anaphor is in the domain of a subject (*Mary*) but is free in the smallest S containing that subject. Although one binding was derived by NP-Movement and the other by semantic interpretation rules deriving LF, they are both subject to the SSC in exactly the same way.

Now, the variable inserted by Quantifier Interpretation must not be subject to the SSC, as the following example shows (cf. chapter 13):

(10)
a. Someone wants to see each of us
b. [each of us_i [$someone_j$ [e_j wants PRO_j to see e_i]]]
c. for every x, x one of us, there is a y, y a person, such that y wants to see x

In (10b), which we will take to be equivalent to the formula in (10c) (see chapter 12 for details), the variable e_i is bound across the subject e_j. That (10a) is grammatical means that we cannot subject the binding of variables to the SSC. The binding of variables by quantifiers is thus parallel to the binding of *wh*-traces, which is not subject to the SSC (section 9.2.3). We therefore conclude that variables inserted by Quantifier Interpretation are not anaphors.

11.4 Bibliographical Comments

On the role of semantics within a generative grammar, see the works listed in chapter 5. The theory to which the current conception of LF is compared in section 11.1 is the semantic theory developed in Katz (1972).

Although a full discussion of model theory falls outside the scope of this book, we have left open the possibility that some syntactic level of representation such as LF might serve as a basis for model-theoretic interpretation. This possibility is explored in Partee (1975b), Cooper and Parsons (1976), and Montague (1974). A good introduction to these works is Dowty, Wall, and Peters (1981). Some critical remarks about model theory are found in Chomsky (1982b).

A more complete discussion of the relation between sentence grammar and text or discourse grammar is contained in Williams (1977).

See the next two chapters for references dealing with the rules and well-formedness conditions of LF, which are discussed more fully there.

Chapter 12
Binding

We have seen that the Specified Subject Condition and the Tensed-S Condition, first formulated as conditions on rule application, are in fact better treated as conditions on representations. Since these conditions determine the proper *bindings* in a representation, they are referred to (along with other conditions that determine proper bindings), as the *binding theory*.

In this chapter we will

A. discuss the development of a more explicit binding theory,
B. explore more consequences of the shift from conditions on rules to conditions on representations,
C. show how the typology of null NPs given in table 9.1 can be extended to nonnull NPs, and examine this typology in light of the binding theory.

Task C will involve reference to the seven types of NPs mentioned so far:

(1)
a. lexical NPs
b. pronouns
c. reflexives and other bound anaphors
d. PRO
e. NP-trace
f. *wh*-trace
g. logical variables

In this chapter we will be concerned only with the first five. (The distinction between the first five and the last two is a principled one, whose import we will discuss in chapter 13 and later chapters.) Furthermore, we will be concerned only with certain aspects of the distribution of these five items, such as binding and the relation of anaphoric items to their antecedents.

12.1 Disjoint Reference

Why is it that in (2) *John* and *he/him* can be construed as referring to the same person, whereas in (3) *John* and *him* cannot be so construed?

(2)

a. *John* hopes that *he* will get the prize
b. *John* wants Mary to like *him* $\Big\}$ coreference possible

(3)

a. *John* likes *him*
b. *John* wants *him* to get the prize $\Big\}$ only disjoint reference possible

The classical transformational solution to this problem involved a transformation of Pronominalization that converted a full NP into a pronoun just in case it was "identical" to another "appropriately" situated NP. The SD of the rule was such that it could not apply to *John likes John,* but it could apply to *John wants Mary to like John.*

In line with the lexicalist approach, however, it is reasonable to assume that pronouns are base-generated and that an LF rule of Coreference, with an SD similar to that of the old-style Pronominalization, assigns the "coreference relation" to pairs of NPs when one of them is a pronoun. This proposal is able to make sense of the fact that pronouns occur in sentences where they could not have been introduced by transformation, such as *He left.*

12.1.1 The Disjoint Reference Rule

A considerable refinement of this proposal comes with the realization that sentence grammar should properly be concerned, not with coreference, but with *non*coreference. This might sound like a rather subtle shift in perspective, but actually it radically changes the problem.

As an analogy, consider phonology. In phonology, natural classes of speech sounds can be labeled with feature complexes, and the fewer the features, the more general the class. Thus, for example, the non-high consonants can be labeled [+cons, −high], and phonological rules can be written that affect all members of this general class. But it would not be so easy to write a rule affecting the complement of this class.

The best we could do would be to specify a union of two classes, the nonconsonantal segments [−cons] and the high segments [+high]. Thus, in phonology it clearly makes a difference in simplicity whether a rule is written to apply to a class or its complement.

The situation is similar with coreference. Is it simpler to specify the environments in which an NP and a pronoun can be coreferential, or the environments in which they cannot be (that is, in which they must be disjoint in reference)? The new insight is that it is simpler to specify where they cannot be coreferential.

12.1.2 Notation

Various proposals have been made for representing the noncoreference relation. We will consider two of these, the one presented in "On Binding" (Chomsky (1980b)) and the one presented in *Lectures on Government and Binding* (Chomsky (1981c)). These two notations appear quite different from each other, but in fact both preserve the insight that it is the noncoreference relation that is to be characterized in sentence grammar, not the coreference relation.

In "On Binding" Chomsky proposes that NPs (specifically, lexical NPs and pronouns) receive two indices, a referential index and an anaphoric index. The anaphoric index is specifically used for stating disjoint reference. It is actually a set of indices: the set of (referential) indices of NPs from which the indexed NP is disjoint in reference. The Disjoint Reference rule then assigns the referential index of certain NPs to the anaphoric index of certain pronouns, namely any pronouns that the NP is disjoint in reference from. This rule might be stated as follows:

(4)
Disjoint Reference
If NP_1 precedes and c-commands NP_2 and NP_2 is a pronoun, then assign the referential index of NP_1 to the anaphoric index of NP_2.

(For the definition of c-command, see (5) of chapter 9.)

Now, let us assume that each lexical NP and pronoun is assigned a referential index in D-Structure. Let us further assume that the anaphoric index of an NP is represented as a set enclosed in square brackets and that in D-Structure and S-Structure this set is empty. Disjoint Reference (4) will convert the s-structure (5a) into the LF-representation (5b):

(5)

a. John$_{i,\ [\ ]}$ likes him$_{j,\ [\ ]}$

b. John$_{i,\ [\ ]}$ likes him$_{j,\ [i]}$

This correctly represents the fact that *John* and *him* cannot be coreferential. (Note that the noncoreference is *not* represented by the fact that *John* and *him* have different referential indices; rather, it is represented by the fact that the anaphoric index of *him* contains the referential index of *John*, namely [i].)

But this rule will assign an incorrect interpretation to a sentence like *John wants Mary to like him:*

(6)

John$_{i,\ [\ ]}$ wants Mary$_{j,\ [\ ]}$ to like him$_{k,\ [i,j]}$

(6) correctly represents the fact that *Mary* and *him* cannot be coreferential, but it incorrectly claims that *John* and *him* also cannot be coreferential. If the pronoun is in the subject position of an infinitive, though, the rule will again apply correctly:

(7)

John$_{i,\ [\ ]}$ wants him$_{j,\ [i]}$ to like Mary$_{k,\ [\ ]}$

This difference between subject and object is already familiar—it reflects the SSC.

One solution to the problem posed by (6) and (7) would be simply to restrict the application of (4) by the SSC. For the facts considered thus far, this would be sufficient. But rule (4) in fact needs to be more general. Consider a sentence in which a pronoun precedes and c-commands a lexical NP:

(8)

He thinks that Mary likes John

Here, rule (4) will wrongly allow *he* and *John* to be coreferential, since (a) it assigns anaphoric indices only to pronouns (and hence will not assign one to *John*) and (b) *he* is c-commanded by nothing (and hence also receives no anaphoric index). Suppose the rule is allowed to assign an anaphoric index to all NPs, or at least to lexical NPs and pronouns:

(9)

Disjoint Reference

Assign the referential index of NP$_i$ to the anaphoric index of all NPs that NP$_i$ c-commands.

If this rule applies to (8), it derives the correct LF-representation (10):

(10)

he$_{i, [\ ]}$ thinks that Mary$_{j, [i]}$ likes John$_{k, [i,j]}$

(10) says that *John* is not coreferential with *he*, that *Mary* isn't either, and that *Mary* and *John* are not coreferential.

But the application of (9) that puts the referential index of *he* in the anaphoric index of *John* violates the SSC. Clearly, it makes a difference whether the second NP is a lexical NP or a pronoun. This difference must be built either into the rule or into the SSC. It might be possible, though perhaps peculiar, to construct a theory along these lines: the SSC inhibits the operation of Disjoint Reference (9) when the second NP is a pronoun, but not when it is a lexical NP. On the other hand, rather than obstructing the application of the rule, it might be better to prohibit the configuration derived by the rule. This will require two definitions:

(11)

a. *Domain-of-a-subject:* X is in the domain-of-a-subject if X is c-commanded by that subject.

b. *Anaphorically free with respect to* i *in X:* An NP is anaphorically free with respect to *i* in X if the anaphoric index of that NP contains *i* and there is no c-commanding NP in X whose referential index is *i*.

Given these definitions, the part of the SSC that governs disjoint reference may be stated as follows:

(12)

Specified Subject Condition

If a pronoun is anaphorically free with respect to *i* in the domain-of-a-subject, then remove *i* from the anaphoric index of that pronoun.

Thus construed, the SSC is an operation on LF that applies after the indexing rule(s). The SSC will thus derive (13b) from (13a):

(13)

a. John$_{i, [\ ]}$ wants Mary$_{j, [i]}$ to like him$_{k, [i,j]}$

b. John$_{i, [\ ]}$ wants Mary$_{j, [i]}$ to like him$_{k, [j]}$

The anaphoric index *i* is erased from *him*, thus correctly predicting that *John* and *him* are not necessarily disjoint in reference. The erasure takes place because the pronoun is in the domain of *Mary* and is anaphorically free with respect to *i* in that domain. If the pronoun is in the subject position of an infinitive, as in (14),

(14)

John$_{i, \, [\,]}$ wants him$_{j, \, [i]}$ to like Mary$_{k, \, [i,j]}$

then no erasure takes place, since the only subject in whose domain *him* falls is *John,* and it is not anaphorically free in that domain. Erasure is also blocked when the lower NP is lexical, since the SSC refers only to pronouns:

(15)

he$_{i, \, [\,]}$ wants Mary$_{j, \, [i]}$ to like John$_{k, \, [i,j]}$

Thus, the distinction between lexical NPs and pronouns is built into the SSC, not into the indexing rule.

12.2 The Interpretation of Indices

The interpretation of the anaphoric index is roughly, "If *i* is in the anaphoric index of an NP, then that NP is not to be taken as coreferential with any NP whose referential index is *i*." When neither of two NPs has the referential index of the other in its anaphoric index, then these two NPs may either be taken as coreferential, or not. In other words, the two NPs are both free in reference, and (the sentence in which they occur may be used in such a way that) they may corefer. Thus, sentence grammar underdetermines coreference. All it says about reference is that certain pairs of NPs may not corefer; it says nothing about whether other pairs of NPs corefer or not.

The next plausible step would be to try to construct a theory that indicates (exhaustively) the coreference relation; that is, a theory that indicates both that certain pairs of NPs cannot corefer and that certain NPs do corefer. This can be done (as in Chomsky (1981c)) by eliminating the anaphoric index from the theory and returning to the traditional notion of coreference wherein two NPs are coreferential if they have the same index and are not coreferential if they do not. Then, assuming that every NP has some index, coreference relations are exhaustively specified.

However, the theory should not include a rule that *assigns* coreference, since the noncoreference relation is much easier to state. Furthermore, a coreference rule would be a strictly unbounded rule, and would deliberately violate the SSC, since it would only apply across subjects. A noncoreference rule would look more like other rules we have examined, in its "local" character.

The procedure would then be to assign indices freely (by a rule that says simply, "Index NPs freely") and subsequently filter out the unwanted cases of indexing. Consider the following two examples, in which indexing has applied freely:

(16)
a.   John$_i$ saw him$_j$
b.   *John$_i$ saw him$_i$

To rule out the second, but not the first, it might suffice to require that a pronoun be *free* (with respect to its index) in a given domain (where an NP is free in X if it is not coindexed with any c-commanding NP in X). Then the SSC may be stated as follows:

(17)
Specified Subject Condition
In the domain of a subject, a pronoun must be free.

This will rule out (16b): him$_i$ is in the domain of *John$_i$*, but it is not free in that domain (it is coindexed with *John$_i$*).

Unfortunately, this version of the SSC will also rule out (18):

(18)
John$_i$ wants Mary$_j$ to like him$_i$

This is an undesired result, since *John* and *him* can be coreferential in such a structure. Since *him$_i$* occurs in the domain of *John$_i$*, it must be free in that domain, by (17). The key difference is that *him* also occurs in the domain of *Mary*, and this second domain is "smaller" than the first. To capitalize on this difference, the SSC may be rewritten as follows:

(19)
Specified Subject Condition
A pronoun must be free in the smallest domain-of-a-subject in which it occurs.

This will work when the second NP is a pronoun. But what if the second NP is lexical?

(20)

*He$_i$ wants Mary$_j$ to like John$_i$

Again, lexical NPs differ from pronouns. Clearly, the rule that says that *he* and *John* cannot be coreferential in this structure is blind to the fact that a subject, *Mary*, intervenes between the two. The following rule is thus needed to account for lexical NP:

(21)

A lexical NP must be free (in all domains-of-a-subject) (or, equivalently, in all domains).

This difference between lexical NPs and pronouns is perhaps the only difference that is relevant to their logical properties. For example, in chapter 13 we will examine the binding of pronouns by quantifier phrases; the fact that lexical NPs cannot be bound by quantifier phrases will follow from the same rule, (21).

(21) applies even to lexical NPs that have antecedents. Thus, for example, *John* can be coreferential with the epithet *the bastard* in (22):

(22)

[$_S$ John arrived late]$_S$ and [$_S$ the bastard had the nerve to criticize Mary]$_S$

Coreference is permitted because *John* does not c-command *the bastard*. When the c-command relation does hold between an NP and an epithet, coreference is not permitted:

(23)

*John thinks that the bastard will win

Principles (19) and (21) are well-formedness conditions on LF. They are quite abstract, but they are invoked in many explanations, as we will see. A theory with these two principles can afford to have the most general (and least interesting) rule of coreference assignment: "Index NPs freely."

12.3 Control, Bound Anaphora, and NP-Trace

Rules (19) and (21) cover two of the five types of NP we are considering here, pronouns and lexical NP. The others—PRO (at least obligatory control PRO), reflexives, and NP-trace—share a property the first two lack: they have obligatory antecedents, and the relation between them and their antecedents is governed by strict structural conditions.

We will begin the discussion with the idea that these items must be bound. The fact that this idea must be stipulated would seem to be an irreducible property of these items, though in part IV we will examine an effort to derive it from more general principles. Next we will consider the conditions that govern the binding of these items, seeking a comprehensive theory. Finally, having examined the properties that these three types of NP share, we will turn to properties that distinguish them. In fact, it will turn out to be arbitrary to divide NPs into the two classes "lexical NP, pronoun" and "PRO, reflexive, NP-trace," since there are properties that cut across this division: reflexives, like lexical NPs and pronouns, are lexical, and case-marking applies both to lexical NPs and pronouns and to reflexives (as well as *wh*-trace). In part IV we will see that the several different types of NP are projections of an abstract set of categories, such as [±anaphoric] and [±case-marked]. Thus, the remainder of this chapter may be regarded as an investigation of the feature [+bound].

12.4 Are There Binding Rules?

Another logical step is to attempt to construct a theory in which there are no binding rules, but only the already needed rule of free coindexing plus conditions on LF that determine the well-formed bindings. In such a theory NP-trace will already be bound to its antecedent at S-Structure. Thus, the LF *rule* "Index NPs freely" will apply neither to NPs that bind NP-traces nor to the NP-traces that they bind; however, general LF *conditions* on binding *will* apply to them, since at LF the bindings determined by NP-Movement will be indistinguishable from bindings determined at LF itself.

We know that NP-Movement, PRO Construal, and Reflexive Interpretation are all governed by the SSC:

(24)
a. *Bill$_i$ is believed Sam to have seen e_i
b. *Bill$_i$ believes Sam to have seen himself$_i$
c. *Bill$_i$ believes Sam to have promised PRO$_i$ to go

But a rule of free indexing will generate all these structures. How, then, are they to be ruled out?

Assuming that NP-trace, PRO, and bound lexical anaphors (such as reflexives) are all anaphors, then the condition that governs the relation of an anaphor to its controller can be stated as follows:

(25)

An anaphor must not be free in the smallest domain-of-a-subject in which it occurs.

This will rule out (24a–c). By itself, it will not be sufficient to determine the distribution of anaphors. Further conditions will be needed for that. However, it is not only a step in the right direction: if correct, it is one of the fundamental laws of language, and one must get down to quite specific details of particular constructions to see what remains to be explained about anaphors. This we will do in due course.

Note that this condition does not specifically refer to the antecedent of the anaphor—rather, it refers to "freeness," where an anaphor can fail to be free only if it is c-commanded by a coindexed NP. But what about reflexives?

(26)

*Himself left

(25) does not rule out (26), since the reflexive does not occur in any domain-of-a-subject, and so of course does not occur free in any domain-of-a-subject. Thus, (25) must operate in conjunction with the requirement that a reflexive must have an antecedent. PRO, on the other hand, whose status with respect to (25) we have not yet determined, can sometimes appear free:

(27)

PRO to leave would be nice

We will return to this problem in a later section.

(25) constrains the distribution of NP-trace in an interesting way. NP-Movement, from which NP-traces arise, can move NPs to positions in which they do not c-command their traces:

(28)

a. For it to rain impressed John
b. *For John$_i$ to rain was impressed e_i

It is immediately clear why (28b) is ungrammatical: since e_i is not c-commanded by John$_i$, it is not bound in the smallest domain-of-a-subject in which it occurs—in fact, it is not bound at all. In sum, then, (25) requires that movement always be to a c-commanding position.

In fact, (25) predicts that all anaphors must be c-commanded by their antecedents. Again, there are some problems with PRO, to which we will return later. There are also problems with reflexives:

(29)

Those pictures of himself$_i$ pleased John$_i$

In (29) the reflexive is not c-commanded by its antecedent *John*. Nevertheless, the sentence is grammatical.

The range of cases where the c-command prediction fails, though, is quite limited. For example:

(30)

*John$_i$'s friends upset himself$_i$

Other cases where c-command fails could be attributed to reanalysis, as discussed in chapter 9:

(31)

a. John talked [$_{PP}$ to Bill]$_{PP}$ about himself

b. John [talked to] Bill about himself

If (31a) is reanalyzed to (31b), then this case is accounted for, since *Bill* does c-command the reflexive in (31b). The reanalysis is warranted in this case, since Passive can apply to (31b).

(32)

Bill$_i$ was [talked to] e_i about himself by John

Furthermore, when reanalysis can be shown to be impossible, then binding of the reflexive is not permitted. For example, when *Wh*-Movement fronts the entire postverbal PP, reanalysis cannot take place:

(33)

[To whom] did John talk [$_{PP}$ e]$_{PP}$ about himself

Here, the reflexive can only be understood as bound to *John,* not to *whom,* whereas (34), in which reanalysis has taken place, is again ambiguous:

(34)

Who did John [talk to] [e] about himself

12.5 PRO

The problem with PRO is that sometimes it behaves like an anaphor and sometimes it does not:

(35)

a. John advised Mary PRO to leave

b. PRO to leave would be nice

In (35b) PRO is free and thus cannot be an anaphor; in (35a) it is not free and in fact cannot be interpreted freely.

It would not be enough to posit an ambiguity between PRO [+anaphor] and PRO [−anaphor]. It would still be necessary to determine how these two types of PRO are distributed. Anaphoric PRO (known as *obligatory control PRO* in the earlier stage of the theory described in section 8.5) is essentially limited to complements. Nonanaphoric PRO (*nonobligatory* or *optional control PRO*) occurs, among other places, in infinitival subjects, infinitival relatives, and infinitival indirect questions.

Perhaps it would instead be more correct to say that there are specific *environments* in which PRO must be anaphoric rather than ascribing the feature [±anaphoric] inherently to PRO itself. Thus, the subject position of infinitival complements of V will be a position of bound anaphora (*V PRO to VP*), but the subject position of an infinitive that is itself a subject will not. Lexical pronouns, like PRO, are not inherently bound, but in certain environments they too function as bound anaphors. For example:

(36)

John lost *his* way

Formulating the theory of bound anaphora in terms of environments of bound anaphora, instead of in terms of anaphoric items, complicates it a good deal. For example, the question immediately arises what the notational system is for specifying bound anaphora. We will not take this up here, but will return to it in chapter 19.

12.6 Summary and Conclusions

We have described a partial theory of the distribution of lexical NP, NP-trace, pronouns, reflexives, and PRO—specifically, the part of the theory that concerns binding and disjoint reference among these items. The system can be summarized as one (trivial) rule and three conditions:

(37)
a. Rule: "Index NPs freely"
b. Conditions:
   i. A bound anaphor (or a potentially anaphoric item in an environment of bound anaphora) must be bound in the smallest domain-of-a-subject in which it occurs.
   ii. A pronoun must be free in the smallest domain-of-a-subject in which it occurs.
   iii. A lexical NP must be free in all domains.

The last two conditions correspond to what was called earlier the Specified Subject Condition. The difference is that these two are conditions on LF, whereas the SSC, as construed earlier, was a condition on the operation of specific rules, namely Disjoint Reference and the rules assigning antecedents to bound anaphors.

We must emphasize that many aspects of the distribution of the five NP types are not determined by these binding conditions. For example, given that the subject of the complement of *promise* is a position of bound anaphora, and given that the reflexive is a bound anaphor, the conditions in (37) will permit the following structure:

(38)
*John$_i$ promised Mary [himself$_i$ to win]

But this is not due to any failure of the binding conditions; in chapter 14 we will see that the reason why the reflexive cannot occur here has nothing to do with binding, but rather turns on the distinction between "lexical" and "nonlexical," a distinction that is irrelevant to binding, according to the theory.

Thus, any comprehensive account of the distribution of these five different kinds of NP will involve several distinct parts of the total theory. Of course, these parts of the theory cannot be evaluated in isolation. From this, though, it does not follow that a single "unified" theory must be constructed. On the contrary, the simplicity that can be achieved in each part of the theory is the prime reason for articulating the theory into subparts in the first place. The explanations for particular facts might turn out to be complicated, involving principles from all of the theories, but sheer "simplicity of explanation" cannot be taken seriously as a goal of theory construction.

12.7 Bibliographical Comments

The binding theory described in this chapter is that of Chomsky (1980b) (a precursor to the binding theory described in chapter 17, namely that of Chomsky (1981c)). In particular, the formalization in terms of a referential and an anaphoric index is developed in the appendix to Chomsky (1980b).

Since we will be discussing more recent proposals concerning the binding theory in part IV, we concentrate here on earlier publications that have played a role in developing it. As far as bound anaphors are concerned, interesting analyses of reflexives are found in Helke (1971) and Jackendoff (1972). For reciprocals, see Dougherty (1970) and Fiengo and Lasnik (1973). For PRO, see the references given in chapter 8.

The literature on pronouns is more abundant. An early transformational analysis is found in Lees and Klima (1963). Many of the facts that are still central to the theory of pronouns were discovered in Lakoff (1968). The first insightful interpretive analysis is Dougherty (1969).

The major breakthrough in the study of binding, however, came with the insight that the binding properties of pronouns should be handled by a disjoint reference rule rather than by a rule assigning coreference. The idea as such originates with Postal's "Unlike Person Constraint" (Postal (1969)). But it was Chomsky (1973) who showed that this rule could be formulated in such a way that it was subject to the same constraints as the rules for bound anaphora (the SSC and the TSC). This approach was extended to cover the full range of pronominal anaphora in Lasnik (1976). Another important analysis of pronominal (non)coreference along these lines is Reinhart (1976). For a diverging view, see Bach and Partee (1980).

Chapter 13
Quantification

Sentence (1a) is ambiguous, its two interpretations being roughly represented by structures (1b) and (1c):

(1)
a. Someone saw everyone
b. For all x, there is a y, such that x saw y
c. There is a y, for all x, such that x saw y

Certainly this is an ambiguity in the meaning of the sentence, and certainly structural properties of sentences affect the interpretation of quantifiers like these. Nevertheless, since LF is not a full representation of meaning, it is by no means clear that the scope of quantifiers is represented there.

We might suppose that at least those aspects of meaning that determine the truth or falsity of a sentence were represented in LF, in which case the scope of quantifiers would also be represented there, since (1b) and (1c) will not be true of the same situations—(1b) is true of a greater range of situations than (1c). This supposition is undoubtedly incorrect within the framework adopted here, since, for example, aspects of word meaning that we explicitly exclude from LF are definitely involved in determining truth and falsity (witness such cases as *unmarried bachelor*). Nevertheless, it has the character of a methodological guideline in the early stages of empirical research, subject to revision as the theory of LF develops.

In this chapter we will outline a theory about the representation of the scope of quantified NPs in LF. The representations will be roughly like those of ordinary predicate calculus. The empirical content of the theory of quantification can be divided into two parts. First, the representations of those aspects of meaning that concern the scope of quantifiers assigned by the grammar must correspond to our intuitions about meaning, or at least where they do not, the theory must explain why not.

Second, even proposals that meet this empirical requirement may leave many questions unanswered—for example, whether LF is the appropriate level of representation for indicating quantifier scope, or whether in fact any level of representation of grammar proper is appropriate. Perhaps only coreference and disjoint reference relations are appropriately represented at LF.

Thus, postulating that quantification and reference relations are represented at the same level of description is an empirical claim, and one that requires demonstration. Evidence bearing on it comes from the phenomenon of *weak crossover* (section 13.5). Before discussing that topic, though, we will outline a theory of LF quantification, including a discussion of the interpretation of structures generated by *Wh-*Movement.

13.1 The Interpretation of *Wh*-Structures

By the hypothesis of previous chapters, the input to the rules deriving LF is S-Structure, in which are represented the bindings derived by movement rules. Among these are the bindings derived by *Wh*-Movement, such as the following:

(2)
Who$_i$ do you see e_i

The relation between a *wh*-phrase and the trace it binds bears a resemblance to the binding of a variable by a quantifier in predicate calculus. This resemblance has been capitalized on to derive the strongest empirical results in the theory of quantification. As a first step toward assimilating *wh*-structures to quantificational structures, suppose that *wh*-structures receive a "quantification"-like interpretation in LF. For example, the s-structure (2) might receive the LF-representation (3):

(3)
For which x_i, x_i a person, do you see x_i

Or, to abbreviate:

(4)
$?x_i[x_i:$ who] do you see x_i

Another type of example involves NPs with *which:*

(5)
a. Which pie did you eat
b. $?x_i[x_i:$ pie] you eat x_i

This notation is the notation of restricted quantification; the material between brackets is a restriction on the quantifier "$?x_i$." One way to paraphrase (5b) is "For which x_i, where x_i ranges over the things that are pies, did you eat x_i?" Reasons for using the notation of restricted quantification for natural language quantification will be given later.

At this point the reasons for translating S-Structure to LF in this way may seem arbitrary, but before we can proceed to justification we must formulate the proposal for translation in more detail. The following rules may be postulated for (4) and (5):

(6)
$[wh\text{-word } N']_i \ldots e_i \ldots \rightarrow ?x_i[x_i: N'] \ldots x_i \ldots$

(7)
$[_{NP} wh\text{-word}]_{NP_i} \ldots e_i \ldots \rightarrow ?x_i[x_i: A] \ldots x_i \ldots$

A = person if *wh*-word = *who*
A = thing if *wh*-word = *what*

Rule (6) is for NPs with *which,* and rule (7) for NPs with *who* and *what.* These rules are explicit enough to give the required representations. Bearing in mind that rules of this explicitness are possible, we will use more informal notation in the discussion that follows.

We now turn to the nature of the variable x_i left by these rules, and the nature of the quantifier phrase itself.

13.2 The Variable and Strong Crossover

Since the variable is an indexed item in LF, is it subject to the opacity conditions? If so, to which one? Example (8) demonstrates that the variable must be "free in all categories," a result partly anticipated in chapter 9. It cannot be understood as anaphoric with any of the pronouns that c-command it (where *anaphoric with* means "instance of the same variable as"):

(8)
a. Who did he think that he said he saw
b. $?x_i[x_i:$ person] he think that he said he saw x_i

If *wh*-variables are taken to be subject to the same constraint as definite NPs and proper names—that is, they must be "free in all categories"—then such representations as (9) will be automatically excluded,

(9)
*?$x_i[x_i$: person] he think that he$_i$ said he saw x_i

since in such a representation x_i is coindexed with a c-commanding phrase, which is not allowed. Of course, the variable cannot be coindexed with any of the c-commanding pronouns in this example.

If the order of pronoun and variable is reversed, an anaphoric relation is possible (though not required):

(10)
a. Who did Jo think said John saw him
b. ?$x_i[x_i$: person] Jo think x_i said John saw him$_i$

Here, *him$_i$* is to be construed as an instance of the same variable as x_i. The intended meaning could be paraphrased as follows:

(11)
Which person is such that Jo thinks that that person said that John saw that person

The fact that the pronoun in (10a) can be construed as anaphoric with the variable follows from the opacity conditions of chapter 12: the pronoun is free to be coindexed with any phrase outside of its minimal domain. It follows as well that a pronoun cannot be coindexed with a variable that is in the smallest domain of the pronoun:

(12)
a. Who$_i$ did Bill say [e_i liked him]
b. *?$x_i[x_i$: person] Bill said [x_i liked him$_i$]

Here the opacity condition on pronouns will prevent the indicated coindexing.

All of these cases are as expected if it is assumed that the variable is subject to the opacity condition on proper names and regular full NPs. Examples like (8) are known as cases of *strong crossover,* since in the derivation the *wh*-phrase that is connected with the variable has "crossed over" the pronoun, and it is in this case that the anaphoric relation is impossible. In the formulation given here, the actual crossing in the derivation is not of foremost importance, since the possibilities of coindexing are stated in terms of structural configurations in LF, rather than in terms of the derivation (of S-Structure or LF), though because of the right-branching nature of English (that is, the fact that trees of English sentences branch on the right more heavily than on the left) and the fact that movement is leftward, crossing will generally occur in the cases where a pronoun and a variable must be disjoint. It must be noted, however, that the theory predicts that the variable would be disjoint from any c-commanding pronouns even if the movement giving rise to the variable were to the right (and thus involved no crossing).

13.3 Reconstruction

So far we have systematically avoided the more complex wh-constructions that involve pied piping:

(13)
a. Which person's mother loves him
b. To whom did you think he wanted Bill to speak
c. Whose mother do you think he wanted Bill to speak to

There are two reasons to believe that the mechanism of variable insertion outlined in the previous section is not appropriate for these examples. First, if variables are simply inserted for the traces of Wh-Movement, the resulting structures do not seem to represent the interpretations of the sentences. In (13c), for example, the question variable corresponds to who; the wh-trace, however, is not the trace of who, but the trace of whose mother. If this lack of correspondence between the moved constituent and the questioned constituent were the only thing at stake, a solution might be to write rules that would sever the connection between trace and variable, to derive representations like (14):

(14)
$?x_i[x_i: \text{person}] [[x_i\text{'s mother}]_j \text{ you think he wanted Bill to speak to } e_j]$

This is not as simple as (15),

(15)
$?x_i[x_i: \text{person}] \text{ you think he wanted Bill to speak to } x_i\text{'s mother}$

but it would still be a viable representation.

But there is another reason to prefer the representation in (15) over the one in (14), again involving strong crossover. Both (14) and (15) predict that he and whose mother cannot be coreferential, or anaphorically linked. In (14) the trace of x_i's mother is c-commanded by he, and so cannot be coindexed with it, if *wh*-trace must be free in all categories; and in (15) x_i's *mother* itself is c-commanded by the pronoun. But another fact must be explained as well—namely, that *who(se)* and *he* cannot be anaphorically linked. That is, (13c) cannot be paraphrased as (16):

(16)
Which person is such that you think that person wanted Bill to speak to that person's mother

In representation (15) this is straightforward: the variable x, which corresponds to *who*, is c-commanded by *he* and thus cannot be coindexed with it, as in the previous section. But in representation (14) there is no way to immediately extend the results of the previous section to account for this gap in anaphoric possibilities—*he* does not c-command the variable x. And this despite the unavoidable conclusion that this is another case of strong crossover, since if the positions of *whose* and *he* are reversed, the anaphoric relation is suddenly possible:

(17)
[Who$_i$se mother]$_j$ do you think e_j wanted Bill to speak to him$_i$

Now, the representation in (15) immediately provides the necessary result, but so far there is no way to derive that representation. It has proved simple enough to provide the appropriate rule. Essentially, the rule for interpreting *wh*-structures will "undo" *Wh*-Movement, when the moved phrase is larger than a *wh*-phrase (that is, a phrase that can be the input to (6) or (7)). Correspondingly, a *wh*-phrase has been defined as the smallest phrase that contains a *wh*-word; thus, *wh*-phrases will be *who, what, which man, whose* (but not *whose mother*). The rule of *Wh*-Interpretation can then be stated as follows:

(18)
Wh-Interpretation (Reconstruction)
[$_{COMP}[_a$ ... [$_b$ ...]$_b$ ...]$_{a_i}$]$_{COMP}$ ... e_i ...
Where b is a *wh*-phrase, replace e_i with a_i, replace b with x_i, and place $?x_i$ N' in COMP, where N' is the head of b. Or, if $b = who$, place $?x_i[x_i:$ person] in COMP.

This rule, more complicated than the earlier rule for *wh*-interpretation, will derive the structures to which disjoint reference rules will apply without further stipulation. Since this rule reconstructs (almost) the pre-*Wh*-Movement structure, it has been called *Reconstruction*.

In sum, then, in order to treat (13c) as a case of strong crossover without complicating the opacity conditions outlined in chapter 12, we have complicated the rule for *wh*-interpretation. We could have done the opposite, as in fact Higginbotham (1980) has proposed; that is, instead of invoking Reconstruction, we could have complicated the rules governing disjoint reference for pronouns. Alternatively, we could impose the coreference conditions before *Wh*-Movement; in that case it would not be necessary to reconstruct the pre-*Wh*-Movement structure. An analysis along these lines is attempted in Van Riemsdijk and Williams (1981). At present, it would seem worthwhile to keep all three possibilities in mind; we have outlined the Reconstruction theory here mainly because of its familiarity.

13.4 Unmoved *Wh*-Words

Since *Wh*-Movement, and in fact all movement, is optional, structures will be generated in which *wh*-words appear in their D-Structure positions. The rule for *wh*-interpretation would then be inapplicable to them, since that rule applies only to *wh* in COMP. It is conceivable that no rule should apply to them. As a result, no interpretation would be assigned to sentences containing them; these sentences would then be effectively filtered out of the language, for lack of interpretation. But in fact there is a rule for interpreting these unmoved *wh*-words, a rule already discussed in chapter 4. We repeat its main features here in order to examine how they fit into the LF framework. It will turn out that the rule interpreting unmoved *wh*-words is the same one as the rule interpreting quantified NPs in general.

There are two different kinds of interpretation that an unmoved *wh*-word might be subject to. First, there is the *echo* sense of *wh*-words, used when communication has failed:

(19)
Speaker A: I saw the . . . in the field today
Speaker B: You saw the *what* in the field today?

Second, unmoved *wh*-words are used to create questions in which more than one position is questioned:

(20)
Who gave what to whom

The echo use of *wh*-words can be distinguished from the second, more "logical" use in a number of ways. In the echo question, the main stress invariably falls on the *wh*-word, the part of the sentence after the *wh*-word is on a constant high pitch, the echo *wh*-word can occur as the only *wh*-word in the clause, and it has the rather narrow discourse function of drawing attention to failed communication. None of these is true of (20), the use we will be exploring here.

Wh-Interpretation (Reconstruction) will give (20) the following partial interpretation:

(21)

$?x_i[x_i$ gave what to whom]

But it does not say how *what* and *whom* are interpreted. Intuitively, the interpretation of such sentences seems to involve a triple, along the following lines:

(22)

For which triple, (x,y,z), x gave y to z

Or, equivalently:

(23)

For which x, for which y, for which z, x gave y to z

This kind of interpretation could be derived from a rule that would apply to unmoved *wh*-words:

(24)

Unmoved Wh-Interpretation

$[\ldots$ *wh*-phrase $\ldots] \rightarrow [?x_i]\ [\ldots x_i \ldots]$

This rule would adjoin the question operator to some S dominating the *wh*-phrase and would place a coindexed variable in the place of the *wh*-phrase. Applying this rule twice to (21) would produce (25):

(25)

$?x_i[?x_j[?x_k[x_i$ gave x_j to $x_k]]]$

(25) is a fairly good approximation to the felt interpretation of the sentence.

However, this rule predicts the existence of ordinary *wh*-questions in which no *wh*-phrase has moved. For example, it would convert (26a) into (26b):

(26)
a. John saw who
b. ?x_i [John saw x_i]

Now, (26a) is certainly interpretable as an echo question, but not as a simple question. In fact, the rule for unmoved *wh* should operate only when there is already a *wh* in the complementizer. This idea could be implemented in a number of ways. It could be written into the SD of the rule, for example. This has a number of disadvantages. Not only does it complicate the rule; it also makes it impossible to consider this rule a special case of Quantifier Interpretation, as it seems we should (see section 13.6). Also, in many languages the restriction on the complementizer would not be valid, because in those languages either questions do not involve movement (as in Japanese, for example) or movement is optional (as in French). The only way to form a question when there is no movement is to apply rule (24). It is perhaps a peculiarity of English, which should not be written into this rule, that only clauses with a *wh*-word in COMP can be interpreted as questions.

13.5 *Wh*-Interpretation and Weak Crossover

We now turn to cases where anaphoric relations fail to hold, but where this failure does not follow from the principles outlined in chapter 12. The principle involved seems to be unique to quantificational structures. Consider the following cases of failed anaphora:

(27)
a. Who does the girl that *he* likes miss x_i
b. Who does *his* mother like x_i
c. Who would the fact that *he* was sick for three days upset x_i

In all of these cases *he/his* cannot be considered to be a bound variable, bound to the *wh*-operator or coindexed with the variable (x_i). But this failure of coindexing does not follow from the opacity conditions, even under the assumption that the variable is "like a name," because the pronoun does not c-command the variable.

It would not do to weaken the structural condition of c-command to cover these cases of failed anaphora, because the failure does not extend to all cases that the Opacity Condition was designed to govern. Consider the following structurally parallel cases:

(28)

a. The girl that *he* likes misses *John*
b. *His* mother likes *John*
c. The fact that *he* was sick for three days upset *John*

In these cases the anaphoric reading is possible. Thus, the restriction exhibited in (27) seems to be limited to variables.

Let us tentatively say that the relevant condition is that a pronoun cannot be coindexed with a variable to its right. This has been called the *Leftness Condition*. As (29) shows, the Leftness Condition must follow some kind of reconstruction:

(29)

Whose mother does his father like e_i

Here, *whose* cannot be coindexed with *his,* but the Leftness Condition cannot apply, because there is no variable to the right of *his* corresponding to *whose.* But *Wh*-Interpretation (Reconstruction) will result in the following structure:

(30)

$?x_i$[his father likes x_i's mother]

Here, the variable x_i is to the right of *his,* and the Leftness Condition can apply to prohibit the pronoun from being coindexed with the variable—the correct result. This provides further evidence for the rule of Reconstruction, though some of the previously mentioned alternatives to Reconstruction would work equally well.

These cases in which coindexing fails are referred to as the *weak crossover* cases. They are distinguished from the strong crossover cases by the fact that only the Leftness Condition, and not the Opacity Condition, applies to them.

Do unmoved *wh*-words show the weak crossover effect? In fact, they do:

(31)

Which newspaper reported that his mother liked which candidate

Though this sentence may be awkward, it seems clear that *his* and *which candidate* cannot be coreferential. But this result will follow from the rules given so far. *Wh*-Interpretation (Reconstruction) and rule (24) for unmoved *wh*-interpretation will give the following LF-representation:

(32)

$?x_i[x_i$: a newspaper] $[?x_j[x_j$: a candidate] $[x_i$ reported that his mother liked $x_j]]$

Here, x_j is to the right of *his*, so (correctly) coindexing is not possible. (33) is a similar case, but one where the Leftness Condition is not applicable:

(33)

Which newspaper reported that its editors liked which candidate

Here, *its* can be coindexed with the variable corresponding to *which newspaper*, since that variable is to the left of *its*.

These constructions provide striking evidence for the level of LF as well as for trace theory. The variables that are subject to the Leftness Condition arise from two different sources: both from *Wh*-Interpretation (Reconstruction) and from the rule for unmoved *wh*-phrase interpretation (24). In S-Structure these two cases are quite different— one has a trace where the other has a *wh*-phrase. In LF, on the other hand, they are similar in that they both have a *variable* in the relevant position. The notions "variable" and "coindexed with" are the key notions in LF. In the next section we will see how the applicability of these notions has been extended.

13.6 Quantifier Interpretation

Returning to the examples with which this chapter began, we may ask again whether there is any evidence that their ambiguity should be resolved at LF:

(34)
a. Someone saw everyone
b. For all x, there is a y, such that y saw x
c. There is a y, for all x, such that y saw x

Let us suppose for the moment that it should, and let us extend the notions "variable" and "binding" introduced in the previous sections to these cases. This can be done by identifying certain phrases as quantifier phrases (QPs), adjoining them to some higher node that dominates them, and leaving a variable in their S-Structure position. The rule that effects this adjunction is *Quantifier Interpretation*, often called the *Quantifier Rule* or *Quantifier Raising* (*QR*):

(35)

Quantifier Interpretation

[$_S$ ... [QP] ...]$_S$ → [$_S$[QP]$_i$ [$_S$ ... x_i ...]$_S$]$_S$

The S that is sister to the QP is the *scope* of the QP. We can for the time being identify a QP as any NP that begins with a quantifier, where Quantifier is a lexical class that includes *many, every, few,* etc.:

(36)

Quantifier Phrase: [$_{NP}$ Q ...]$_{NP}$

Applying Quantifier Interpretation to both of the QPs in (34a) will derive either of the following LF-representations (depending on how the rule applies), corresponding to the felt ambiguity:

(37)

a. Someone$_i$ [everyone$_j$ [x_i saw x_j]]

b. Everyone$_j$ [someone$_i$ [x_i saw x_j]]

This rule is nearly identical to the rule for unmoved *wh*-phrase interpretation (24): in both cases a phrase is adjoined to a containing S and a variable is left in its place. If in fact *wh*-words are simply identified as quantifiers, then rule (24) can be eliminated, since Quantifier Interpretation will do its work. In effect, then, the rule for unmoved *wh*-phrase interpretation is a special case of Quantifier Interpretation.

The use of variables and binding as the mechanism for indicating the meaning of quantified expressions has an immediate, interesting empirical consequence, namely that pronouns anaphorically related to these quantified expressions should show weak crossover effects.

First, observe that a singular pronoun in the scope of *everyone* can be coindexed with the quantifier and can be interpreted as an "instance of the same variable" as the one in the position of the quantifier in LF:

(38)

a. Everyone thinks that he is the fastest

b. Everyone is here. He thinks he will leave soon

c. Everyone is here. They think they will leave soon

In (38b) this relation is not possible, since scope cannot be larger than a single utterance. Hence, the singular *he* in (38b) cannot refer to *everyone;* only a plural pronoun is possible, as in (38c).

Next, observe the effects of the Leftness Condition:

(39)

a. That *he* was sick upset *everyone*

b. *His* mother likes *everyone*

In neither of these is the anaphoric relation indicated in italics possible. Deriving the LF-representations for them and coindexing the pronouns with the quantifiers will show why:

(40)

a. Everyone$_i$ [[that he$_i$ was sick] upset x_i]

b. Everyone$_i$ [his$_i$ mother likes x_i]

Both structures contain a pronoun coindexed with a variable to its right; hence, the Leftness Condition rules them out.

   This is an encouraging result. We have now seen three kinds of cases to which the Leftness Condition applies: the structure resulting from the interpretation of structures in which *Wh*-Movement has taken place, the interpretation of unmoved *wh*-phrases, and the interpretation of quantifiers. The Leftness Condition applies in all three cases because all three involve a variable in LF. This constitutes indirect evidence for the existence of LF, in the sense that it constitutes evidence for the existence of a level of representation in which both quantificational binding and coindexing of anaphorically related items are represented.

   There is one further construction where the Leftness Condition seems to be involved. A stressed NP does not seem to permit pronouns anaphoric to it to its left:

(41)

a. That *he* was sick upset *JOHN*

b. The man that *he* knew gave *JOHN* the money

(Capital letters indicate the position of main sentence stress.) Apparently, the indicated coreference is not possible, even though the antecedent to the pronoun (*John*) is not a QP.

   However, if the sentence is assigned an interpretation in terms of *Focus* and *Presupposition,* in which main sentence stress serves to mark the Focus constituent, then these facts can be assimilated to the previous argument. Suppose that the *Focus* of a sentence is any constituent that contains the main sentence stress on its right branch. Then let us define the *Presupposition* to be what is left of a sentence when the Focus is removed; more specifically, let us define it as what is derived from S-Structure, given an identification of the Focus, by removing the

Focus and replacing it with a variable. Thus, if *JOHN* is the Focus in (41b), the Presupposition is as shown in (42):

(42)

Focus x_i = *John;* Presupposition = *the man that he knew gave x_i the money*

Now, if the Focus-Presupposition structure derived in this way is a feature of LF, then the facts of (41) are accounted for: the Leftness Condition will prevent the pronoun from being coindexed with the variable.

13.7 Summary

This chapter concludes our outline of the properties of LF and its relation to the rest of the grammar. To summarize: LF is derived from S-Structure by a Markovian derivation involving the free indexing rule ("Coindex NPs freely"), Quantifier Interpretation, and *Wh*-Interpretation (Reconstruction). LF, then, is a very "syntactic" representation, not containing any new notations not contained in S-Structure—Quantifier Interpretation bindings are like the *wh*-bindings in S-Structure, and the bindings that arise from free indexing are like the NP-Movement bindings. LF is then subject to well-formedness constraints—in particular, the binding conditions and the Leftness Condition on variables.

13.8 Bibliographical Comments

The notation used in the LF-representations of sentences in this chapter is essentially that of predicate logic, a form of logic developed in the nineteenth century by the German mathematician Gottlob Frege. A good collection of his writings is Frege (1980). Readers unfamiliar with logic can acquaint themselves with basic notions by consulting Allwood, Andersson, and Dahl (1977).

On the interpretation of *wh*-structures, see the references given in chapter 4.

Crossover phenomena play a central role in the argumentation for LF. The first linguist to explore such phenomena in any detail was Postal (1971). The analysis in terms of trace theory was first considered in Wasow (1972, 1979), where the terms *strong crossover* and *weak crossover* were introduced. Other studies of crossover phenomena include Jacobson (1977) and Milner (1978).

Reconstruction was first discussed in Chomsky (1977a). The main alternatives to the rule of Reconstruction that was proposed there are found in Higginbotham (1980) and Van Riemsdijk and Williams (1981). The Leftness Condition, which plays an important role in the treatment of weak crossover, was introduced in Chomsky (1976), and a more complete account was offered in Higginbotham (1980). A more recent proposal, which dispenses with the Leftness Condition but presupposes the theory to be developed in part IV, is Koopman and Sportiche (1982).

The proposal to account for the behavior of quantified NPs by means of an LF analogue to *Wh*-Movement (here called Quantifier Interpretation) is due to May (1977, 1985). May calls this rule *Quantifier Raising* (QR). Several alternative accounts and modifications have appeared, some of which we will mention in later chapters. But an important alternative analysis that does without Quantifier Interpretation has been developed in Reinhart (1976, 1979, 1983).

Part IV

THE MODULES

Chapter 14
Case Theory

The empirical idea that the descriptive devices of the transformational component of grammar should be highly reduced, in fact trivialized, has led to the quest for a linguistic theory consisting of relatively autonomous modules, each characterized by a small number of simple, universal, but in some cases parametrized principles—a quest embodied in the stage of the grammatical theory to be presented in the next five chapters, the *Government-Binding Theory*. In this chapter we will examine the logic of this quest for modularity.

The route from reduction in transformational descriptive options to modularity has been this: It has been proposed that the descriptive devices of the transformational part of the grammar should be reduced to near zero. Essentially, the transformational component of a grammar consists of two universally available rules, "Move *wh*" and "Move NP," or perhaps of a single rule, "Move α," whose structural descriptions are specified universally, and any conditions on their application, such as Subjacency (also universal). Languages may perhaps differ with regard to whether they have movement at all or not; if they have movement, they may perhaps differ with regard to the bounding node for Subjacency, choosing either S or S'. Still, these universal and language-particular elements can only combine to yield three distinct possible transformational components for the languages of the world:

I. No movement
II. Movement; S is the bounding node for Subjacency
III. Movement; S' is the bounding node for Subjacency

Movement theory would thus predict a three-way typology of languages: I = Latin, etc.; II = English, etc.; III = Italian, etc. However, since there is clearly more to systematic linguistic variation than this typology indicates, movement must be relevant to only a very limited portion of this variation, and the rest must fall within the province of some other "subtheory" of the theory of grammar.

The same is true of variation between constructions within a given language. For example, given that *Wh*-Movement is involved in numerous constructions in English (questions, relative clauses, topicalization, etc.) and given that *Wh*-Movement is the same rule across all of these constructions, how are the various differing properties of these constructions to be accounted for? It is no longer possible to describe each construction completely in a transformational rule for its formation, since such rules are barred. The properties of the different constructions (in fact, the very existence of the different constructions) must be accounted for by the interaction of the transformational component (one might say, the "movement module") and whatever other modules there are.

The idea that the grammar is modular raises many interesting questions. How many modules are there? What are they? How are they related to one another? And so on. If the movement module is typical, we might expect the others to be simple, each allowing a very limited range of linguistic variation. Such a theory goes a long way toward explaining the central problem of language acquisition. It suggests that the problem the child faces is simply that of fixing certain parameters within each module, each of which takes only a limited range of values and all of which taken together determine a finite number of possible grammars to choose from. This is surely an improvement over a theory that takes the problem the child faces to be the writing of rules in a relatively unrestricted rule-writing system.

For example, relative clauses and questions in English differ considerably in their surface details. Given that the same base rules and transformations are used for both, how are we to account for the differences? For instance, how are we to account for the fact that a (substantive) question must have a *wh*-word in COMP, whereas a relative clause need not?

(1)

a. *$[_{\text{COMP}} \emptyset]_{\text{COMP}}$ did I see $\begin{Bmatrix} e_i \\ \text{who} \end{Bmatrix}$

b. the man$_i$ $[_{\text{COMP}}$ that$]_{\text{COMP}}$ I saw e_i

One solution would be to posit a filter that would rule ungrammatical any question that does not have a *wh*-word in COMP. Since such a filter would be language-particular (for example, Japanese, which does not have movement in questions, cannot have such a filter), a general theory of filters would be needed to specify under what circumstances they are available to languages, the notation in which they are written, how they interact with the rest of the grammar, etc. Another solution would be to propose that (1a) is ungrammatical because some rule of interpretation cannot interpret it as a substantive question. Since languages would again differ with regard to whether they have such a rule (Japanese clearly would not), a general theory of such rules of interpretation would be needed to specify such things as the range of descriptive options these rules made available to the linguist or language learner.

14.1 Case-Marking

Beginning with another look at NP-Movement, let us see how this research strategy leads to case theory. Passive and Raising appear to be optional relations since, for example, there is a passive sentence related to every active sentence. However, NP-Movement, which is the movement component in our account of these sentences, appears to be obligatory:

(2)
a. * — was seen John
b. * — seems John to be sick
c. * — was believed John to be sick

Since NP-Movement has no structural description or other means to determine when it can, cannot, and must apply, some other means must be developed to accomplish this. Furthermore, since *Wh*-Movement must be optional and since NP-Movement and *Wh*-Movement are both instances of "Move α," the rule must be optional. How, then, to account for the fact that it must apply in (2)?

(2a) aside, (2b) and (2c) would seem to reflect a general fact about infinitives, namely, that they do not have overt subjects. This is true not only of English but also of human languages in general; in fact, the restriction is more severe in many other languages than in English, where there are exceptions. It might be well, then, to base our explanation of (2b) and (2c) on this general fact about infinitives. If some module of grammar has as a consequence the prohibition of lexical (i.e., phonetically realized) subjects of infinitives, then (2b) and (2c) require no further comment: NP-Movement is obligatory so as to evade that prohibition. This is simple enough, but again it leaves open certain important questions: Which module accomplishes this? Why are there exceptions? How are these exceptions to be characterized? What is the status of (2a)?

As we saw in chapter 10, it has been proposed that there is a filter governing (2), a filter that directly prohibits subjects of infinitives. Since the avoidance of infinitive subjects appears to be universal, we might posit a universal filter (3a), whose English instantiation would be (3b) (see (25) of chapter 10):

(3)
a. *[NP *to* VP] where NP is lexical.
b. *[NP *to* VP]

$$\text{except in the context } \begin{cases} V \underline{\hspace{1cm}} \text{ (i.e., exceptional verbs)} \\ P \underline{\hspace{1cm}} \text{ (i.e., } for\text{)} \end{cases}$$

Since the filter in its general form is universal, certain questions, such as what descriptive options are available in the general theory of such filters, do not arise.

This filter rules out (2b) and (2c) and in addition embodies an important generalization about the world's languages: their infinitives do not have overt subjects. Moreover, the effect of the filter goes well beyond the conditioning of NP-Movement. It explains the obligatory presence of PRO in a number of constructions:

(4)
a. *[Bill to leave] was expected
b. *I tried [Bill to leave]
c. *What I want is [Bill to leave]
d. *the man [Bill to talk to]

In each of these cases it is the presence of an overt subject that makes the sentence ungrammatical. (Though there are examples very similar to these that do allow a lexical subject. We will turn to these shortly, but for the moment let us assume that filter (3) holds with full force.)

Now, why should such a filter as (3) hold? What is special about the subject position of an infinitive, that it cannot contain a lexical item? As Rouveret and Vergnaud (1980) recognized, the special thing about this subject position is that it is not associated with a *case-assigner*—that is, the single item in the environment of a given NP that licenses (validates the appearance of) the case in question:

(5)

Position	Case	Case-assigner
subject of tensed clause	nominative	tensed VP
possessive NP in an NP	genitive	noun
object of verb	accusative	verb
object of preposition	accusative	preposition
subject of tenseless clause	—	—

(In what follows we will leave the genitive out of consideration.)

Now, suppose that all overt (i.e., lexical, phonetically realized) NPs must have case. Then if the subject position of an infinitive is not a position to which case can be assigned, it cannot contain a lexical NP. This then explains why the NP-*to*-VP Filter holds.

This is a very satisfying rationalization of the NP-*to*-VP Filter, since it explains the filter in terms of a module of grammar, the theory of case, that must be worked out in any event. It leaves open the same questions that the filter did, but it suggests different routes to answering them. Thus, linguists have dropped the filter and have assumed that its effects are to be derived from the theory of case and from the fact that overt NPs must have case. This fact has been expressed in the Case Filter (see Chomsky (1981, 49)):

(6)
Case Filter
*NP, where NP has no case

The Case Filter is more appealing than the NP-*to*-VP Filter because a theory of case is needed independently, but the NP-*to*-VP Filter is not. But is it in fact true that a theory of case is independently necessary? In what sense do the English Ns *John* and *table,* which show no case distinctions, need case? And yet they are as ungrammatical in the subject position of an infinitive as the few English Ns (the pronouns) that do show case distinctions:

(7)
a. *[John to be there] would be nice
b. *[The table to be there] would be nice
c. *[He to be there] would be nice

Clearly, it must be claimed that such NPs as *the table* and *John* receive case even though it is not morphologically realized. Since the case these NPs bear is not realized, it has been called *abstract*. Abstract case is nothing more than ordinary case, with case distinctions morphologically neutralized; hence, it is not something new, but is a part of the general theory of case. A language could neutralize all case distinctions (that is, it could have no distinctive word endings at all that reflected different cases) and still have the Case Filter. Although properties of abstract case (such as the Case Filter) might not determine the particular properties of "real," or morphologically realized, case, they cannot be incompatible with them, for they are both part of the same system, the theory of case.

As (5) indicates, case (both real and abstract) is assigned to NPs in particular syntactic environments. For many cases, a particular terminal element of the environment can be identified as the determinant of case-assignment. For example, the direct object of a verb can be said to "get its case from" the verb, and similarly for the object of a preposition. Since nominative case is assigned to subjects of tensed (and subjunctive) clauses, the tense morpheme has been identified as the case-assigner for nominative case:

(8)
Case-assignment

Environment	Case
[V ____]	accusative
[____ tense VP]	nominative
[P ____]	accusative

The case-assigners share certain properties. First, none are phrasal elements. Second, they are either lexical (V and P) or tense, which may not be lexical in a strict sense, but is not phrasal. Third, each is the head of the phrase that most immediately contains the NP that is assigned case, at least if it is legitimate to regard tense as the head of a tensed sentence, as has been suggested. Observe, however, that not all heads are case-assigners because (in most languages) N and A cannot assign accusative case.

Case-assignment can take place only when the case-assigner and the NP to which it assigns case bear a structural relation to one another known as *government*. A preliminary definition of this relation is as follows:

(9)

Government: X governs Y if Y is contained in the maximal
$\bar{\text{X}}$-projection of X, X^{max}, and X^{max} is the smallest maximal projection
containing Y, and X c-commands Y.

For example, V governs NP in (10a) but not in (10b-i), (10b-ii), and
(10b-iv). In (10b-iii) V governs NP_1 but not NP_2.

(10)
a. $[_{VP}$ V NP$]_{VP}$
b. i. $[_{VP}$ V $[_{PP}$ P NP$]_{PP}]_{VP}$
    ii. $[_{VP}$ V $[_{S'}$ NP VP$]_{S'}]_{VP}$
    iii. $[_{VP}$ V NP_1 $[_{PP}$ P $NP_2]_{PP}]_{VP}$
    iv. $[_S$ NP $[_{VP}$ V$]_{VP}]_S$

Consequently, V can assign case to NP only in (10a). In (10b-i) and
(10b-ii) the NP is contained in a smaller maximal projection than the VP
(PP in (10b-i) and S' in (10b-ii)). In (10b-iii) NP_1 is governed by V but
not by P, since P is contained in a maximal projection (PP) that does not
contain NP_1. Furthermore, P does not c-command NP_1. Similar considerations apply to (10b-iv), assuming that VP is the maximal projection of V. Thus, the V of a sentence will not govern the subject NP.

The government relation is not unique to case theory but in fact per-
vades all modules of the grammar. Since the notion of government
must be formulated carefully to meet the needs of each of these modules, the definition given in (9) will be subject to revision. This is a
desirable result, since it leads to an extremely "tight" theory—any ad-
justment in the definition of government has far-reaching consequences
and can thus easily be checked against fact.

If case is assigned under government, and if every lexical N must
have case, then every lexical NP must appear in a position in which it is
governed by some case-assigner. Thus, in general, a lexical NP cannot
appear as the subject of a nontensed S:

(11)
*[[The boy] to win] tense would [upset me]

In this structure, the NP *the boy* is governed by the infinitive marker *to,*
but this marker, unlike "tense," is not a case-assigner. "Tense" in the
main clause is a case-assigner, but it does not govern *the boy.* Finally,
win (the verb of the infinitive) cannot assign case to *the boy* (its subject
NP), since, as discussed above, it does not govern it. Hence, the NP is
assigned no case, and the sentence is ungrammatical. This is the preliminary fact we wanted case theory to account for, and it has done so.

What happens if a case-assigner governs a nonlexical phrase, such as trace or PRO? Clearly, PRO *need not* have case, since it appears exactly in the environment that has been termed caseless: the subject position of an infinitive. In fact, if it were assumed that PRO *cannot* appear in a case-assignment position, then PRO would automatically be excluded from the subject position of tensed clauses. We will return to this later.

Trace bears on the original goal in constructing case theory—that is, explaining the obligatoriness of NP-Movement in the configurations (12a–c) (= (2a–c)):

(12)
a. * — was seen John
b. * — seems [$_{S'}$ John to be sick]$_{S'}$ (cf. *John seems to be sick*)
c. * — was believed [$_{S'}$ John to be sick]$_{S'}$ (cf. *John was believed to be sick*)

If the subject position of an infinitive is caseless, then we have an explanation for (12b) and (12c): the NPs must move, since they must acquire case. This requires that case-assignment must take place after movement, that is, at S-Structure. This explanation will do for now, though it will have to be complicated shortly, when we consider exceptional case-marking.

(12b–c) are ill-formed in another way as well: the matrix subject position is unfilled. Perhaps this, rather than the failure of case to be assigned to the postverbal position, is the reason the postverbal NP must move. Thus, consider the following cases:

(13)
a. * — seems that John was sick
b. It seems that John was sick
c. * — was believed that John was sick
d. It was believed that John was sick

The ungrammaticality of (13c) cannot be ascribed to the failure of case to be assigned to *John,* so it must be ascribed to the fact that the subject position of the matrix is unfilled. (13d) confirms this view, since in this case the subject is filled. Perhaps the subject position must be filled because the case associated with tense "must be assigned" in some sense and the expletive *it* stands in for this purpose. Similar remarks hold for (13a–b).

But in fact this does not explain the ungrammaticality of (12b–c), because even when the matrix subject is filled in with *it*, the structures are still ungrammatical:

(14)
a. *It seems John to be sick
b. *It was believed John to be sick

For these cases we must return to the original analysis: that they are ungrammatical because no case has been assigned to the postverbal NP.

(12a) is still mysterious: if *seen* is a case-assigner, then, since *seen* governs the NP *John*, *seen* should assign case to *John*, and it is not clear why *John* must move. But suppose that passive participles such as *seen* are *not* case-assigners. Then the object (here, *John*) will be forced to move. Perhaps the elimination of the case-assigning property is part of the derivation of the passive participle.

This assumption gains naturalness from the long-observed facts that the passive participle is more "adjectival" than the active verb—for example, in many languages the passive participle takes adjectival agreement markers—and that adjectives are not case-assigners in English and many other languages:

(15)
a. *John is proud Mary
b. *It was seen John

If this line of reasoning is correct, then (12a–c) are all ungrammatical for the same reason: the postverbal NP *John* fails to receive case. In (12a) this is because *seen*, which governs *John*, is not a case-assigner; in (12b–c) it is because *seems* and *believed* do not govern *John*, being separated from it by a maximal projection (S'), and because *John* is not governed by any case-assigner in its own clause. (Actually, the insertion of *of* can "rescue" such cases as (15a), but not (15b):

(16)
a. John is proud of Mary
b. *It was seen of John

It is not known why this remedy is not available for passive participles.)

Note that (12c) (* — *was believed [John to be sick]*) is now ruled out for two reasons. *Believed* cannot assign case to *John* because (a) under the definition of government it does not govern *John*, and (b) being a passive participle, it is not a case-assigner.

To sum up, then, the following elements of case theory are needed to explain the obligatoriness of NP-Movement observed in (12):

(17)
a. Every lexically headed NP must receive case from a case-assigner.
b. Case-assignment requires that the case-assigner govern the NP to which it assigns case.
c. Tense, V, and P are case-assigners.
d. The infinitive marker *to* and the passive participle are not case-assigners.

(12a) is ungrammatical because *seen,* a passive participle, is not a case-assigner. It can be improved by movement of *John* to the subject position, which is a case-assignment position, being governed by the case-assigner "tense." (12b) is ungrammatical because *seems* does not govern *John,* since *John* is contained in a maximal projection that does not include *seems.* Finally, (12c) is ungrammatical for two reasons: *believed* does not govern *John,* nor is it a case-assigner in any event.

We will soon see the need to revise these assumptions and explanations about (12b) and (12c), but first it is necessary to examine the phenomenon of exceptional case-marking.

14.2 Exceptional Case-Marking

English infinitives can have lexical subjects in certain exceptional circumstances (chapter 10). In the approach that includes case theory, these are known as cases of *exceptional case-marking* (ECM):

(18)
a. Bill believes [John to have left]
b. [For John to have left] would be good

It would be undesirable to attribute the subject's ability to appear to the infinitive itself, since in general infinitives cannot take subjects. In each instance there is a case-assigner in the vicinity of the subject in need of case: the verb *believes* in (18a) and the complementizer *for* in (18b). To account for (18b) it has been proposed that *for* be called a case-assigner, since it looks like a preposition and prepositions generally are case-assigners. This should not raise eyebrows, although generally complementizers do not seem to assign case.

(18a) poses a different problem. On the one hand, there is no reason not to consider *believes* to be a case-assigner, since it is an active verb. On the other hand, *believes* should not assign case to *John* because it does not govern it, if the complement clause is an S', since maximal projections block government.

Since (18a) is very much the exception, rather than the rule, especially in the context of the world's languages generally, we should not expect the correct solution to have the flavor of a natural phenomenon in language. It should have the flavor of the unusual.

One proposed solution is to say that verbs have the option of subcategorizing for S' or S (S' being the unmarked option and S the marked option) and that active *believe* subcategorizes for S. Since government is blocked only by maximal projections, it will therefore not be blocked in (18a). The unusualness of this construction can then be attributed to the unusualness of verbs, like *believe,* that subcategorize for S, given the reasonable assumption that subcategorization is for maximal projections in the "unmarked" case and that other possibilities are available only as marked options, which must be learned on a case-by-case basis. (This solution, which implies the absence of COMP, has certain consequences for Subjacency and successive cyclic *Wh*-Movement. For this reason a slightly different solution has been proposed, which we will discuss below and more extensively in chapter 18.)

If *believe* takes S in the active, then it would be simplest to assume that the passive participle *believed* inherits this subcategorization. Hence, the passive participle actually governs the subject of the infinitive complement in (19) (= (12c)):

(19)
* — was believed [$_S$ John to be sick]$_S$

This eliminates one of the reasons developed earlier for the ungrammaticality of this construction and leaves only the notion that the passive participle is not a case-assigner. Thus, (12a) and (12c) are accounted for identically, and (12b) is the only construction where the NP does not receive case because it is not governed.

The solution we have just outlined gains some plausibility from the fact that although there are Vs like *believe,* there are no adjectives like *believe*—that is, there are no adjectives that take infinitive clauses with overt subjects:

(20)

*John is desirous [Bill to leave]

This is because adjectives are never case-assigners. There are, however, adjectives that allow (in fact, require) Raising:

(21)

a. * — is certain [John to win]
b.   John is certain [e to win]

Certain cannot be a case-assigner, since it is an adjective; therefore, NP-Movement must move the NP to a position where it can receive case.

In sum, then, giving certain verbs in English the marked option of subcategorizing for S instead of S' accounts for the exceptional subject-taking infinitives in English. In particular, in conjunction with case theory, it predicts an important feature of the distribution of the exceptional subject-taking property: it occurs only when the subject of the infinitive is in a position in which it is governed by a case-assigner.

To conclude this section, it will be useful to consider a slight variant on the above theory of ECM—a variant that solves a certain problem with Subjacency and will better support the discussion of these phenomena in later chapters, especially chapter 18.

We have adopted the notion that ECM verbs exceptionally subcategorize for S, instead of S'. Since these Ss will not have COMPs, this theory predicts that extractions from them will be blocked:

(22)

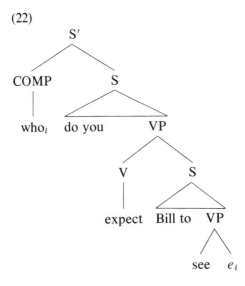

The movement of *who* from the trace position to the higher COMP is blocked by Subjacency, because two S-nodes intervene. Furthermore, there is no way to break this movement into two parts, each of which obeys Subjacency, since the lower S has no COMP. But the sentence is completely grammatical and has nothing of the flavor of a Subjacency violation.

We must therefore retreat to a theory in which the complement of ECM verbs is a full S', with a COMP. But we still will not want this S' to block the assignment of case by the matrix verb to the embedded subject. And we still want these verbs, and their complements, to be "exceptional." Therefore, let us suppose that the ECM verbs do subcategorize for S' after all, but that the complements of these verbs are marked as *transparent to government,* in order to permit case-assignment. The verbs will then still be exceptional, in that they assign the feature of transparency to their complements. The ECM configuration will then look like this, where superscript t indicates a transparent S':

(23)

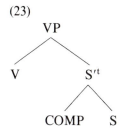

We will return to this notion of S' transparency in chapter 18.

14.3 Case, PRO, and *Wh*-Trace

In concluding this discussion of case, we will briefly outline the case status of PRO and *wh*-trace.

As we have seen, PRO need not have case, since it occurs regularly as the subject of infinitives. If PRO *could* take case, we might expect it to occur in alternation with lexical NP. This does not appear to happen, however; in fact, PRO and lexical NP seem to occur in complementary distribution:

(24)

John believes $\left\{\begin{array}{c} \text{*PRO} \\ \text{Bill} \end{array}\right\}$ to be sick

Such complementary distribution would follow from the assumption that PRO *cannot* receive case—a natural assumption, if the presence of case is associated with being phonetically realized, and the absence of case with being phonetically unrealized.

Wh-trace, on the other hand, seems to require case. First, the positions in which *wh*-trace is found seem always to allow lexical NPs as well:

(25)
a. Who$_i$ do you believe e_i to have left
b. I believe John to have left

Second, *wh*-trace seems to be in complementary distribution with NP-trace:

(26)
a. *Who$_i$ is it believed [e_i to have left]
b. John$_i$ is believed [e_i to have left]

(27)
a. Who$_i$ did you see e_i
b. *John$_i$ saw e_i

A natural account of these facts is that *wh*-trace needs case and that NP-trace cannot have case. At this point we simply note this difference; it will play a fundamental role in characterizing some of the important features of LF in chapters 16 and 17.

14.4 Bibliographical Comments

The main text in which the Government-Binding stage of the theory is developed is *Lectures on Government and Binding* (Chomsky (1981c)), often referred to as "LGB" (or as the "Pisa Lectures," since it is based on lectures given by Chomsky after the 1979 GLOW conference at the Scuola Normale Superiore in Pisa). Since it treats all of the topics that will be covered in the rest of part IV, it is the central reference for chapters 15 through 18 as well.

An overwhelming number of publications have appeared on various aspects of Government-Binding Theory in the few years since the Pisa lectures. We will list only a small number of them here, and we refer the reader to chapter 19, in which we discuss important current theoretical developments and provide a more liberal bibliography.

A good overview of the modular conception of linguistic theory is found in Chomsky (1981b).

Case theory, as described in this chapter, is due to Jean-Roger Vergnaud and is developed in Rouveret and Vergnaud (1980) and Vergnaud (1982).

The theory of case developed here is a theory of abstract case, not (or not primarily) one of morphological case. Though the two notions of case must be compatible, the actual relation between them is complex and has not attracted a great deal of attention. Some of the problems pertaining to this issue are discussed in Van Riemsdijk (1983).

Although the notion of government is central to Government-Binding Theory, its precise formal definition is a hotly debated issue. For a good overview of alternative formulations and some empirical considerations pertaining to them, see Aoun and Sportiche (1983).

Chapter 15
θ-Theory

θ-theory (theta-theory) concerns the fundamental logical notion "argument of," a notion (like case) that any theory of grammar must account for. Within Government-Binding Theory, θ-theory takes a specific form that could not be anticipated on the basis of the logical notion "argument of" alone; it has specific empirical content, and in its interaction with case theory and NP-Movement it provides considerable deductive explanation. In this chapter we will look at the basic principles of θ-theory, including the θ-Criterion and the Projection Principle, and we will explore the interaction of θ-theory and case theory in the description of several constructions, including raising, passive, and clitic constructions.

15.1 Argument Structure

The notion "argument of" has great intuitive force; our theorizing about argument structure is largely based on this more or less unanalyzed intuition of what is and what is not an "argument of" what. For example, there is widespread agreement that in (1) the verb *love* has two arguments, the NPs *John* and *Mary:*

(1)
John loves Mary

A logician might symbolize this as follows:

(2)
Loves (John, Mary)

Unfortunately, there are cases where intuition is unreliable. For example, are manner adverbs arguments? Are time and place adverbs arguments? Different speakers will answer differently. The study of *selectional restrictions* is an attempt to discover some empirical basis for the distinction between arguments and nonarguments, the idea being that a verb will have selectional restrictions on its arguments and not on anything else.

Varying the surface subject of a raising verb like *seems* does not change the acceptability of the sentence, so long as the embedded verb can be varied appropriately:

(3)
a. The sail   seems to luff
b. The hour   seems to elapse
c. The mole   seems to die
d. The train   seems to derail

According to the theory of selectional restrictions, the fact that *seems* does not "select for" its surface subject—that is, the fact that there are no restrictions on what the surface subject of *seems* can be—suggests that its surface subject is not one of its arguments. On the other hand, the fact that the selection of the surface subject of *seems* does appear to depend on the particular verb embedded under *seems* suggests that the subject is an argument of the embedded verb. This translates intuitions about "argument of" into intuitions about the acceptability of sentences, a kind of intuition that linguists are more comfortable with; unfortunately, the selectional restriction test is ultimately probably no better than the unanalyzed intuitions that it replaced.

The θ-theory within Government-Binding Theory is thus another attempt to account for the relation between verbs and their arguments. It has come to be known as θ-*theory* because θ stands for *thematic;* the terms θ-*role* and *thematic relation* are synonyms for *argument.*

One of the fundamental tasks of θ-theory is to determine the circumstances under which an NP can be an argument of a verb. To designate different arguments of a verb, terms such as *agent, patient* (or *theme*), and *goal* are commonly used. This terminology implies a system of argument *types,* in that, for example, it implies that the agent arguments of two different verbs have something in common. Although this may be true, θ-theory as outlined here is not committed to this idea.

The relation "argument of" is very local; certainly there are no cases in which a verb takes an NP in a lower or an upper clause to be its argument at D-Structure:

(4)
NP ... [$_S$ ... V [$_S$ NP ...]$_S$ ...]$_S$

Neither NP in (4) is available as an argument of the V. This is not to say, however, that all of the arguments of a predicate are located inside the maximal projection of the predicate. A signal exception is the subject; if VP is a maximal projection, then the subject, when it is an argument of the verb (as it is in all but a few cases), is external to the maximal projection of the verb. A verb can have only one such *external* argument; the rest of its arguments must be *internal* to the maximal projection:

(5)
[$_S$ NP [$_{VP}$ V NP PP PP PP ...]$_{VP}$]$_S$

The internal arguments are therefore governed by the verb. In fact, though, government seems too weak a restriction, given that government holds between the italicized V and NP in the following construction:

(6)
John *believes* [*Bill* to be sick]

Bill is not an argument of *believes,* even though *believes* gives *Bill* its case. This is one of the circumstances in which case-assignment and θ-role assignment diverge.

On the other hand, the verb does not govern its external argument (subject). However, there is a sense in which the subject is the subject of the VP, and only by virtue of that relation subject of the V; and the VP does govern the subject. If this is the correct view, then all θ-roles are assigned under government (that is, all of a verb's arguments are in the structural relation "government" with that verb).

15.2 The θ-Criterion

Let us suppose that a verb intrinsically takes a certain number of arguments, and that it appears in a sentence with a certain number of NPs. One might then expect the arguments and the NPs to match up one to one. That they indeed do so is the intent of the θ-Criterion, which we have already encountered, though in different wording, in the context of control theory (chapter 8):

(7)
θ-Criterion

Every NP must be taken as the argument of some predicate; furthermore, it must be so taken at most once.

The first clause of the θ-Criterion rules out sentences like (8):

(8)
*The hour elapsed John

Since the intransitive verb *elapse* can take only one argument (here, *the hour*), then, by the θ-Criterion, the second NP *John* cannot also be construed as one of its arguments.

The second clause of the θ-Criterion applies to sentences like (9),

(9)
John believes [Bill to have left]

where *Bill* cannot be an argument of *believes* because it is already an argument of *have left*. It also prevents an NP from being taken as two arguments of the same verb:

(10)
John recommended Mary

(10) cannot mean "John recommended Mary to herself."

Every NP must be taken as the argument of some predicate, but must every argument be associated with some *syntactically realized* NP? For example, if *eat* is a verb that takes two arguments, then what are we to make of (11), where it appears with only one?

(11)
John ate

Two distinct solutions have been proposed to account for such (exceptional) cases: either it is not necessary for every argument to be syntactically realized; or it is necessary, and *eat* has two lexical entries, as a one-argument verb and a related two-argument verb. We will not present arguments here to decide between these two solutions.

Let us now consider how θ-roles are assigned to NPs that have been moved. According to previous chapters, the passive construction has the following derivation:

(12)

D-Structure: e was admired John by the men

S-Structure: John$_i$ was admired e_i by the men

Two connected questions present themselves: What is the level of representation at which θ-roles are assigned? and What is the manner of assignment?

First, since *the men* is in a *by*-phrase in both representations, it must acquire its θ-role by virtue of being there, whatever the relevant level of structure. Let us assume, then, that the preposition *by* marks agents or experiencers of verbs (or whatever thematic roles are assigned to subjects by active verbs). That is, an NP in a *by*-phrase is assigned the subject θ-role of the verb that governs the *by*-phrase. Assuming that *admire(d)* takes two arguments, this leaves one more to be assigned, which we may call the *theme* argument.

If θ-role assignment takes place in D-Structure, then the assignment of the θ-role "theme" to *John* in (12) is straightforward, assuming that the passive participle assigns theme in the same way as the active verb; in D-Structure *John* is in the direct object position and can receive the θ-role directly.

But suppose that θ-role assignment were to take place at S-Structure. If we again assume that the active verb and the passive participle assign θ-roles identically, then the theme role will be assigned to the trace in (12). However, since *John* is coindexed with this trace through movement, we may assume that *John* inherits the θ-role from the trace. Thus, *John* will receive the theme role in any event.

So far we have no reason to choose D-Structure or S-Structure assignment. This is a delicate matter, since D- and S-Structure are so similar, and the decision will not be easy.

The s-structure of (12) presents a special problem: it has two NPs for one θ-role, since the theme is associated with both *John* and the trace of *John*. This may appear to be a pseudoproblem, since *John* and its trace are coindexed, but it reveals a lack of precision in defining "NP" in statement (7) of the θ-Criterion. What counts as one NP? Clearly, an NP and its coindexed trace should count as one, and not two, NPs, since in this example that pair is assigned only one θ-role.

It might seem possible to avoid this problem by assigning θ-roles in D-Structure, where there are no traces. Despite this inviting prospect, we will explore the idea that θ-roles are instead assigned in S-Structure, precisely because the ultimate goal is that θ-theory will participate in explaining the distribution of S-Structure traces. Therefore, it is necessary to modify the θ-Criterion to take traces into account.

To facilitate this, the notion of *chain* has been introduced:

(13)
Chain: A chain consists of an NP (called the *head* of the chain) and the traces coindexed with that NP.

Here we will take *chain* to mean "maximal chain"—that is, a chain that is not a subpart of any other chain. By this definition, the set (John$_i$, e_i) in (12) is a (maximal) chain, and so is the set (the men).

Actually, (13) will give the wrong result for a certain kind of case:

(14)
John$_i$ was told e_i that he$_i$ was chosen e_i

As will become clear, such cases are best analyzed, not as one chain consisting of a head *John* and two traces, but as two chains, one headed by *John* and the other by *he*. This result has been achieved by redefining *chain* as follows:

(13$'$)
Chain: A chain consists of an NP (the head) and a set of locally bound traces, where *locally bound trace* means either a trace whose nearest c-commanding binder is the head, or a trace whose nearest c-commanding binder is a locally bound trace.

The second trace in (14) cannot form a chain with *John,* since the nearest c-commanding binder is *he*. Now the θ-Criterion can be defined in terms of chains:

(15)
θ-Criterion
Every chain must receive one and only one θ-role.

At first glance, it might appear that *Wh*-Movement gives rise to a chain as well. For example, it might appear that the *wh*-phrase in COMP in (16) acquires its θ-role from the trace in object position, and that (who$_i$, e_i) form a chain:

(16)
Who$_i$ did [George see e_i]

In fact, though, there are good reasons to exclude material in COMP from θ-role assignment.

First, no verb takes an argument in COMP the way it takes an argument in subject or object position. An argument of a verb may appear in COMP if it has been moved there by *Wh*-Movement, but a θ-role is never assigned to COMP directly by a verb.

Second, there are constructions in which a *wh*-phrase binds two traces (the "parasitic gap" constructions; see chapter 16 for more discussion):

(17)
Which books$_i$ did you read e_i before filing e_i

If a *wh*-phrase in COMP could head a chain, then (17) would be a counterexample to the θ-Criterion, since the chain (which books$_i$, e_i, e_i) receives two θ-roles, one from *read* and one from *filing*. If each trace constitutes its own chain in (17), then no θ-Criterion violation exists. This result can be achieved by excluding COMP from chains. Note that no comparable examples can be constructed with NP-Movement:

(18)
*The book$_i$ was read e_i before filing e_i

Since the NP *the book* is not in COMP, it is not excluded from the chain (the book$_i$, e_i, e_i), and this chain violates the θ-Criterion.

The exclusion of material in COMP from chains is not simply a device for solving the problems just mentioned. If the intent of the θ-Criterion is considered to be to restrict the assignment of arguments, it could only be this way. Material in COMP in general corresponds to logical operators; in describing standard logic, it would be inappropriate to refer to the operator ($\forall x$) below as an argument of F, even though it is "coindexed" with x:

(19)
($\forall x$ (Fx))

NP-trace binding has no analogue in standard logic; if *wh*-binding corresponds to quantifier binding of an argument, then NP-binding is "below" the level of arguments.

How exactly is material in COMP to be excluded from chains? In the examples discussed so far, it is necessary to exclude COMP from a complex chain with traces and to prevent material in COMP from inheriting a θ-role from a trace. Recall, though, that COMP is a position in which an NP cannot be assigned a θ-role *directly,* either. Thus, it has been proposed that phrase structure positions in which arguments can appear at D-Structure be referred to as *argument positions* (A-positions) and that phrase structure positions in which no argument can appear at D-Structure be referred to as *nonargument positions* ($\overline{\text{A}}$-positions). *Chain* may then be redefined once again as follows:

(20)
Chain: A chain is an NP and its locally bound traces, all in A-positions.

In early transformational work, it was understood that the difference between control and movement structures was a difference in argument structures: in a control structure, there were two arguments, but in a movement structure, only one. This was reflected in the differences in underlying structures for the two constructions:

(21)
Control structure: John wants [John to leave]
(two instances of *John*)

(22)
Movement structure: *e* was seen John by Fred
(one instance of *John*)

The analogue of this distinction must be reconstructed in the stage of the theory described here. With NP-Movement two positions are involved, the movement target site and the trace, but because of the definition of chain this pair corresponds to only one argument position.

   Since the definition of chain refers to traces, and not to PRO, an (NP, PRO) pair will not constitute a chain; NP and PRO will each constitute a different chain and will therefore receive a different θ-role. This is the desired result. However, so far it has been reached merely by stipulation, since the definition of chain could have as easily been written to refer to "coindexed empty categories" rather than traces, in which case trace and PRO would not have been distinguished. We will carry over to the next chapter this unsolved theoretical problem.

   Reflexives, like PRO, do not count as "traces" in the definition of chain. Hence, a reflexive and its antecedent are assigned two θ-roles:

(23)
John saw himself

Here, *John* is assigned the subject θ-role of *saw,* and *himself* the object θ-role. An interesting set of exceptions to this will be discussed later in this chapter.

Returning now to the passive construction, recall that in a passive sentence like (24) the agent receives its θ-role by virtue of being in a *by*-phrase, and the derived subject receives its θ-role by virtue of being coindexed with the trace in object position, with which it forms a chain:

(24)
John$_i$ was killed e_i by Bill

An important feature of this construction that distinguishes it from the active is that the passive participle assigns no θ-role to the subject position:

(25)
a. Active: Bill saw John
b. Passive: John$_i$ was seen e_i by Bill

If a θ-role were assigned to the subject in (25b), then the chain (John$_i$, e_i) would receive two θ-roles, violating the θ-Criterion.

The passive participle must differ from the active verb, then, in θ-role assignment. That is, they both have the same θ-roles to assign, but they assign them differently: the active verb takes one internal and one external (subject) argument and assigns a θ-role to each, whereas the passive participle takes two internal arguments (and no external (subject) argument) and assigns a θ-role to each. For the passive participle, then, the subject position is "dethematized."

We saw in chapter 14 that the passive participle, unlike its active counterpart, does not assign case to the object position. Thus, the passive participle and the active verb differ in two important ways, summarized in table 15.1. We will assume that the rules of the lexicon that relate active verbs and passive participles are responsible for this difference, where by "rules of the lexicon" we mean rules that state systematic relations among lexical items.

We also saw in chapter 14 that it is the failure of passive participles to assign case to object position that makes NP-Movement *obligatory* for them—the object NP must move to a position where it can receive

Table 15.1
Properties of active verb and passive participle

	Assigns case to object	Assigns θ-role to subject
Active verb	yes	yes
Passive participle	no	no

case. Now we see that it is the failure of passive participles to assign a θ-role to subject position that makes NP-Movement *possible* for them.

Clearly, the other verbs that trigger NP-Movement, the raising verbs, must have the same properties as the passive participle; that is, they must not assign case to the postverbal NP, and they must not assign a θ-role to the subject position. In (26), then, *seems* both fails to assign case to the postverbal NP and fails to assign a θ-role to the subject position, with the result that NP-Movement takes place:

(26)
e seems [John to be sick]

There are other constructions in which a θ-role is not assigned to a subject. Not surprisingly, one is based on the verb *seems* — but with a tensed clause:

(27)
It [seems that Bill has gone]

The subject of a sentence with *seems* is never.assigned a θ-role, as (28) shows:

(28)
*A disaster seems

The VP headed by *seems* has no external argument. It would appear, then, that (27) violates the θ-Criterion, since the NP subject (*it*) is assigned no θ-role. It has been proposed, however, that *it* is a special NP that need not be assigned a θ-role—in fact, it cannot be assigned one, since it is inherently nonreferential.

Another NP to which no θ-role is assigned is the NP *there* of existential sentences:

(29)
There is a God

Given the existence of NPs that do not receive θ-roles, and given that there are verbs, such as passive participles, that do not assign θ-roles to their subjects, we might expect to find the following sentence:

(30)
*It was bitten John

(30) obeys the θ-Criterion. Of course, we know why (30) is ungrammatical in English: the passive participle does not assign case to the

direct object in English; thus, *John* receives no case. But is (30) a possibility for language in general, even though it is excluded in English? It appears not to be, a fact that led Burzio (1981) to formulate the following "law":

(31)
Burzio's Generalization
If a verb assigns case to its object, then it assigns a θ-role to its subject.

From this it will follow that sentences like (30) will be impossible in any language. However, this generalization as stated here is dissatisfyingly arbitrary; it is to be hoped that further research will uncover a more explanatory principle from which it proceeds.

This generalization is also asymmetrical: it says nothing about the subject position in case a verb has no object. For example, a regular intransitive verb, such as *dance,* assigns a θ-role to its subject and no case to its nonexistent object; and a verb like *seem* assigns no θ-role to its subject and of course no case to its nonexistent object. Since there is no object in such instances, and no case assigned or assignable to it, Burzio's generalization is compatible with there being no θ-role assigned to the subject position. Theoretically, then, sentences like (32) ought to be possible, and indeed they are in other languages, as (33a–b) attest:

(32)
*It was danced

(33)
a. Es wurde getanzt (German)
   it was danced
   'There was dancing'
b. Il a été tiré sur le bateau (French)
   it was fired on the boat
   'The boat was fired upon'

Since Burzio's generalization allows for this construction, and since it occurs in other languages than English, its absence in English must be accidental. The peculiarity of English passive participles seems to be that they can be formed only from transitive verbs; in this respect, they are different from the French and German passive participles. But the passive construction in all three languages obeys the θ-Criterion, Burzio's generalization, and the Case Filter.

The French passive shows an interesting use of the θ-Criterion. The reflexive clitic in French, *se,* moves from object position and attaches itself to the verb, as in (34):

(34)

a. Jean lave   se   *
   Jean washes himself

b. Jean se$_i$ lave e_i
   'Jean washes himself'

Now, suppose that it were possible to passivize a verb to which a reflexive clitic was attached; the derived structure would look like (35). Note that the clitic *se* is in an Ā-position:

(35)

NP$_i$ [se$_i$ est pass. part. e_i e_i]

Such a structure violates the θ-Criterion, since each of the traces in the chain (NP$_i$, e_i, e_i) is in a θ-position. In fact, such cases are ungrammatical:

(36)

a. Jean a   présenté   Pierre à   Marie
   Jean has introduced Pierre to Marie

b. Jean s$_i$'   est présenté   Pierre e_i
   Jean to himself has introduced Pierre
   'Jean introduced Pierre to himself'

c. Pierre$_i$ a   été   présenté e_i à   Jean
   Pierre   has been introduced   to Jean

d. *Pierre$_i$ s$_i$'   est été   présenté e_i e_i
   Pierre   to himself has been introduced
   'Pierre has been introduced to himself'

15.3 The Projection Principle

We have assumed throughout that the θ-Criterion applies at S-Structure, and this assumption has figured crucially in some of the explanations offered (for example, in the explanation for the failure of passivization in French reflexive sentences).

In all of the sentences considered so far, the θ-Criterion has been satisfied at D-Structure as well:

(37)

a. *e* was seen John by Bill

b. *e* seems [John to be sick]

The θ-role assignments are marked; in each case, one and only one θ-role is assigned to each NP. The difference between D- and S-Structure θ-role assignment is that in D-Structure every chain consists simply of an NP, since there are no traces.

In some sense, it is simpler to assign θ-roles to D-Structure—the notions "chain" and "trace" are not needed. θ-role assignment to S-Structure requires traces; one might say that the existence of traces is implied by the assignment of θ-roles at S-Structure.

It has been proposed that θ-role assignment be required to apply at both D-Structure and S-Structure, and that it must apply "identically" at each level—that is, the lexical properties of verbs that determine what arguments they take and where their arguments are located are observed identically at both levels. This restriction, which we first encountered in section 9.1.3, has some important consequences that we will examine here. It is formulated as follows:

(38)
Projection Principle
The θ-Criterion holds at D-Structure, S-Structure, and LF.

The first important consequence of the Projection Principle is that traces must exist, in order for θ-role assignment at S-Structure to match θ-role assignment at D-Structure, even though NPs have been moved between D-Structure and S-Structure. For example:

(39)
a. *e* was killed John by Fred
   Theme: John; Agent: Fred
b. John$_i$ was killed e_i by Fred
   Theme: (John$_i$, e_i); Agent: Fred

(39a) is the d-structure of the s-structure (39b). Because of the trace at S-Structure, the θ-role assignments are the same in each case, thus allowing the θ-Criterion to hold at both levels as the Projection Principle requires.

The second important consequence of the Projection Principle is that even with traces, it imposes strong restrictions on the relation between D-Structure and S-Structure, restrictions that otherwise would not necessarily hold. For example, it prohibits a transformational operation that exchanges two NPs, leaving no traces:

(40)
John broke the jar $\rightarrow$
The jar broke John

Such an exchange is prohibited because the θ-role assignments would be different in the two structures.

The Projection Principle also prohibits movement of an NP from a $\bar{\theta}$-position (a non-theta position—that is, a position to which no θ-role is assigned) to a θ-position. In such a case the θ-role assignments would be different in D-Structure and S-Structure: in D-Structure the NP would not receive a θ-role, but in S-Structure it would:

(41)
a. e wants [$_S$ John to seem that Bill is here]$_S$
b.   *John$_i$ wants [$_S$ e_i to seem that Bill is here]$_S$

The subject of *wants* is a θ-position, and the subject of *seems* is a $\bar{\theta}$-position. (41b) is ruled out, even though it meets the θ-Criterion, because its d-structure does not meet the θ-Criterion. Generalizing this result somewhat, the Projection Principle implies that in a chain with traces, only the lowest trace *will* be in a θ-position and furthermore it *must* be in a θ-position.

The Projection Principle can be extended to include LF as well. In that case, the derivation of LF from S-Structure is constrained in the same manner as the derivation of S-Structure from D-Structure. The result is an extremely cohesive relation among the three levels.

15.4 Bibliographical Comments

The θ-Criterion is due to Freidin (1978).

As outlined in the text, the θ-Criterion is a purely formal principle that is not sensitive to the actual semantic content of the various θ-roles. Although distinctions between agent and patient, source and goal, etc., are familiar from traditional grammar and a variety of non-generative frameworks, the substantive side of θ-theory has received relatively little attention within generative grammar. Two exceptions are Gruber (1965) (later published as Gruber (1976)) and Jackendoff (1972). And occasionally syntactic principles are proposed that do refer to the content of θ-roles, as in Keenan and Comrie (1977). The correctness of such principles being an empirical issue, counterarguments are possible, and such a counterargument to Keenan and Comrie's proposal is found in Cinque (1981).

The systematic link between θ-role assignment (to the subject) and case-assignment (to the object) is established in Burzio (1981), with the result that it is referred to as "Burzio's generalization."

Though we will not explore existential constructions here, there is an extensive subliterature on the topic. The main "early" analyses are Milsark (1974) (summarized in Milsark (1977)) and Jenkins (1975). More recent analyses include Safir (1982) and Williams (1984).

The argument from reflexive clitics in French presented in section 15.2 was discovered by Riny Huybregts and Edwin Williams (perhaps among others), though never published by them. An account along slightly different lines is presented in Rizzi (1983).

Chapter 16
NP-Types and NP-Positions

Case theory, θ-theory, and government create a typology of NP-*positions*, such as case-marked and caseless. Several subtheories create a typology of NP-*types*, such as [±pronominal] in terms of the binding theory (see chapter 17) and case-marked vs. caseless in terms of case theory. In this chapter we will explore the relation between these two typologies.

16.1 A Modular Classification of NP

For the purposes of all the chapters in this section, NPs can be grouped into the following classes:

(1)
a. reflexives and reciprocals
b. pronouns
c. lexical NPs
d. *wh*-words
e. *wh*-trace and trace of quantifier phrase
f. NP-trace
g. PRO

Of course, it is not enough to list these and give their properties. Various NP classes group together, and such a list would not express their common properties. In fact, however, it is not enough even to list the *groups* and their properties, since the NP classes group together differently with respect to different properties. For example, *wh*-trace and NP-trace pattern alike in being subject to Subjacency, but they pattern differently in the context of the binding theory, where *wh*-trace is treated like lexical NP and NP-trace is not.

Showing how the list in (1) is cross-classified by various properties would no doubt come close to a satisfactory theory of NP-types. Most satisfying of all, of course, would be rational and simple theories of each of the properties themselves that would explain the distribution of the types. This is the goal that linguists have in constructing case theory, θ-theory, binding theory, bounding theory (the theory of movement and Subjacency), and so forth.

Case theory provides a classification of (1) according to the distinction case-marked vs. caseless:

(2)

Case-marked:	reflexives and reciprocals
	pronouns
	lexical NPs
	wh-words
	wh-trace and trace of quantifier phrase
Caseless:	NP-trace
	PRO

A rational explanation is already available for most of this classification: if it is a property of phonetically realized nouns that they must have case of some kind, then all but the classification of *wh*-trace and the trace of quantifier phrase can be explained simply in terms of morphology.

On these grounds, there is no reason to expect empty categories (ECs)—*wh*-trace and trace of quantifier phrase, NP-trace, and PRO—to have or not have case. They might equally be expected to be case-marked obligatorily, optionally, or not at all. As it turns out, some are case-marked and some are caseless, so further principles are needed to explain why they divide as they do on this property.

We will take up PRO in chapter 17, where we will see that it can occur only in ungoverned positions. Since case can only be assigned to a position that is governed by a case-assigner, PRO will therefore never appear in a position to which case is assigned and will never receive case.

NP-Movement is obligatory in passive constructions because the object position of passive participles is not assigned case, and the lexical NP that appears there must have case. When NP-Movement takes place, it leaves behind an NP-trace in the object position. Thus, we know that NP-trace can appear in caseless positions:

(3)
a. was seen Fred
b. Fred$_i$ was seen e_i

But is it also true that NP-trace cannot appear in case-marked positions? At the moment, it would be difficult to give reasons for excluding NP-trace from such positions. The examples that would prove that it must be excluded would have the following form:

(4)

NP	[V	NP]
Fred	case-	e
	assigner	

Such cases are inconsistent with Burzio's generalization: since the verb is a case-assigner, it assigns a θ-role to its subject position; but the D-Structure–S-Structure pair that underlies (4) violates the Projection Principle, since θ-role assignment to the subject position is possible in S-Structure but not in D-Structure:

(5)
D-Structure: V Fred
S-Structure: Fred$_i$ V e_i

Thus, NP-trace will not appear in case-marked positions, if we accept Burzio's generalization.

The surprise in (2) is probably that *wh*-trace appears in case-marked positions—a surprise since this fact cannot be derived from any need to have morphological case, *wh*-trace being an EC. It is quite easy to show that *wh*-trace can appear only in case-marked positions; it is more difficult to explain why.

The caseless positions are all occupied by either NP-trace or PRO, these being the only NPs that can get by without case. The following examples show that in the constructions containing these two ECs, the substitution of a *wh*-trace into the caseless position always leads to ungrammaticality:

(6)
a.   John$_i$ tried PRO$_i$ to leave
    *Who$_i$ did John try e_i to leave
b.   John$_i$ seems e_i to leave
    *Who$_i$ does it seem e_i to leave
c.   John$_i$ was hit e_i
    *Who$_i$ was it hit e_i

Interestingly, *wh*-words moved to COMP do not appear in case-marked positions generally. COMP is not governed by a case-assigner, under the assumptions made here about government; the S' boundary protects COMP from government by anything *outside* of the clause, and since COMP c-commands everything and is not c-commanded by anything in the clause, it is not governed by anything *inside* the clause either:

(7)

... [s' COMP [s ...]s]s'

There is no way to account for the case on the *wh*-word in COMP, then, if case is assigned in S-Structure.

With respect to case, then, *Wh*-Movement and NP-Movement are opposed to each other in two ways, as shown in table 16.1. Perhaps the fact that the moved-to position of *wh*-words is caseless has something to do with the fact that the position of *wh*-trace is a cased position; in effect, the *wh*-word in COMP must acquire its case from the position occupied by its trace.

Certain simple schemes of case-assignment are not compatible with the data in table 16.1. Uniform assignment of case in D-Structure will assign case correctly to *wh*-words, but not to the (surface) subjects (deep objects) of passive participles, since these will not be in case-assignment positions in D-Structure. Uniform assignment in S-Structure, on the other hand, will not assign case to *wh*-words in COMP.

Let us assume (as in chapter 14) that case is assigned uniformly in S-Structure and that a *wh*-phrase (though not a quantifier phrase) acquires its case by agreement with the trace it binds. This will generate both the facts represented in table 16.1 and the fact that *wh*-phrases generally have the case that would be assigned to their D-Structure position. This is not the only way to derive the facts in table 16.1; another would be free assignment of case in both D-Structure and S-Structure, subject to the Case Filter.

We will return to the discussion of *wh*-trace, and the fact that it appears in case-marked positions, at the end of this chapter.

Table 16.1
Case properties of *Wh*-Movement and NP-Movement

	Moved-to position	Moved-from position
Wh-Movement	caseless	case-marked
NP-Movement	case-marked	caseless

θ-theory gives a somewhat different classification of the NP-types. Since all of the items in (1) can be assigned a θ-role and can occupy a θ-position, the distinctions drawn by θ-theory involve the argument status of the antecedents of these items.

First, there is the distinction, partly independent of θ-theory, concerning whether or not an item has an antecedent. There are three possibilities: an antecedent may be obligatory, impossible, or possible but not obligatory (table 16.2). As the table shows, the classification according to antecedent requirements is independent of case distinctions. Among the NP-types that take antecedents, there is the further distinction concerning whether or not the antecedent is in an argument position (A-position). Among the NP-types whose antecedents appear in A-positions, there is the further distinction concerning whether or not the antecedent is necessarily in a $\bar{\theta}$-position.

What is the difference between A-positions and θ-positions? Consider the three positions COMP, subject, and object. COMP is never a position to which a θ-role is assigned. Subject is a position to which a θ-role is generally assigned, but not always (recall that raising verbs and passive participles do not assign θ-roles to their subjects). Object position (we may assume for the moment) is a position to which a θ-role is always assigned. (These distinctions are displayed in table 16.3.) COMP is never assigned a θ-role because it is not governed by the verb,

Table 16.2
Antecedent and case properties of NP-types

Type	Antecedent			Case-marked	Caseless
	Obligatory	Impossible	Possible		
Reflexive	✔			✔	
Wh-trace	✔			✔	
NP-trace	✔				✔
Lexical NP		✔		✔	
Wh-word		✔		✔	
Pronoun			✔	✔	
PRO			✔		✔

Table 16.3
θ-role assignment to COMP, subject, and object positions

	θ-role assigned
COMP	Never
Subject position	Sometimes (depending on verb)
Object position	Always

and θ-roles are always assigned under government. In other words, the reason why COMP never receives a θ-role is strictly structural and does not depend on the choice of verb or other lexical items. The status of the subject position is quite different, since subject position is accessible to θ-role assignment, but the assignment depends on the verb.

A position that is *structurally inaccessible* to θ-role assignment is called a *nonargument position* ($\overline{A}$-position). A position that is not assigned a θ-role *in a particular sentence* is called a *$\overline{\theta}$-position*. Clearly, an $\overline{A}$-position will always be a $\overline{\theta}$-position—if a position is structurally inaccessible to θ-role assignment, then of course no θ-role assignment can take place. The reverse does not hold, however, because there are A-positions (notably the subject position) that are, given the right choice of verb, $\overline{\theta}$-positions.

Given these distinctions, NPs may be classified as shown in figure 16.1 according to whether their antecedents are in A- or $\overline{A}$-position and—for the ones whose antecedents are in A-position—according to whether those antecedents are in θ- or $\overline{\theta}$-position. Again, we have a partial explanation for some of this. The antecedent of an NP-trace is necessarily in a $\overline{\theta}$-position, because of the θ-Criterion and the Projec-

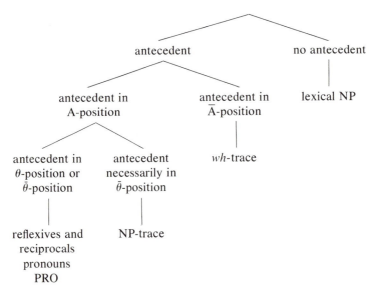

Figure 16.1
Classification of NP-types according to antecedent properties

tion Principle. The antecedent of a reflexive (or pronoun, or PRO) will have a θ-role independent of the θ-role of the reflexive, since the antecedent does not form a chain with the reflexive; therefore, the antecedent can be in either a θ- or a $\bar{\theta}$-position.

We have seen that since *wh*-trace arises through *Wh*-Movement and since *Wh*-Movement is to COMP (intrinsically an $\bar{A}$-position), the antecedent of *Wh*-Movement will always be in an $\bar{A}$-position. However, although this is a reason why the antecedent of a *wh*-trace is in an $\bar{A}$-position, it is not a reason that follows from any more explanatory principle. The fact that *Wh*-Movement is to COMP is stipulative in a way it perhaps need not be. Why does *Wh*-Movement not move *wh*-words to subject position, for example? The remainder of the chapter will address this question.

The distinction between *wh*-trace and NP-trace ultimately rests on a distinction familiar from predicate logic, the distinction between variables and quantifiers (or operators). In predicate logic, variables fill argument positions of predicates to give propositional forms; quantifiers are affixed to these forms to give further propositional forms:

(8)
$$\forall x \quad (\exists y \quad (F \quad (x \quad y)))$$
quantifiers   variables

The quantifier/variable system is apparently appropriate for the analysis of the semantics of natural language (see chapters 13 and 17).

Wh-Movement bears several similarities to a rule of quantifier scope assignment. First, it moves an item to an $\bar{A}$-position on the periphery of a clause; in other words, to a position very similar to the position of the quantifiers in (8). Second, it leaves a coindexed trace in the position from which movement has taken place; in this way, it is like the binding of variable (= *wh*-trace) by quantifier (= *wh*-word) in (8). Third, the *wh*-trace, like a variable, is in the argument position of a predicate:

(9)

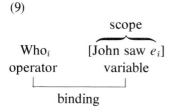

In essence, *Wh*-Movement does in syntax (or in S-Structure) what Quantifier Interpretation does in logic (or LF).

NP-Movement also leaves a trace in the argument position of a predicate, so it may at first appear that NP-Movement also creates a quantifier/variable structure. In fact, though, there is good reason *not* to analyze the structures created by NP-Movement as having the same logical status as those created by *Wh*-Movement.

16.2 Parasitic Gaps

The distinction between NP-trace and *wh*-trace was already firmly established in section 9.2. Further evidence for this distinction comes from a study of *parasitic gap* constructions, in which two traces are bound by a single *wh*-word:

(10)
a. What$_i$ did you read e_i [before PRO filing PG$_i$]
b. Who$_i$ did you give pictures of PG$_i$ to e_i
c. Who$_i$ did pictures of PG$_i$ upset e_i
d. Who$_i$ did the fact that Mary had seen PG$_i$ upset e_i

(We use *PG* for the parasitic gap for expository reasons to distinguish it from the *wh*-trace e_i.) Here, the two gaps count as "instances of the same logical variable," as in the predicate logic expression (11),

(11)
$\forall x(\text{F}x\ \&\ \text{G}x)$

where the two instances of x are bound by the quantifier $\forall x$.

Parasitic gap constructions have a marginal status at best—most speakers judge them semigrammatical, especially the cases like (10b) where the two gaps are in the same clause. We will return to the semigrammatical status of parasitic gaps later in this chapter, but we will soon see that their semigrammaticality has nothing to do with how much insight into grammar they provide.

How the two-gap structure in (10) arises is interesting in itself. The trace (e_i) can be assumed to arise through movement of the *wh*-word, since the relation between it and the *wh*-word appears to be governed by Subjacency. As (10c–d) show, however, the relation between the *wh*-word and the parasitic gap (PG$_i$) is not. We may speculate, then, that the parasitic gap is base-generated and is coindexed with the *wh*-phrase that binds it by a rule deriving LF. It shares with the *wh*-trace two important properties: it must be in a case-marked position, and it must receive a θ-role, in fact a θ-role completely independent of that received by the trace:

(12)

a. *Who did you see e_i [because it seemed PG_i to have left]

b. *Who$_i$ did you see e_i [because PG_i seemed that George left]

Most important for present purposes is the fact that NP-Movement does not give rise to the double gap structures; it does not "license a parasitic gap":

(13)

*The book$_i$ was read e_i before we filed PG_i

In fact, we already have an explanation for the ungrammaticality of (13): it violates the θ-Criterion, since the chain (the book$_i$, e_i, PG_i) receives two θ-roles (one from *read* and one from *filed*).

The parasitic gap construction shows several interesting things about how the modules interrelate. It is especially revealing where the movement module is concerned, since the parasitic gap is similar to a *wh*-trace but does not arise through movement.

First, the reason (10a–d) do not violate the θ-Criterion is that the two traces each constitute a separate chain—the *wh*-phrase that binds them is in an $\overline{A}$-position and thus cannot be part of a chain, since *chain* is defined to include only A-positions. Separately, the two traces do not violate the θ-Criterion, since each is assigned one and only one θ-role. In effect, then, the θ-Criterion says that each chain is associated with one and only one θ-role.

Second, the fact that the parasitic gap is case-marked shows that the fact that *wh*-trace must be case-marked cannot be explained by the theory of movement, since *wh*-trace and the parasitic gap differ precisely in that one is moved and the other is not. They must share some other property, then, from which it follows that they both have case. Returning to the idea that the *wh*-trace and the parasitic gap function as variables, in the logical sense, variables may be required to have case, ultimately perhaps as a matter of definition:

(14)

A variable must be case-marked.

Third, the fact that the parasitic gap is assigned a θ-role shows that this feature of *wh*-trace is also best divorced from movement and instead attributed to the fact that the *wh*-trace is a variable. This suggests another requirement:

(15)
A variable must receive a θ-role.

This is reminiscent of the θ-Criterion, which says that a chain must receive a θ-role. To simplify, the notions "variable" and "chain" may be identified with one another in the following way:

(16)
A variable is the head of a chain.

From this two things follow: first, that variables will be case-marked, since (as a result of considerations that are irrelevant here) it is the head of a chain that is case-marked; and second, that the variable will receive a θ-role, since the θ-Criterion requires that every chain receive one (and only one) θ-role.

To see how these definitions work, consider (17):

(17)
Who$_i$ e_i was believed [e_i to have left]

Here, the chain (e_i, e_i) receives one θ-role (the subject θ-role of *left*) and one case (the subject nominative case in the matrix). Since it has case and a θ-role, it qualifies as a variable (or, interchangeably, its head does); this variable is bound by the operator *who* in COMP.

Given the further definitions that *wh*-words are intrinsically operators and that an operator must bind a variable (see (23)), we can answer the two questions with which this discussion began: why is the *wh*-trace case-marked, and why does *Wh*-Movement move elements to COMP, and not to subject position?

The reason the *wh*-trace is case-marked is this: since the *wh*-word must bind a variable, and a variable must have case, and the *wh*-trace is a variable, it follows that the chain headed by the *wh*-trace must receive case. Then, since a chain realizes its case on its head, *wh*-trace is case-marked.

The fact that the *wh*-word moves to COMP, and not to a subject (or other) position, again involves the notion "variable." If a variable must head a chain, and a *wh*-word must bind a (whole) chain, then the *wh*-word cannot be a part of the chain. However, if the *wh*-word is moved to any A-position, it will be a part of some chain by the definition of chain; therefore, it must move to an $\overline{\text{A}}$-position.

At this point too much should not be made of the *direction* of these deductions. They could just as easily run the other way: for example, if a variable must have case, then it follows that it will always head a chain.

It is important to understand the very technical nature of the definition of variable that is involved here, since it does not coincide exactly with the logician's use. This is especially clear for the parasitic gap. Perhaps the most striking fact about parasitic gaps is that they cannot be c-commanded by the gap that "licenses" them:

(18)
a. *Who$_i$ did you [tell e_i that you liked PG$_i$]
b. Who$_i$ did you [hit e_i] because you liked PG$_i$

This is a strange restriction, since pronouns can occur in the position of the second (parasitic) gap in (18a), with the interpretation intended for (18a)—that is, the pronoun is understood to be a second instance of the same variable as e_i:

(19)
Who$_i$ did you tell e_i that you liked him$_i$

The argument for disqualifying (18a) takes the following form: the second EC in (18a) must be construed as one of the possible ECs (that is, NP-trace, PRO, or variable); if the theory can be modified so as to exclude all these possibilities, and if there are no more, then (18a) will be ruled out.

The job is already mostly done. The EC cannot be PRO, since it is in a governed (not to mention case-marked) position, which (as we will see in chapter 17) PRO may not occupy. It also cannot be interpreted as NP-trace, since an NP-trace in that position would (a) be case-marked, which NP-trace cannot be, and (b) violate the Opacity Condition (see chapter 17).

The difficulty is that there is no reason why this EC cannot be construed as a variable bound by the *wh*-operator. This construal can be blocked, though, by defining *variable* and *binding* in the right way.

In all of the cases of binding discussed so far the operator c-commands the variables that it binds. We might formulate a definition of *binding* and *variable* that incorporates this insight:

(20)
a. *Binding:* X binds Y if X and Y are coindexed and X c-commands Y.
b. *Variable:* A variable is an EC bound by an operator in an $\bar{A}$-position. ("A variable is an $\bar{A}$-bound EC.")

This definition of binding is no doubt connected to a definition of *logical scope* — the scope of an operator is the subtree that it c-commands, just as in symbolic predicate logics. (20) reflects ordinary logical practice and theory; it will prevent all sorts of pathological representations, for example those in which a *wh*-word has been lowered:

(21)
$*e_i$ wonders [who$_i$ Bill saw Mary]

So far, we still have no way to distinguish between (18a) and (18b); by the definitions, the second EC in both is a variable. But, since the first EC c-commands the second in (18a) but not (18b), we can now at least state the difference between them: in (18a) the second EC is bound by both the *wh*-word and the first EC; in (18b) the second EC is bound only by the *wh*-word.

Suppose we now revise the definition of variable in the following way:

(22)
Variable: A variable is an EC whose closest binder is in an $\bar{A}$-position. ("A variable is 'locally $\bar{A}$-bound.' ")

By this definition, the second EC in (18a), but not (18b), is a variable. Since all other interpretations of the second EC in (18a) are already ruled out, (18a) is judged ill-formed, as desired.

This definition of variable has a surprising connection to a set of problems involving pronouns: the weak crossover phenomenon. As mentioned earlier, sentences with parasitic gaps are semigrammatical, not gathering enthusiastic assents from native speakers; nevertheless, they are a part of the language in some sense. We may take this to indicate that the parasitic gap violates a relatively weak principle of grammar; weak compared to the θ-Criterion or Subjacency, for example. Since parasitic gap sentences are simply sentences with two variables bound by a single quantifier, it has been proposed that some principle of grammar weakly militates against such binding:

(23)

The Bijection Principle

a. Weak half: A quantifier can bind only one variable.
   (Violation results in semigrammaticality.)
b. Strong half: A quantifier must bind a variable.
   (Violation results in ungrammaticality.)

(23a) (weakly) rules out parasitic gap constructions.

Apart from parasitic gap constructions, though, the Bijection Principle might seem at first glance to do more harm than good. If pronouns as well as ECs can be variables, then we have seen numerous cases where a quantifier binds two variables. For example:

(24)

a. Everyone thinks that he is sick
   LF: Everyone$_i$ [x_i thinks that he$_i$ is sick]
b. Who$_i$ e_i thinks that he$_i$ is sick

Actually, though, these examples *do not* violate the Bijection Principle, because of the special definition of variable given in (22). The closest binder of the pronoun in (24a) is the variable x_i (in an A-position), and the closest binder in (24b) is the e_i in subject position. Therefore, the pronoun is not a variable in either case, and the Bijection Principle is not violated.

One way to construct examples that are like (24) except that the pronoun is not locally bound by the variable is to place the pronoun in such a position that it is not c-commanded by the variable; in that case its closest binder will be the operator. Of course, we want to ensure that the pronoun does not c-command the variable either, since the variable would then not be a variable, its closest binder being a pronoun in an A-position. If we construct examples in which neither c-commands the other, exactly the cases of "weak crossover" result:

(25)

?Who$_i$ did the picture of him$_i$ upset e_i

Both e_i and the pronoun count as variables in (25), since the only binder for either is the *who* in $\overline{\text{A}}$-position; thus, (25) violates the Bijection Principle, which assigns "weak" ungrammaticality. That native speakers judge these cases to be only weakly ungrammatical, as the Bijection Principle would predict, confirms the general approach in an interesting way. (25) should be compared with cases of strong cross-over, in which the pronoun does c-command the variable:

(26)
*Who$_i$ did he$_i$ think that Bill liked e_i

Such cases violate not the Bijection Principle (since the e_i cannot be a variable, its closest binder being *he*), but the binding theory.

We emphasize again that the term *variable* is used here in a highly particular way, and picks out only a subset of the cases a logician would call variables in English. For that reason, perhaps the term *variable* is not entirely appropriate. Certainly, linguists do not mean to imply, by their use of the term, that the two pronouns in (27a–b) have different interpretations in a model-theoretic, or some other, sense:

(27)
a. Who$_i$ thinks that he$_i$ is sick
b. ?Who$_i$ does his$_i$ mother think is sick

Leaving aside the fact that (27b) is semigrammatical, we see no reason that (model-theoretic) interpretation cannot proceed identically for these two cases; in both, the pronoun counts as a variable in the logician's sense. Nevertheless, only the pronoun in (27b) counts as a variable in the sense defined here.

16.3 Bibliographical Comments

For section 16.1, which is largely a summary of chapters 14 and 15, see the references given there. For diverging approaches concerning the level of representation at which case-assignment applies, see Chomsky (1980b) and Van Riemsdijk and Williams (1981).

The existence of parasitic gaps was discovered as early as Ross (1967). More recently, they have been analyzed in Taraldsen (1981) and Engdahl (1983). Taking these analyses as his point of departure, Chomsky (1982a) develops in detail the analysis sketched in the text. Crucial in this account are the Bijection Principle and the definition of *variable* proposed in Koopman and Sportiche (1982).

A warning note is in order here. The works by Taraldsen, Engdahl, Chomsky, and Koopman and Sportiche are based on an interpretation of the notion "empty category" that is slightly different from the one presented here. Our account assumes that the differential properties of ECs are, as it were, inherent. (Thus, for example, the EC in (4) would

inherently possess some case feature.) The EC, with its inherent properties, is then subject to the various well-formedness conditions outlined in these chapters. A somewhat different approach would be to say
that all ECs are inherently alike and that their differential properties are
determined contextually. This approach, which has come to be called
the *functional interpretation of empty categories,* was first explored in
chapter 6 of Chomsky (1981c). As a brief illustration, consider an example of strong crossover like *Who_i did he_i say you saw e_i.* Here e_i is
A-bound. As a result, the sentence violates two principles: first, the
θ-Criterion, since he_i and e_i form a chain that receives two θ-roles; and
second, the Bijection Principle, since e_i cannot be a variable (who_i is
not its closest binder and hence does not have any variable to bind).
This distinction is not crucial to the presentation of the Government-
Binding Theory given in the text, but it is worth bearing in mind in
sampling the literature.

Chapter 17
The Binding Theory

17.1 A-Binding vs. Ā-Binding

In chapters 14 through 16 we have outlined a partial theory about the distribution of NP-types and NP-positions in terms of two modules: case theory and θ-theory. In case theory some properties of an NP are determined by the presence vs. absence of a governing case-assigner. In θ-theory an NP is, or is not, assigned argument status with respect to some predicate. In both cases the property may sometimes be transmitted to the NP from its trace. Trace theory itself determines a good deal about the behavior of NPs. In particular, the binding relations described in chapter 12 must be incorporated into the comprehensive modular theory of NPs. In the sections to follow we will see how this has been done.

Recall that the perspective on binding adopted here has shifted subtly. In the first half of chapter 12 we spoke in terms of actual binding *rules:* rules that "look for an antecedent," "coindex NPs," "assign disjoint reference." In the second half of chapter 12, however, we explored, in a preliminary fashion, the possibility of assuming free coindexing plus a set of conditions on representations (chapter 12, (37b)). These conditions were essentially a reformulation of the Specified Subject Condition, previously defined in chapter 7. Let us start by reexamining these conditions:

(1)
a. A bound anaphor must be bound in the smallest domain-of-a-subject in which it occurs.
b. A pronoun must be free in the smallest domain-of-a-subject in which it occurs.
c. A lexical NP must be free in all domains.

In light of the discussion in chapter 16, (1) raises many questions, of which the following are most important:

(2)

a. Can the notion "domain-of-a-subject" be made more precise, and, in particular, can it be assimilated to the notion "government"?

b. Can these conditions be extended to the full range of NP-types?

c. Does the notion of binding involved in (1) refer to A-binding (being bound to an A-position), to $\overline{\text{A}}$-binding (being bound to an $\overline{\text{A}}$-position), or to both?

We can dispense with the last question rather quickly. The conditions in (1) involve A-binding only. At several points we have discussed the reasons for saying that the SSC and TSC do not apply to the relation between a moved *wh*-phrase and its trace (see chapters 9 and 13). One of these involves the strong crossover effect, in which *wh*-traces can be seen to behave like names; that is, they obey (1c):

(3)

a. Who$_i$ does he$_{*i/j}$ think e_i left

b. He$_{*i/j}$ thinks John$_i$ left

The trace in (3a) behaves with respect to *he* exactly like *John* does in (3b). But if we want to say that the trace in (3a) must be free in all domains, it is clear that *free* can only refer to A-binding, since that trace is $\overline{\text{A}}$-bound to *who*. Though the consequences of the conclusion that the binding theory is limited to A-binding are not uncontroversial, we will maintain that conclusion here.

In the following sections we will address questions (2a) and (2b).

17.2 The Notion of Governing Category

The reason for using the term *domain-of-a-subject* earlier was that the subject of certain infinitival complement clauses behaves in a special way, as we have often seen. Consider (4), for example:

(4)

John expects himself to win

Without such cases, it would be possible to maintain an optimally simple binding theory wherein an anaphor must be bound in its minimal clause and a pronoun must be free in its minimal clause. But *himself* in (4) is bound in the next clause up. In terms of the earlier approach, the smallest domain-of-a-subject *himself* is in is the clause of which *John* is the subject. Recall, now, that the behavior of *himself* is exceptional not only with respect to binding, but also with respect to case-marking. In chapter 14 we considered the exceptional case-marking of lexical subjects of infinitivals and saw that it can be accounted for in terms of government and subcategorization for S (not S'). Not to integrate the two cases would be to miss a generalization.

Adopting this perspective, compare (4) with (5):

(5)
*John expects that himself will win

The main difference in terms of case is that *himself* is governed by tense in its S' in (5), whereas it is governed from outside its S by *expects* in (4), the S' being absent or transparent. This fact might be translated into the following intuitive domain statement: A reflexive must be bound in the smallest clause that contains its governor.

This idea has been stated more precisely by defining *governing category* as follows:

(6)
Governing category: α is the governing category for X if and only if α is the minimal NP or S containing X and a governor of X.

On the basis of (6), the binding condition for reflexives can be formulated in a very simple way:

(7)
A reflexive must be bound in its governing category.

Let us briefly address some details in the formulation of (6). First, notice that it refers to S, not S'. The reason for this choice is to be found in the behavior of *for*-infinitivals. Consider (8):

(8)
John wants very much for himself to win

Here *himself* is governed by the preposition-like complementizer *for*. As a result, *himself* is governed inside its "own" S':

(9)

$[_{S_1}$ John wants very much $[_{S'_2}$ for $[_{S_2}$ himself to ...

But given the formulation in (6), the *minimal* S containing a governor for *himself* is S_1; hence, *himself* can be bound by *John*.

Consider next the addition of NP in (6). This works rather well in cases such as (10):

(10)

John$_i$ expected [$_{NP}$ Bill's$_j$ stories about himself$_{*i/j}$]$_{NP}$ to be discredited

The bracketed constituent in this example is the minimal NP containing the governor of the reflexive (i.e., *about*). In (10) that NP contains a potential antecedent. By virtue of (7), *Bill* can, but *John* cannot, be a binder for *himself*.

Unfortunately, problems arise in view of examples like the following:

(11)

a. John expected [pictures of himself] to be on sale

b. John expects that [pictures of himself] will be on sale

In both cases the reflexive has no antecedent in its governing category. Nevertheless, both are grammatical with *John* construed as the binder of the reflexive. In the next subsection we will explore a possible solution to this problem.

17.3 Accessible SUBJECTs

First we must digress to reconsider the structure of the English auxiliary system and to introduce some machinery. Within generative grammar the auxiliary system has usually been analyzed as in (12) by means of a phrase structure rule (12a) and a transformation (12b). (It may be possible to make the rule of Affix Hopping more consistent with "Move α," but this is a task we will not undertake here.)

(12)

a. AUX $\rightarrow$ [±tns] (M) (*have* + *en*) (*be* + *ing*)

b. *Affix Hopping*

X – AFFIX – VERB – Y

SD: 1 2 3 4 $\rightarrow$

SC: 1 $\emptyset$ 3+2 4

where AFFIX = [±tns], +*en*, +*ing*

VERB = V, M, *have*, *be*

In (12) the reference to [±tns] is the most imprecise part. Several other features are involved, including features to indicate what tense (e.g., [±past]) and features (such as those for number and person) establish-

ing agreement between the subject of a tensed clause and the finite
verb. Taken together, these have been called an *inflectional component*
of AUX, or *INFL*. Accordingly, (12a) can be revised to (13):

(13)
AUX → INFL (M) (*have + en*) (*be + ing*)

Since we will be concerned here only with the INFL part of AUX, for
ease of exposition we will use simplified structures like (14):

(14)
[$_s$ NP INFL VP]$_s$

The inflectional features are of two kinds. The tense features are
contextually related to the VERB only. The agreement features are
contextually related not only to the VERB (by Affix Hopping) but also
to the subject NP by some rule of agreement. In addition, the agreement features are contextually dependent on the presence of the feature [±tns]. It has been assumed, therefore, that there are two types
of INFL (where α, β, and γ are variables ranging over the values that
these features can take: present vs. past, singular vs. plural, and
masculine-feminine-neuter):

(15)
a. INFL   b.   INFL

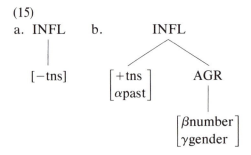

The agreement relationship between the agreement node AGR and the
subject can be expressed by coindexing:

(16)
[$_s$ NP$_i$ [$_{INFL}$[±tns] AGR$_i$]$_{INFL}$ VP]$_s$

Returning now to the problematic contrast between (5) and (11b) (repeated here),

(17)
a. *John expects that himself will win
b. John expects that pictures of himself will be on sale

we may try to capitalize on the fact that *himself* in (17a) is coindexed with the AGR node of the complement clause, whereas *himself* in (17b) is not because it is the containing NP (*pictures of himself*) that agrees with the verb.

To see how this can be done, observe that AGR has basically nominal characteristics since it carries typically nominal features and can be coindexed with NPs. Consequently, in a structure like (16) there is a sense in which AGR_i is just as much the subject of S as NP_i. Going a little further, suppose that AGR_i, when present, is considered the most *prominent part* of the "discontinuous subject" consisting of NP_i and AGR_i. (Of course, when there is no AGR_i, NP_i is automatically the most prominent subject of S.) The notion "most prominent subject" has been given the name *SUBJECT:*

(18)
SUBJECT: The SUBJECT of a clause is $[AGR_i, S]$ if there is one, otherwise $[NP_i, S]$ or $[NP_i, NP]$ (where $[X,Y]$ means "the X immediately dominated by Y" (modulo such nodes as INFL and AUX)).

With this tool it is possible to reintroduce the earlier notion "smallest domain-of-a-subject." Consider again the core cases:

(19)
a. NP_i $[_{INFL}$ $[+tns]$ $AGR_i]_{INFL}$ VP
b. ... V $[_{S'}$ for *NP* to VP$]_{S'}$
c. ... V $[_S$ *NP* to VP$]_S$ (ECM)
d. $[_{NP}$ *NP*'s$_i$ N ...$]_{NP}$

Now, an *opaque domain* can be defined as the c-command domain of the SUBJECT (indicated in (19) by italics). Observe, incidentally, that this unifies the SSC and the TSC: if *specified subject* is replaced by SUBJECT in the definition of the SSC, then the SSC subsumes the TSC.

Now *governing category* may be reformulated as follows:

(20)
Governing category: α is the governing category for X if and only if α is the minimal category containing X, a governor of X, and a SUBJECT accessible to X.

Before we define the notion of accessibility used in (20), notice that this formulation has the major advantage over (6) of avoiding the stipulative reference to S or NP: PP and AP are automatically excluded since they have no subject at all, and NP counts only when it has one. It is not necessary to refer to S rather than S′ in a case like (9) since the first clause containing both the governor (for) and the SUBJECT (here, the AGR node of S_1) is S_1, as required.

Accessibility is defined as follows:

(21)

a. *Accessibility:* α is accessible to β if and only if α c-commands β and the assignment of the index of α to β does not lead to a violation of the *i*-within-*i* Condition.

b. *i-within-i Condition*
   $*[_\gamma \ldots \delta \ldots]_\gamma$
   where γ and δ have the same index

The *i*-within-*i* Condition is independently necessary to exclude cases like (22a–b):

(22)

a. *[a proof of itself$_i$]$_i$

b. *[his$_i$ friend]$_i$

Given definition (21a), consider again the crucial cases:

(23)

a. *John expects that himself will win

b. John expects himself to win

c. John wants very much for himself to win

d. John$_i$ expects Bill's$_j$ pictures of himself$_{*i/j}$ to be on sale

e. John expects pictures of himself to be on sale

f. John expects that pictures of himself will be on sale

These sentences have the following structures:

(24)

a. $[_{S_1}$ NP$_i$ AGR$_i$ V $[_{S_2'}$ that $[_{S_2}$ himself$_i$ AGR$_i$ VP]$_{S_2}]_{S_2'}]_{S_1}$

b. $[_{S_1}$ NP$_i$ AGR$_i$ V $[_{S_2}$ himself$_i$ to VP]$_{S_2}]_{S_1}$

c. $[_{S_1}$ NP$_i$ AGR$_i$ V $\ldots$ $[_{S'}$ for $[_{S_2}$ himself$_i$ to VP]$_{S_2}]_{S'}]_{S_1}$

d. $[_{S_1}$ NP$_i$ AGR$_i$ V $[_{S_2}[_{NP}$ NP's$_j$ pictures of himself$_{i/j}]_{NP_k}$ to VP]$_{S_2}]_{S_1}$

e. $[_{S_1}$ NP$_i$ AGR$_i$ V $[_{S_2}[_{NP}$ pictures of himself$_i]_{NP}$ to VP]$_{S_2}]_{S_1}$

f. $[_{S_1}$ NP$_i$ AGR$_i$ V $[_{S_2'}$ that $[_{S_2}[_{NP}$ pictures of himself$_i]_{NP_j}$ AGR$_j$ VP]$_{S_2}]_{S_2'}]_{S_1}$

How does the revised definition of governing category given in (20) apply to (24a–f)? The reflexive in these examples corresponds to X in (20). The governor is AGR (of the embedded clause) in (24a), the matrix verb in (24b), the complementizer *for* in (24c), and *of* in (24d–f). What is crucial, then, is where the closest accessible SUBJECT is. In (24a) it is the lower AGR_i, since no *i*-within-*i* Condition violation can arise. Consequently, S_2 is the minimal category containing X, its governor, and a SUBJECT accessible to X. Since the reflexive is not bound inside S_2, the sentence is ungrammatical. In (24b) and (24c) the closest accessible SUBJECT is AGR_i of the matrix clause, yielding S_1 as the governing category and NP_i as the binder for the reflexive. In (24d) the closest accessible SUBJECT is $NP's_j$, so the NP is the governing category. Therefore, the reflexive must be bound by $NP's_j$ and cannot be interpreted as being coreferential with NP_i. In (24e), where the NP has no SUBJECT, the closest accessible SUBJECT is again AGR_i of the matrix, and NP_i is a legitimate binder of the reflexive. In (24f) the *i*-within-*i* Condition selects AGR_i as the SUBJECT. AGR_j cannot be the SUBJECT because it is inaccessible: assigning the index *j* to the reflexive would result in structure (25):

(25)
$[_{NP}$ pictures of $himself_j]_{NP_j}$

Thus, introducing the notion "accessible SUBJECT" into the definition of governing category has a number of empirical and conceptual advantages.

17.4 A New Binding Theory

Given the new definitions, (1a–c) can be reformulated as (26a–c):

(26)
a. A bound anaphor must be bound in its governing category.
b. A pronoun must be free in its governing category.
c. A lexical NP must be free.

This is the binding theory as given in Chomsky (1981c, 188). Now, can this binding theory be extended to the full range of NP-types?

(27)
a. bound anaphors (reflexives and reciprocals)
b. pronouns
c. lexical NPs
d. *wh*-words
e. *wh*-trace and trace of quantifier phrase
f. NP-trace
g. PRO

As it stands, (26) applies only to (27a–c). What can be said about the other NP-types? As far as *wh*-words are concerned, moved *wh*-words must be distinguished from unmoved *wh*-words. Moved *wh*-words (in COMP) are outside the domain of the binding theory, since COMP is an $\overline{\text{A}}$-position. Unmoved *wh*-words, such as those in multiple *wh*-questions, behave like logical variables. Since we already know that variables behave like lexical NPs in crossover-like situations, we can assimilate that case of (27d) to (27c). The same is true of (27e). NP-trace, on the other hand, behaves like a bound anaphor. This is the essential insight of trace theory. (27f) is therefore assimilated to (27a). What about PRO? PRO—at least obligatory control PRO—shares one feature with anaphors: it must be bound. But PRO also shares one feature with pronouns: it can never be bound in its minimal clause. Furthermore, PRO can only occur in the subject position of infinitivals. PRO, then, appears to be problematic.

This distribution of properties has led to positing the two features in (28), which interact to produce the classification of NP-types given in (29):

(28)
[±anaphoric], [±pronominal]

(29)
a. $\begin{bmatrix} +\text{anaphoric} \\ -\text{pronominal} \end{bmatrix}$ bound anaphors
NP-trace

b. $\begin{bmatrix} -\text{anaphoric} \\ +\text{pronominal} \end{bmatrix}$ pronouns

c. $\begin{bmatrix} -\text{anaphoric} \\ -\text{pronominal} \end{bmatrix}$ lexical NPs
logical variables

d. $\begin{bmatrix} +\text{anaphoric} \\ +\text{pronominal} \end{bmatrix}$ PRO

Given this classification, the binding theory has been reformulated as follows:

(30)
Binding Theory
A. A [+anaphoric] NP must be bound in its governing category.
B. A [+pronominal] NP must be free in its governing category.
C. A [−anaphoric, −pronominal] NP must be free.

Observe first that principle C in some sense ruins the symmetry of principles A and B, since one would hope that the binding properties of lexical NPs would follow from their being exempt from principles A and B. But they do not. Although proposals have been made to eliminate principle C from the binding theory, we will not pursue this matter here.

At first sight, PRO still appears to be problematic. In effect, (29d) says that PRO must be simultaneously subject to binding principles A and B. But how could any element be both free and bound in its governing category? The answer is surprising and simple. An element can satisfy principles A and B at the same time *only if it has no governing category*. The only way an NP-position can fail to have a governing category is for it to be ungoverned, and the only NP-position that is systematically ungoverned is the subject position of an infinitival S′. And that, of course, is exactly the position to which PRO is limited. In other words, it is possible to *derive* the distribution of PRO from the binding theory. Therefore, this result is often referred to as the *PRO-theorem*.

17.5 Pied Piping, Reconstruction, and Point of Application

In the remainder of this chapter we will address two important questions:

(31)
a. Where in the grammar does the binding theory apply?
b. How does pied piping under *Wh*-Movement interact with the binding theory?

We will begin with the latter question, since it bears on the former. Though we have discussed this problem before (section 13.3), it must be considered anew in the context of the present formulation of the binding theory. The implicit assumption in chapter 13 was that *Wh*-

Movement creates structures that correspond in a trivial one-to-one fashion to their LF-representations. Consider (32), for example:

(32)

a. Who$_i$ did you say Bill killed e_i

b. For which x_i, x_i a person, did you say Bill killed x_i

But as soon as pied piping is taken into account, this correspondence breaks down. Consider:

(33)

[Whose$_i$ brother]$_j$ do you think he$_{*i/*j/k}$ hates e_j

Here, the crossover effect obtains both between *he* and *whose brother* and between *he* and *whose*. The former case is straightforwardly accounted for by taking e_j to be a variable, as before. The latter case, however, is so far unexplained. It would be explained, if the following LF-representation could be assigned to (33):

(34)

For which x_i, x_i a person, do you think he hates x_i's brother

In (34) the variable x_i's must be free. But how are we to get from (33) to (34), since there is no one-to-one correspondence? It appears that the LF-representation (34) reflects, in some sense, the premovement structure of the *wh*-phrase. For this purpose a rule of *Reconstruction* is assumed, which moves all of a pied-piped phrase back into the position of its trace—except for the operator element, for which a variable is substituted. This rule can be written as follows:

(35)

Reconstruction

$[_\alpha \text{ X OP}_i \text{ Y}]_{\alpha_j} \ldots [e]_j \ldots \rightarrow \text{OP}_i \ldots [_\alpha \text{ X vbl}_i \text{ Y}]_{\alpha_j} \ldots$

(where *OP* stands for *operator* and *vbl* for *variable*)

Reconstruction must apply after S-Structure is derived and before the binding principles apply. It seems clear that adopting Reconstruction is conceptually rather awkward, since its sole purpose is to undo most of what *Wh*-Movement has previously done. Alternatives, however, have been found to have far-reaching and controversial effects. For these we refer the reader to the bibliographical section at the end of this chapter.

Given these remarks, we already have a partial answer to (31a). The binding theory applies after Reconstruction and hence after S-Structure. The remaining question concerns the ordering between the binding principles and the rule of LF-Movement (called Quantifier Rule or QR in chapter 13) that assigns scope to operators. Take, for example, (36):

(36)
a. *He$_i$ loves everyone$_i$
b. [$_S$ Everyone$_i$ [$_S$ he$_i$ loves e_i]$_S$]$_S$
c. [$_S$ For every x_i, x_i a person, [$_S$ he$_i$ loves x_i]$_S$]$_S$

Principle C of the binding theory will rule out such a structure regardless of whether it applies to the pre-LF-Movement structure (36a) or to the post-LF-Movement structure (36b–c). Potential evidence comes from examples like (37):

(37)
a. He watched every movie that John had directed
b. I am not sure who said that he hated which movie that John had directed

In both examples *he* and *John* must be disjoint in reference. The evidence is weak, however, since it is related to the question of whether there is pied piping under LF-Movement. If there is, then the binding principles must precede LF-Movement. This is so because pied piping of the relative clause reverses the binding properties, as in (38):

(38)
Which movie that John had directed do you think he hates

Here, *he* may be coindexed with *John*. But since there appears to be no reason to assume that LF-Movement involves pied piping, the question remains open. We will therefore assume the organization of the grammar shown in figure 17.1. This leaves (38) as a problem: the only way to

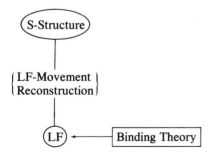

Figure 17.1
The place of the binding theory in the grammar

account for this sentence straightforwardly would be to assume that the binding principles apply before Reconstruction, an option that is excluded in view of the strong crossover cases that motivated Reconstruction in the first place. The only viable alternative, at this point, is to simply stipulate that pied-piped relative clauses are exempt from Reconstruction. This is not a solution, just a way out. Further research will have to address this problem.

17.6 Concluding Remarks

As the preceding section has shown, linguists have not solved all the problems that arise in connection with the binding theory. Nevertheless, this binding theory constitutes a significant improvement over previous accounts of binding. These improvements are both empirical and conceptual in nature. On the empirical side, this binding theory accounts for the cases of bound anaphors embedded in a subject NP by means of the notion "accessible SUBJECT." Conceptually, it allows the fact that PRO is restricted to the subject position of infinitival S's to be derived as a theorem, and it unifies the Specified Subject Condition and the Tensed-S Condition.

17.7 Bibliographical Comments

Since this chapter presents a reformulation of the binding conditions outlined in chapter 12, we refer the reader to the works cited there in connection with binding.

Alternatives to the binding theory have been proposed by Aoun (1981a), Huang (1982), Koster (1984), Brody (1984), and Sportiche (1983), as well as by Higginbotham (1983) and Montalbetti (1984), who advocate the so-called linking approach inspired by Evans (1980).

As the domain of facts to be covered by the binding theory is broadened, complications arise that call for revisions either of existing analyses or of the theory. An account of a number of apparently exceptional usages of bound anaphors is offered in Lebeaux (forthcoming). So-called *donkey*-sentences (sentences of the type *Every man who owns a donkey beats it,* in which the pronoun *it* is bound by the non-c-commanding NP *a donkey*) are analyzed in Haïk (1984).

Considerable work is being done on the subject of so-called long reflexives—that is, cases in which reflexives are seemingly bound outside their governing category. Such phenomena occur in the Scandinavian languages, Dutch, German, Russian, Chinese, Korean, and Japanese, among others. Since most of this work is still in the research stage, we will mention only Yang (1983), which presents a useful overview of such phenomena in a variety of languages.

Chapter 18
The Empty Category Principle

The previous chapters of this part have outlined a full-fledged modular theory of the behavior of the different types of NPs in syntax and LF. We have seen that the principles of several modules, in particular case theory, specify the context in which each type of NP may appear. The interaction of several modules, principally θ-theory and the binding theory, predicts the relations that may hold between a given NP and other NPs in a sentence. Conversely, given an NP-position, its context, and its coindexing properties, these theories can predict with great certainty what type of NP can, must, or cannot occur in that position.

The main distinctions among NP-types are as follows:

(1)
a. $\pm$case-marked
b. $\pm\theta$-marked
c. antecedent in A-position or $\bar{\text{A}}$-position
d. $\pm$locally $\bar{\text{A}}$-bound
e. $\pm$anaphoric
f. $\pm$pronominal

It is remarkable that these (partly overlapping) distinctions cut across one of the most straightforward and obvious distinctions among NP-types: phonologically realized vs. phonologically null. None of the distinctions in (1) is coextensive with this distinction. This observation suggests an important question: Does the notion "empty category" constitute a significant grammatical generalization?

There are three types of phonologically unrealized NPs:

(2)

a. NP-trace

b. *wh*-trace (or, more generally, variable)

c. PRO

However, this chapter is only about the first two. Though at first glance it seems arbitrary to draw the distinction in this way, we will see that there is in fact a generalization that holds for both kinds of traces and, taking parasitic gaps into account, for all empty categories except PRO. Thus, in the sense of this chapter the term *empty category* is restricted to [$_{NP}$ e]$_{NP}$, PRO being excluded from its domain.

To see the generalization that holds for empty categories, we must retrace our steps historically and pursue the fate of two separate lines of research that suddenly clashed in the late 1970s to produce a paradox—a paradox from which the Empty Category Principle was born.

18.1 A Paradox

The first line of research concerns the reformulation of the Tensed-S Condition (TSC) as the Nominative Island Condition (NIC) and culminates in the possibility of deriving the *That*-Trace Filter from the NIC. This presupposes that *wh*-trace is subject to the NIC. The second line of research concerns the discovery that *wh*-trace does not behave like an anaphor but rather like a variable with name-like properties. This presupposes that *wh*-trace cannot be subject to the NIC. The paradox, then, is that *wh*-trace both must be and cannot be subject to the NIC.

The TSC, together with the Specified Subject Condition (SSC), was established to restrict anaphoric relations across a clause boundary to relations with the subject of an infinitival clause (chapter 7):

(3)

a. *Tensed-S Condition*

No rule may relate X and Y in the structure

... X ... [$_\alpha$ ... Y ...]$_\alpha$ ...

where α is a tensed clause.

b. *Specified Subject Condition*

No rule may relate X and Y in the structure

... X ... [$_\alpha$ ... Z ... W$_1$ Y W$_2$ ...]$_\alpha$ ...

where Z is the subject of W$_1$ Y W$_2$.

These constraints overlap in a great number of cases. Consider (4a–b).

(4)

a. *John$_i$ expected [that Mary would write to himself$_i$]
b. *John$_i$ appears [that Mary hates e_i]

Both examples are ruled ungrammatical by both constraints, since the anaphor (*himself$_i$* in (4a) and e_i in (4b)) is in a tensed clause and since *Mary* is the specified subject of the predicate to which it belongs. An initially promising but ultimately untenable attempt to avoid this redundancy by reformulating one of the constraints in a more specific way was presented in Chomsky (1980b). Chomsky's idea was this: If the SSC remains constant, then the only remaining case that is uniquely handled by the TSC is the subject of a tensed clause:

(5)

a. *John$_i$ expected [that himself$_i$ would win]
b. *John$_i$ seemed [that e_i would win]

Since case theory was developed at the same time, it seemed reasonable to express the generalization "subject of a tensed clause" in terms of case—that is, as "nominative NP." Given this insight and the fact that the relevant constraint does not apply to all NPs but only to anaphors, the TSC could be reformulated as follows:

(6)

Nominative Island Condition (NIC)

A nominative anaphor must be bound inside its clause.

This formulation properly characterizes the anaphoric subject of a tensed clause as opaque.

The NIC made one interesting prediction and gave rise to a fascinating extension. The prediction involved anaphors embedded in a nominative NP. Consider (7):

(7)

They$_i$ said [that [$_{NP}$ pictures of [each other]$_i$]$_{NP_j}$ were on sale]

The reciprocal anaphor can be bound to the matrix subject *they$_i$*. The TSC rules this out, but the NIC does not, since NP$_j$ is not an anaphor but is nominative, whereas *each other$_i$* is an anaphor but is not nominative. In this respect, then, the NIC is superior to the TSC.

Much more far-reaching, however, was the extension of the NIC that was discovered by several researchers as soon as the formulation of the NIC became available. This extension concerned the *That*-Trace Filter (see chapter 10):

(8)

That-*Trace Filter*

*$[_{S'}$ *that* $[_{NP}$ $e]_{NP}$ ...$]_{S_i}$

unless S_i' (or its trace) is in the context $[_{NP}$ NP ____$]_{NP}$

This filter is required to account for the following contrast:

(9)

a.   Who$_i$ do you think e_i saw Bill
b.   Who$_i$ do you think Bill saw e_i

(10)

a.   *Who$_i$ do you think that e_i saw Bill
b.   Who$_i$ do you think that Bill saw e_i

(8) is highly suggestive because it involves one of the main ingredients of the NIC: the *That*-Trace Filter is really about a nominative NP.

The question then arises: Can the NIC be used to exclude (10a)? It can indeed, given the following two assumptions:

(11)

a.   *Wh*-traces are anaphors.
b.   The presence of *that* prevents the trace from being bound in its clause.

Let us simply assume (11a) for the moment and consider how (11b) can be derived from the theory. There are several ways to do this; we will describe just one. Recall that COMP has two positions, one for a *wh*-phrase or its trace and one for a lexical complementizer such as *that*. Hence, when both positions are realized, COMP is branching. But when COMP is branching, the *wh*-trace in COMP no longer c-commands the *wh*-trace in the subject position. Therefore, that nominative *wh*-trace will not be (properly) bound inside its clause, if S' is taken to be the category that is relevant for the NIC. In other words, (9a) and (10a) essentially have the following structure:

(12)

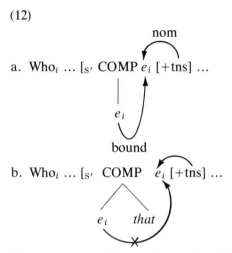

a. Who$_i$ ... [$_{S'}$ COMP e_i [+tns] ...

bound

b. Who$_i$ ... [$_{S'}$ COMP e_i [+tns] ...

Thus, it was possible to derive the effect of the *That*-Trace Filter from the NIC. Needless to say, the unification of two such divergent principles was a highly significant result.

But assumption (11a), on which this unification rests, is incompatible with the theory about *wh*-trace, as outlined in parts II, III, and IV of this book. One of the main arguments to the effect that *wh*-trace cannot be subject to the opacity conditions (i.e., the SSC and TSC) and hence not to the NIC (which replaces the TSC) is that Rizzi's account of *wh*-island violations in Italian cannot be maintained if *wh*-trace is subject to Opacity (see section 9.2.3). This fundamental distinction between *wh*-trace and anaphors, which is further supported by such phenomena as strong crossover, is one of the core properties of the Government-Binding system. Indeed, the realization that *wh*-trace is subject to principle C of the binding theory and not to principle A is another major result of linguistic research in the late 1970s.

How is the paradox to be resolved? It appears that there is no way to save both results, so one of them must be sacrificed and hopefully salvaged in some other way. It seems impossible to go back on the second result. The NIC has now been solidly incorporated into the binding theory. A vast body of evidence, from crossover phenomena, parasitic gaps, etc., would be unaccounted for if the notion that *wh*-trace is a variable were dropped. The only choice, then, is to give up the idea that the *That*-Trace Filter can be derived from the NIC or, ultimately, from the binding theory. Once that step has been taken, there are two options: either to reintroduce the *That*-Trace Filter or to search for a new, more general, and more interesting account of those aspects of the distribution of traces that the NIC and the binding theory cannot handle. In the remainder of this chapter we follow the linguistic developments that have resulted from the latter course of action. Faced with a domain of data that the NIC cannot handle (known as the *residue of the NIC*), linguists began searching for some principle (to be called *RES(NIC)*) capable of dealing with the *that*-trace phenomena in an insightful way.

18.2 From RES(NIC) to ECP

One might try to save the essential insight of the NIC account of *that*-trace phenomena in the following way. If the essential insight is taken to be that the trace in the subject position is somehow not licensed by its syntactic environment, then on the NIC account the licensing factor is being properly bound by some coindexed element in COMP. This account could simply be taken over, generalized, and incorporated into a first approximation of RES(NIC):

(13)
RES(NIC) (First approximation)
$[_{NP}\ e]_{NP}$ must be locally coindexed with a c-commanding NP.

Observe, now, that the *that*-trace phenomena discussed so far have been restricted to cases of *Wh*-Movement. But (13) generalizes our account of them to trace in general. (13) suggests, then, that we look for an NP-trace phenomenon parallel to the *that*-trace effect. Such a phenomenon can indeed be found:

(14)
a. *[The theorem]$_i$ was discovered $[_{S'}$ why $[_S[e]_i$ to be unsolvable$]_S]_{S'}$
b. *[John]$_i$ was tried $[_{S'}[_S[e]_i$ to be promoted$]_S]_{S'}$
c. *[Bill]$_i$ is useful $[_{S'}[_S[e]_i$ to be there$]_S]_{S'}$

None of these examples are ruled out by the theories developed so far. They do not violate θ-theory, since the two coindexed positions form a chain that has a single θ-role. They do not violate case theory, since the trace is caseless, whereas the moved NP receives nominative case in the matrix clause. They do not violate the bounding theory (Subjacency), since only one S-boundary is crossed. Finally, they do not violate the binding theory, since—being ungoverned—they have no governing category and hence are free (like PRO) to take an antecedent in the next clause up.

Furthermore, the notion of local c-command embodied in (13) constitutes the core structural notion in the concept of government. This suggests trying to restate (13) in terms of government:

(13')
RES(NIC) (Second approximation)
$[_{NP} \, e]_{NP}$ must be governed.

Unfortunately, (13') does not by itself account for the *that*-trace cases. Consider again the two relevant situations:

(15)

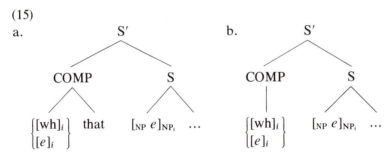

The goal here is to express the idea that the structural relation between the *wh*-phrase (or its trace) in COMP and the trace in the subject position is one of government. To the extent that c-command is incorporated in the definition of government, (13') gives the right result. However, two problems arise. First, we must specify that the trace in the subject position and the element in COMP be coindexed, because otherwise the complementizer *that* or some *wh*-phrase (or its trace) with a different index could serve as governor. Second, the trace in the subject position has case since it is the subject of a tensed clause—and according to the normal definitions of case theory, nominative case is assigned under government by the tense element. More precisely, nominative case is assigned to an NP that is governed by an INFL-node that is headed by [+tns]. Thus, we are faced with the following situation:

(16)

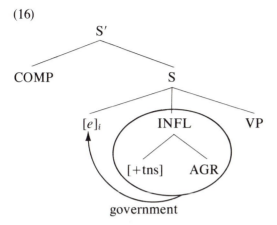

government

Both problems arise because the subject trace is potentially governed by governors that we don't want to count as such.

The solution, then, must be to factor out the defining properties of government and introduce some variation in one of these factors. The main distinction to be drawn is that between the structural relation on the one hand and the definition of what counts as a governor on the other hand:

(17)
Government: X governs Y if and only if Y is contained in the maximal $\overline{X}$-projection of X, X^{max}, and X^{max} is the smallest maximal projection containing Y, and X c-commands Y.

(18)
Governors
a. X^0 (i.e., V, N, A, P)
b. $[_{INFL} [+tns] AGR]_{INFL}$
c. NP_i, where Y (the governee) = NP_i

The null hypothesis would be that all of (18a–c) count as governors for all modules of the theory. But in fact (16) shows that one of the governors, (18c), does not count for case-assignment, and that another, (18b), does not count for the *that*-trace phenomenon (RES(NIC)). Governors must therefore be defined as follows:

(19)
a. *Governors for binding theory and case theory:* (18a), (18b)
b. *Governors for RES(NIC):* (18a), (18c)

This extension of governors to the lexical categories (N, A, V, P) predicts that direct objects, unlike subjects, will not be sensitive to the presence or absence of *that,* since direct objects are governed by the verb and need not depend on being governed by the coindexed NP in COMP to satisfy (19b). This is indeed the case:

(20)
Who$_i$ do you think [$_S$[$_{COMP}$ e_i (that)]$_{COMP}$ Bill saw e_i]$_S$

Even with *that* present in (20), the object trace is governed by a governor permitted under (19b), since it is governed by the verb *saw.* We will therefore adopt the extension to lexical governors embodied in (19b).

The notion of government consisting of the conjunction of (17) and (19b) has come to be called *proper government,* and the ensuing principle was finally termed not RES(NIC), but the Empty Category Principle (ECP).

(21)
Proper government: X properly governs Y if and only if X governs Y (as in (17)) and X is either X^0 (i.e., V, N, A, P; (18a)) or NP$_i$, where Y = NP$_i$ ((18c)).

(22)
Empty Category Principle (ECP)
[*e*] must be properly governed.

Observe that this formulation is not restricted to [$_{NP}$ *e*]$_{NP}$ but applies to other empty categories as well. Since it is not entirely clear that this generalization is warranted, the discussion below will restrict itself to empty NPs.

Let us now examine other cases where X^0 acts as a proper governor. The exceptional case-marking phenomena ought to be relevant here, since these are cases where the subject position of an infinitival clause is governed by the matrix verb. Consider the following example involving exceptional case-marking:

(23)
Who$_i$ do you expect [$_{S''}$ [$_S$ e_i to be there]$_S$]$_{S''}$

In this example the transparent S'-node (S''^{t}) permits government of the trace by *expect.* In other words, *expect* is a proper governor that licenses the subject *wh*-trace.

A problem arises in connection with NP-trace in the subject position of an infinitival clause. Consider the following examples:

(24)
a. John$_i$ seems [$_{S'}$[$_S$ e_i to have left]$_S$]$_{S'}$
b. Bill$_i$ is certain [$_{S'}$[$_S$ e_i to have left]$_S$]$_{S'}$
c. Mary$_i$ is expected [$_{S'}$[$_S$ e_i to be there]$_S$]$_{S'}$

Note that we have been assuming that S' is not transparent in these instances since case need not, indeed must not, be assigned to the NP-trace. But now a problem arises in view of the ECP. The sentences in (24) are perfectly well-formed despite the fact that in each of them the NP-trace is *not* properly governed. We must therefore revise our previous assumptions about these examples by assuming that they too have a transparent S' (S'^{t}) and by attributing the failure of case-assignment to lexical properties of the governor. In the case of (24b) and (24c) this need not be stipulated separately, since we have already concluded that passive participles and adjectives are not case-assigners. For raising verbs like *seem* in (24a) we will just stipulate this property. But this is perhaps not an unnatural stipulation since raising verbs are like intransitive verbs in that they only take one argument (except for an optional *to*-phrase). In accordance with this revision, (24a–c) can be reanalyzed as (25a–c):

(25)
a. John$_i$ seems [$_{S''}$[$_S$ e_i to have left]$_S$]$_{S''}$
b. Bill$_i$ is certain [$_{S''}$[$_S$ e_i to have left]$_S$]$_{S''}$
c. Mary$_i$ is expected [$_{S''}$[$_S$ e_i to be there]$_S$]$_{S''}$

In each case the trace is governed by the matrix predicate, and hence properly governed.

Observe that the structure in (23) is simplified, because the trace in COMP has been omitted. If, in accordance with the theory of successive cyclic movement, there is a trace in COMP, there are two consequences. First, the trace in the subject position is governed not only by the verb *expect* but also by the trace in COMP. Second, and more generally, we must ask if the trace in COMP itself is properly governed. In (23) it is, since the S' is transparent. But the problem arises equally with nontransparent S's from which a *wh*-phrase has been extracted:

(26)
Who$_i$ do you think [$_{S'}$[$_{COMP}$ e_i that]$_{COMP}$ [$_S$ Bill saw e_i]$_S$]$_{S'}$

As things stand now, (26) will be ruled out by the ECP because the trace in COMP is not properly governed. This problem cannot be solved by simply restricting the ECP to empty categories in A-position, because in fact (as we will see) there are ways in which it applies to $\bar{A}$-positions. Thus, a different strategy is needed. Observe, first, that there are languages that are extremely resistant to long *Wh*-Movement of the type exemplified in (26). Russian and certain northern varieties of High German are often cited as languages in which long movement is virtually impossible, and even in English it is excluded with many verbs. Consider (27), for example:

(27)
a. *Who$_i$ did you quip [$_{S'}$[$_{COMP}$ e_i that]$_{COMP}$ [$_S$ Bill saw e_i]$_S$]$_{S'}$
b. *What$_i$ did Sally whisper [$_{S'}$[$_{COMP}$ e_i that]$_{COMP}$ [$_S$ she had secretly read e_i]$_S$]$_{S'}$

For English it has been suggested that long movement is only possible with a specific set of verbs called *bridge verbs*, such as *say* and *think*. We could then say that traces in COMP are subject to the ECP and that long movement is therefore excluded in the normal case. This of course requires introducing a special provision for bridge verbs—namely, that such a verb can properly govern the trace in the COMP of a complement S' that it governs. In essence, this means introducing a second way in which S' can become transparent. We cannot use the usual notion of S'-transparency because we must avoid a situation in which a verb like *say* can govern the subject position of its complement clause:

(28)
*Who$_i$ was John$_j$ said [$_{S''}$[$_{COMP}$ e_i that]$_{COMP}$ [$_S$ e_j had seen e_i]$_S$]$_{S''}$

In (28) the trace in subject position would now be properly governed, an unwanted result, since (28) is ungrammatical. Observe that under the notion of transparency introduced above e_j is governed by the matrix verb *said* as well as by the embedded AGR. Hence, the matrix S counts as a governing category, and (28) cannot be ruled out by principle A of the binding theory.

The salient property of the notion of transparency needed for raising and exceptional case-marking is that only the subject—an A-position—becomes accessible to external government. In the case of bridge verbs only COMP, but not the subject position—in other words, only an $\bar{A}$-position—becomes accessible. Accordingly, we may introduce the notions of A-transparency and $\bar{A}$-transparency and distinguish the two by the superscripts At and $\overline{At}$, respectively. The two cases are thus distinguished as follows:

(29)

a. ...   V $[_{S'At}$ COMP $[_S \; e_j$ ...

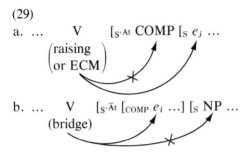

(raising
or ECM)

b. ...   V $[_{S'\overline{At}} \; [_{COMP} \; e_i$ ...$]$ $[_S$ NP ...
   (bridge)

Much of this is tentative, of course, and the diacritics are somewhat arbitrary, but at least the analysis begins to give an account of bridge verbs and allows us to maintain that the ECP applies to all empty categories.

The ECP is definitely a great improvement over the *That*-Trace Filter. For one thing, the formulation is now highly general and has a good chance of being universally valid. More important, the empirical domain of the principle has been extended to encompass cases like (14a–c). On the other hand, one cannot help being somewhat dissatisfied at having to sacrifice the simple and unitary definition of government. One may wonder, in fact, to what extent the three classes of governors in (18) constitute a natural class, and to what extent certain partitionings of (18) do.

In fact, the situation is even more complex, since the classes of governors listed in (18a) and (18b) are as yet incomplete. For example, in section 18.3 we will see that INFL can act as a proper governor in some languages. Moreover, notice that different subsets of the set of categories denoted by X^0 in (18a) (i.e., N, V, A, P) determine different cases. V assigns grammatical objective case. In impoverished case systems P may also assign objective case, though in richer systems it assigns oblique cases. N and A essentially govern no case at all, or at best some highly oblique ones.

In the case of the ECP, we should also ask if all X^0 categories can actually act as proper governors. Clearly, V is a proper governor, since empty categories are permitted in direct object position. A must be a proper governor because raising adjectives govern the subject trace in the complement, as in (30a); and N is probably also a proper governor, because of examples like (30b):

(30)

a. John$_i$ is certain [$_{S''}$[$_S$ e_i to be there]$_S$]$_{S''}$

b. [$_{NP}$[the city's]$_i$ destruction e_i]$_{NP}$

Whether or not N is a proper governor is not easy to decide, because the genitive NP also qualifies as a proper governor, since it is coindexed with the trace and governs it. We leave the matter open here.

Finally, consider P. To the extent that preposition stranding is possible in a language, we might want to say that P is a proper governor, and this might indeed be the right solution for English. But if we make this assumption, it will not be easy to account for the restrictions and asymmetries discussed in section 9.2.1. Consider (31), for example:

(31)

a.   John$_i$ was taken advantage of e_i

b.   *Dinner$_i$ is drunk brandy after e_i

If both *of* and *after* are proper governors, why should these two sentences differ in grammaticality? The Reanalysis rule, which applies to (31a) but not to (31b), will not make any difference. But notice that if we assume that P is not a proper governor, then Reanalysis will turn *take advantage of* into a V and hence create a proper governor for the trace. The trace in (31b) cannot be rescued in this way.

Whether stranding by *Wh*-Movement in English can be handled along similar lines is a more difficult question that we will not discuss in the present context. The situation is clearer in Dutch, where stranding is essentially possible only via the rule of *r*-Movement (section 4.4). Prepositions in Dutch generally do not tolerate an inanimate pronoun as object. Instead, a clitic-like pronominal element, an *r*-pronoun, is substituted and moved to a special position to the left of the preposition:

(32)

a. *op het → er   op
    on it   there on

b. *voor dat → daar voor
    for that   there for

c. *in wat → waar in
    in what   where in

The PPs to the right of the arrows can be assumed to have essentially the following structure:

(33)

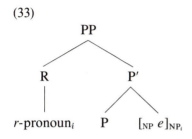

Stranding is possible only with r-pronouns that are moved either into the clitic position (between the subject and the VP) or into COMP:

(34)

a. . . . dat ik niet op hem vuur
         that I   not   at him fire
    '. . . that I do not fire at him'

b. *dat ik hem$_i$ niet op e_i vuur
         that I   him   not   at   fire

(35)

a. . . . dat ik niet [$_{PP}$ er$_i$ op e_i]$_{PP}$ vuur
         that I   not   it   at   fire
    'that I do not fire at it'

b. . . . dat ik er$_i$ niet [$_{PP}$ e_i op e_i]$_{PP}$ vuur
         that I   it   not   at   fire

(36)

a. . . . of hij gisteren   op wie vuurde (*)
         if he   yesterday at who fired
    'whether he fired at who yesterday'

b. *. . . wie$_i$ hij gisteren   op e_i vuurde
          who he   yesterday at   fired

(37)

a. . . . of hij gisteren   [$_{PP}$ waar$_i$ op e_i]$_{PP}$ vuurde (*)
         if he   yesterday   what   at   fired
    'whether he fired at what yesterday'

b. . . . waar$_i$ hij gisteren   [$_{PP}$ e_i op e_i]$_{PP}$ vuurde
         what he   yesterday   at   fired

Assuming that P is not a proper governor will partially account for these facts. Only when an *r*-pronoun or its trace occupies the R-position in the PP will the trace in the object position be properly governed. But what about the trace in the R-position? Here we must take into account a second important fact about stranding in Dutch.

Stranding by *r*-Movement works only when the PP in question is an argument of the verb (or at least closely linked with it as with instrumental adverbials), and furthermore when this PP is inside the VP. Stranding with extraposed PPs, for example, is excluded. This suggests that the trace in the R-position must be governed by the verb. An analysis along the lines of the analysis of bridge verbs suggests itself. Let us assume that the PP-node becomes Ā-transparent when the PP is closely linked to the verb. We do not want to say that the PP becomes A-transparent, of course, since we would then lose the explanation for why it is necessary to use the R-position as an "escape hatch." (It is conceivable that in languages like English A-transparency rather than Ā-transparency is involved. We will not pursue this possibility here, however.) The core case of stranding in Dutch can thus be represented as follows:

(38)

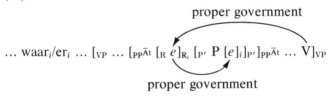

proper government

... waar$_i$/er$_i$ ... [$_{VP}$ ... [$_{PP^{\bar{A}t}}$ [$_R$ e]$_{R_i}$ [$_{P'}$ P [e]$_i$]$_{P'}$]$_{PP^{\bar{A}t}}$ ... V]$_{VP}$

proper government

Thus, preposition stranding can be accounted for in terms of the ECP if it is assumed that P is not a proper governor.

The existence of variation and unclear cases shows, then, that it is a complex matter to determine correctly the list of proper governors. Future research will have to shed more light on these questions.

18.3 The Pro-Drop Parameter

In many languages (for example, Spanish, Italian, Greek, and Hebrew) the pronominal subject of a tensed sentence may remain unexpressed. Italian has paradigms such as the following:

(39)

a. io	parlo	'I talk'	b. parlo	(1st pers. sg.)
tu	parli	'you talk'	parli	(2nd pers. sg.)
lui	parla	'he talks'	parla	(3rd pers. sg.)
noi	parlamo	'we talk'	parlamo	(1st pers. pl.)
voi	parlate	'you talk'	parlate	(2nd pers. pl.)
loro	parlano	'they talk'	parlano	(3rd pers. pl.)

The verbal morphology appears to be rich enough to make the subject pronouns in some sense redundant and recoverable.

As we saw in chapter 10, Perlmutter (1971) discovered that such languages, often called *pro-drop* or *null-subject* languages, systematically lack the *that*-trace effect. Long movement of a subject across a lexical complementizer is perfectly grammatical in Italian, for example:

(40)

Chi$_i$ credi   che e_i verrà
who do-you-believe that   will-come
'Who do you believe will come'

A first hypothesis briefly mentioned in chapter 10 was that pro-drop languages have a rule that optionally deletes subject pronouns. If this rule can also delete subject traces, then structures like (40) will escape from the *That*-Trace Filter and the correlation between (39b) and (40) will be explained. According to this analysis, languages like English lack the deletion rule and hence exhibit the *that*-trace effect.

This account could simply be maintained under the ECP explanation of *that*-trace phenomena. But such an account has several unattractive properties. In particular, why should the grammar contain any deletion rules at all? In the midst of elaborating a comprehensive theory of empty categories, the introduction of pronoun deletion rules that extend to empty categories would seem to undercut the theory in potentially dangerous ways: whenever an empty category with the wrong properties was found in the wrong place, it would be possible to devise a (language-particular) rule to delete it. Let us therefore investigate whether the ECP analysis of *that*-trace phenomena suggests a better way of dealing with pro-drop languages.

Before we turn to technical questions, however, what are some of the predictions that such an account will make? There will have to be some factor F other than a coindexed *wh*-phrase or its trace in COMP that properly governs the subject. But if there is such a factor F, then subjects should be missing in a variety of constructions, not only in cases like (39b). It turns out that this informal prediction is correct: subjects may be absent in the pro-drop language Italian in the following constructions (but not in a non-pro-drop language like English):

(41)

a. Missing subject pronoun:

EC parlano   di linguistica
they-speak of linguistics
'They talk about linguistics'

b. Subject freely postposed from subject position:

i. Le brigate   rosse hanno telefonato
the brigades red   have   called
'The red brigades have called'

ii. EC_i hanno telefonato le brigate rosse
'The red brigades have called'

c. Apparent violation of the *That*-Trace Filter:

Chi_i credi che EC_i verrà   (= (40))
'Who do you believe will come'

d. Subject extraction out of a *wh*-island:

la   donna che_i non so   quando EC_i abbia telefonato
the woman who not I-know when   has   called
'the woman about whom I don't know when she has called'

e. Null resumptive pronoun:

il   professore che_i non so   chi   abbia detto che EC_i sia
the professor who not I-know who has   said   that   has
arrivato
arrived
'the professor about whom I don't know who said that he has arrived'

We have already discussed (41a). (41b) shows that subjects can freely be moved to a position inside, or adjoined to the right of, the VP. Note that French, a non-pro-drop language, also has subject inversion, as in (42a), but it always requires a trigger (*quand* in (42a)) and is not free, as (42b) shows:

(42)

a. Quand EC arrivera   le   professeur
   when   will-arrive the professor
   'When will the professor arrive'

b. *EC est arrivé le professeur

In Italian, however, inversion is free (i.e., not dependent on a trigger). (41c) again illustrates the absence of the *that*-trace effect, and (41d) illustrates the same observation with respect to a violation of the *Wh*-Island Constraint. We have seen that S′ is the bounding node for Italian and hence that certain *wh*-island violations can occur. In (41d) the lower COMP is filled with the *wh*-phrase *quando;* therefore, the subject must have moved directly to the higher COMP. Consequently, the lower COMP does not contain a proper governor for the EC—yet the sentence is grammatical. Finally, consider (41e). This sentence could not have been produced by movement, since movement would have required crossing two S′-nodes, violating Subjacency. But Italian can employ a *resumptive pronoun strategy* (a strategy whereby the gap in a relative clause is replaced by a pronoun), as in (43):

(43)

il   professore che$_i$ non so   chi abbia detto che   non
the professor who not I-know who has   said that not
gli$_i$/*EC$_i$ appartiene questo libro
to-him belongs   this   book
'the professor about whom I don't know who said that this book
doesn't belong to him'

But (41e) shows that in the subject position of a tensed sentence an empty resumptive pronoun will suffice to avoid the Subjacency violation.

We thus have a cluster of five properties that can be reasonably assumed to be due to factor F. What, then, is factor F? We have seen that there is a certain amount of variability about what counts as a proper governor for the ECP. In particular, [$_{\text{INFL}}$ [+tns] AGR]$_{\text{INFL}}$ does not count as a proper governor for the ECP but does count as a governor for case-marking and the binding theory. Suppose now that pro-drop languages differ minimally from non-pro-drop languages in that [$_{\text{INFL}}$ [+tns] AGR]$_{\text{INFL}}$ can properly govern the subject position. This, then, is what has been called the *pro-drop parameter:* a minimal binary difference among languages from which the whole cluster of properties (41a–e) follows automatically.

The idea can be formally implemented as follows. AGR is really a set of agreement features including specifications for gender, number, and person. These features must agree with the subject NP and are (eventually) realized on the verb. Let us express the agreement relation by coindexing AGR and the subject:

(44)

COMP NP_i $[_{INFL}$ [+tns] $AGR_i]_{INFL}$ VP

We may then either assume that AGR_i c-commands NP_i and hence can govern it, or that INFL "inherits" the subscript from AGR_i and acts as the governor. On the former assumption, which we adopt here, we must say either that INFL does not branch, [+tns] being just a feature of INFL, or that it does branch but that this does not matter because the branches do not dominate any lexical material. Without pursuing these options further, we simply assume that AGR_i can c-command NP_i and hence can, in a pro-drop language, properly govern the NP_i in the subject position.

What makes the AGR_i of a pro-drop language different from the AGR_i of a non-pro-drop language? It has been suggested that this relates to the "richness" of the expression of its features on the verb. Though the correlation is neither precise nor complete, pro-drop languages tend to have richer verbal morphology than non-pro-drop languages, as illustrated in (39). We could say, then, that AGR_i acts as a proper governor when rich. Since the choice between rich and poor is made not at the level of each structure but at the level of the grammar of the language, we must identify some formal correlate of "rich" vs. "poor." One possibility is to say that AGR may or may not have categorial features. Since AGR has the typically nominal features for gender, number, and person, it has been suggested that AGR actually is a noun (i.e., [+N, −V]) when rich. Accordingly, the classification of governors in (18) may be revised as follows:

(45)

Governors

a. X^0

b. $[_{INFL}$ [+tns] $AGR]_{INFL}$

c. N_i or NP_i, where Y (the governee) = NP_i

(46)

Proper governors for the ECP: (45a) and (45c)

This system makes it possible for AGR_i to be a proper governor when it has nominal features.

The pro-drop parameter amounts to the choice at the level of the grammar between having AGR with or without nominal features. At this point we should go back to the EC in the subject position in (41) and determine its identity. Clearly, it cannot be PRO since it is governed. Therefore, it must be $[_{NP} \, e]_{NP_i}$. This EC will sometimes arise by movement, as in (41b), (41c), and (41d), and will sometimes be base-generated, as in (41a) and (41e). But in all cases it will be case-marked and $\overline{A}$-bound by AGR_i. No problems with the binding theory ensue.

In conclusion, the ECP, supplemented with the parametrized definition of AGR, yields a highly general and simple account of an entire cluster of properties by which pro-drop languages differ from non-pro-drop languages. As with the S/S' parameter for the bounding theory, the choice that a language makes in the setting of a single abstract binary parameter—here, a choice between nominal and nonnominal AGR—predicts the language's behavior with respect to a wide variety of constructions, and predicts as well how that language will differ with respect to those constructions from a language that makes the opposite choice. Thus, the theory is acquiring a truly deductive structure of considerable depth, unmatched by any other previous or current linguistic theory. Though many details of such parametrized accounts of abstract language typology may still look messy and stipulative, future research will certainly remedy this. The important thing is to continue the search for such abstract parameters for the light they shed on the process of acquiring the grammatical structure of a language. Instead of acquiring a complete set of rules to account for the facts in (41), this theory predicts that the child learning Italian need only hear enough data (Italian utterances) to be able to determine which way Italian fixes the nominal/nonnominal AGR parameter, a determination that can easily be made on the basis of the elementary and abundant sort of evidence given in (39). Everything else follows from the theory—that is, from innate Universal Grammar.

18.4 ECP and Logical Form

One important task that remains is to determine the level of the grammar at which the ECP applies. Essentially, there are three possibilities.

First, the ECP could apply in the phonology, after deletions, just like the *That*-Trace Filter that it replaces. It would then be possible to retain the assumptions outlined in chapter 10 about free deletion in COMP.

Second, if the *That*-Trace Filter can be derived from the NIC, which applies at LF, perhaps the ECP applies at LF as well. In section 18.1 we ignored the consequences of the analysis presented there for the interaction with deletion. Essentially, free deletion in COMP cannot be maintained under that analysis since pairs like (47a–b) cannot be distinguished at S-Structure or LF:

(47)
a. *Who do you think that left
b. Who do you think left

This is so because both start out with *that*-trace at D-Structure, *that* being deleted in (47b) only in the phonology. The alternative is straightforward: to assume that insertion of *that* into COMP is optional at D-Structure and that there is no deletion of *that* in COMP. Under this assumption, (47a) and (47b) are distinct at all levels of representation.

A third logical possibility is that the ECP applies at S-Structure. The consequences for deletion are the same. However, we will not pursue this possibility here.

Here we will explore the consequences of choosing the second assumption, leaving the other two aside. If the ECP applies at LF, then traces left by the rule of LF-Movement must be subject to it. Since the object, but not the subject, is always properly governed under the ECP, this analysis would predict the existence of subject-object asymmetries between quantified NPs. Richard Kayne (1981a) has indeed discovered asymmetries of this sort. Consider first (48) and (49):

(48)
a. J'ai   exigé   que personne ne   soit arrêté
   I have required that nobody (not) be   arrested
   'I have required that nobody be arrested'

b. J'ai   exigé   qu'ils   n'   arrêtent personne
   I have required that they (not) arrest   nobody
   'I have required that they not arrest anybody'

(49)

a. *Je n'ai   exigé   que personne soit arrêté

   I (not) have required that nobody   be   arrested

b. ?Je n'ai   exigé   qu'ils   arrêtent personne

   I (not) have required that they arrest   nobody

In (48) the negated NP has narrow scope and in (49) it has wide scope, as indicated by the scope marker *ne* (or *n'*). (49b) has a question mark because apparently it is always somewhat awkward to interpret negated NPs with wide scope; nevertheless, there is a contrast between (49a) and (49b). This contrast, which is absent in the narrow-scope cases in (48), is immediately accounted for if we assume that the ECP applies at LF—that is, after LF-Movement. This can be seen in the following LF-representations of these four sentences:

(50)

a. J'ai exigé $[_{S'}$ que $[_S$ personne$_i$ $[_S$ e_i ne soit arrêté$]_S]_S]_{S'}$

b. J'ai exigé $[_{S'}$ que $[_S$ personne$_i$ $[_S$ ils n'arrêtent $e_i]_S]_S]_{S'}$

(51)

a. *$[_S$ Personne$_i$ $[_S$ je n'ai exigé $[_{S'}$ que e_i soit arrêté$]_{S'}]_S]_S$

b. $[_S$ Personne$_i$ $[_S$ je n'ai exigé $[_{S'}$ qu'ils arrêtent $e_i]_{S'}]_S]_S$

The trace of *personne$_i$* is properly governed in all cases except (51a). It is governed by the verb in the (b)-sentences and by the moved NP itself in (50a).

Sentences with wide-scope negation in English also exhibit a slight asymmetry:

(52)

a. *In all these weeks, he's suggested (that) not a single term paper be written

b. ?In all these weeks, he's suggested (that) they write not a single term paper

The presence vs. absence of *that* makes no difference, because presumably LF-Movement is not subject to the bounding theory and hence is not successive cyclic.

Finally, a subject-object asymmetry shows up in multiple *wh*-questions. Again the object version is not perfect to start with; yet there is a clearly detectable difference in grammaticality:

(53)

a. I don't remember who believes whom to have read the book

b. I don't remember who believes John to have read what

(54)

a. *I don't remember who believes (that) who read the book

b. ?I don't remember who believes (that) John read what

In these cases it is important to clearly distinguish the multiple *wh*-reading from the echo question reading. On the latter interpretation the asymmetry disappears, a phenomenon consistent with the fact that the *wh*-phrase in echo questions does not undergo LF-Movement.

There is some evidence, then, that the ECP applies at LF. But it is not unproblematic. For one thing, the grammaticality contrast between the subject and nonsubject cases is slight, certainly much slighter than in the canonical *that*-trace cases such as (47a–b). Why this difference in grammaticality should arise remains mysterious. Moreover, there are many types of quantifiers that are generally thought to undergo LF-Movement but do not evidence any kind of asymmetry on wide-scope readings. Consider (55a–b), for example:

(55)

a. They didn't require that anyone register

b. They didn't require that we register anyone

On the perfectly plausible wide-scope interpretation in (56) the trace in subject position should be excluded by the ECP:

(56)

a. $[_S$ Not anyone$_i$ $[_S$ they required $[_{S'}$ that e_i register$]_{S'}]_S]_S$

b. $[_S$ Not anyone$_i$ $[_S$ they required $[_{S'}$ that we register $e_i]_{S'}]_S]_S$

Yet there does not appear to be any difference in grammaticality.

The situation, then, is this. Either it must be assumed that the ECP applies in the phonology or at S-Structure and that the LF asymmetries discussed above are due to some other factor, or it must be maintained that the ECP does apply at LF and an independent explanation must be sought for why the contrast is so weak in the LF cases and why it shows up with some quantifiers but not with others.

The latter alternative, which most researchers prefer, leads to an interesting problem for the pro-drop parameter. The analysis given earlier would predict no subject-object asymmetries with LF-Movement in pro-drop languages like Italian, because the trace would always be properly governed by the nominal AGR. However, it turns out that an asymmetry does show up. Consider (57a–b), for example:

(57)

a. Non pretendo che nessuno ti   arresti
   not I-require that nobody you arrest

b. Non pretendo che tu   arresti nessuno
   not I-require that you arrest nobody

The predicted interpretations are (58a) and (59a) for (57a), and (58b) and (59b) for (57b).

(58)

a. I do not require that nobody arrest you
b. I do not require that you arrest nobody

(59)

a. There is no one such that I require that he arrest you
b. There is no one such that I require that you arrest him

This prediction is only correct for (57b). An asymmetry arises through the fact that (57a) cannot have the wide-scope interpretation (59a). Italian, then, is just like the non-pro-drop language French as far as LF-Movement is concerned.

In view of this we must reconsider the earlier analysis of the pro-drop parameter and the cluster of properties it applies to. In doing so, we will roughly follow the analysis of Rizzi (1982), but we will do no more than outline it, leaving many details unspecified.

The earlier account of pro drop leaves a number of important questions unanswered:

(60)

a. How does the postverbal subject NP in cases like (41b-ii) acquire its nominative case?
b. What is the status of the relation between the postverbal subject and the empty category in the preverbal subject position in terms of the binding theory?
c. If there are postverbal subjects, how do we know whether the *wh*-phrase in a sentence like (40) (*Chi credi che verrà*) was moved from the postverbal position?

Briefly, questions (60a) and (60b) are not limited to the pro-drop problem but occur in similar ways with existential constructions in which a dummy element appears in preverbal position and the "real" subject in postverbal position. Consider (61), for example:

(61)
There$_i$ are [two solutions]$_i$ to this problem

Here too we must assume that the postverbal NP somehow receives nominative case and that the relationship between the preverbal and postverbal positions is allowed under the binding theory. What distinguishes sentences of this sort from the structurally similar reflexive construction in (62)?

(62)
John$_i$ put himself$_i$ on the list

The difference is that in (62) each coindexed NP has its own θ-role, whereas in (61) the two positions have only one θ-role. We may say, then, that the postverbal subject receives both its case and its θ-role from the preverbal position. Furthermore, we will simply assume that the structures in question are legitimate under an appropriate modification of the binding theory (see Rizzi (1982) for extensive discussion).

Question (60c) is the one we will capitalize on in solving the problem caused by (57a–b). Suppose, in fact, that all extractions of some operator from subject position are ruled out by the ECP. We can then assume that apparent *that*-trace violations like (40) are really not violations at all but the result of movement from postverbal position. There is direct and convincing evidence for this assumption. For if this approach is correct, then negated NPs like *nessuno* should be able to receive the wide-scope interpretation. This prediction is borne out:

(63)
a. Non pretendo che nessuno sia arrestato
   not I-require that no-one   be arrested

b. Non pretendo che sia arrestato nessuno

Again, (63a) is unambiguous. It has only the meaning on which *nessuno* takes narrow scope and *non* is an independent negation in the matrix clause. (63b), however, is ambiguous. In addition to the narrow-scope interpretation it can also have the wide-scope interpretation on which *non* is a scope marker. This fact offers strong confirmation for the idea that the extraction of operators from postverbal position is possible. We may assume, then, that the postverbal position is inside the VP and hence properly governed under the ECP.

We thus have the following situation:

(64)

a. Null subject pronouns—(41a), (41e)
   ^{ok}COMP e INFL VP

b. Postposed subjects—(41b)
   ^{ok}COMP e_i INFL [$_{VP}$ V ... NP$_i$ ...]$_{VP}$

c. Operators (wh and Q)—(41c), (41d)
   i. *Op$_i$ ... COMP e_i INFL VP
   ii. ^{ok}Op$_i$ ... COMP e_i INFL [$_{VP}$ V ... e_i ...]$_{VP}$

On the basis of this, we can conclude that the grammaticality of (64c-ii) can be reduced to that of (64b), and that the ECP is responsible for the ungrammaticality of (64c-i). The main problem then is to explain how the empty subjects in (64a) and (64b) can escape from the ECP. Several authors including Rizzi present various complex theories to accomplish this. Here we simply state the problem as such and recommend the further reading at the end of the chapter.

18.5 Concluding Remarks

This discussion of the ECP concludes our survey of the principal modules of the grammar. Let us now take a final look at the structure of the grammar that has developed, and at the place and role of the modules in it.

The system has four levels of representation (D-Structure, S-Structure, LF, and PF) and three rule systems that relate these levels ("Move α"; LF-Movement, control theory, Reconstruction; deletion, filters, phonological rules). In addition it has a number of separate modules that act like conditions on rule application (as in the case of Subjacency) or like well-formedness conditions on representations (as in the case of most other modules) or on rules (as in the case of $\overline{X}$-theory). This results in the model depicted in figure 18.1.

18.6 Bibliographical Comments

The Nominative Island Condition was introduced in Chomsky (1980b). Immediately and independently, three proposals to derive the *that*-trace effect from the NIC were advanced: Kayne (1980), Pesetsky (1982a), and Taraldsen (1978b).

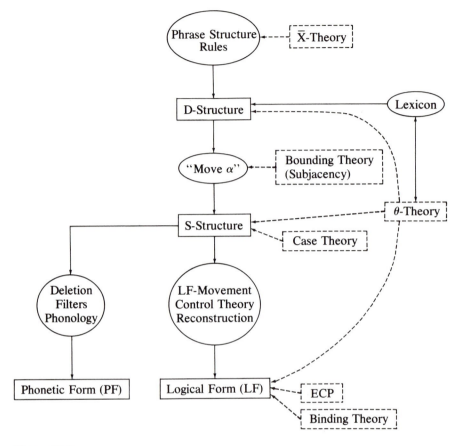

Figure 18.1
The organization of the modules of Government-Binding Theory

Most of the principles discussed in this book have been formulated in several different ways in the literature. This is particularly true of the notions of government and proper government. In fact, Chomsky himself discusses several alternative formulations in LGB. For a recent contribution, see Lasnik and Saito (1984). The notions of A-transparency and Ā-transparency are introduced in this text in order to avoid the many confusions that arise from the notion of S'-deletion, which has never been made sufficiently precise in the literature. Ā-transparency, as applied here to PP for example, is close in spirit to the revised notion of Subjacency proposed in Belletti and Rizzi (1981). For references on preposition stranding, which is analyzed here in terms of Ā-transparency, see chapter 9.

The pro-drop parameter has been another fertile source of contributions to the literature. The two main works on the subject are Jaeggli (1982) and Rizzi (1982) (especially chapter 4).

The extension of the ECP to certain classes of LF phenomena is due to Kayne (1981a) and chapter 4 of Rizzi (1982). More evidence is presented in Huang (1982) and Pesetsky (1982b), but the point remains controversial; see, for example, Haïk (1984) and Van Riemsdijk and Williams (1981).

Since the bounding theory presented in chapter 4 has been incorporated as such into the Government-Binding framework, we have not included a separate chapter on the movement/bounding module in part IV. That is not to say, however, that there are no developments to report. Particularly interesting is the proposal of Kayne (1981b) (countered in Aoun (1981b)) to derive the effect of Subjacency from the ECP. Huang (1982) deals with the question of whether LF-Movement is subject to the bounding theory. On this topic, see also May (1977) and Aoun, Hornstein, and Sportiche (1980).

EPILOGUE

Chapter 19
Current Developments

In this final chapter we survey some of the areas on which research in the theory of grammar is currently focused. It is a chapter that will certainly call for revision as time goes on, since the work we report here is truly "in progress" and insufficient time has passed to sort out the important from the unimportant, identify dead ends, recognize approaches that converge, and so on. We present this survey to give some idea of the wide range of interesting questions currently under study and to introduce the reader to at least some of the most recent literature.

Never before has there been so much progress on so many theoretical fronts in linguistics as there is now. One reason is that the range of data that theoretical linguists take into account has broadened tremendously. Until very recently, the theory was based on a detailed analysis of English, a somewhat less detailed analysis of French, and fragmentary analyses of and isolated facts from a few other languages. In the past decade the situation has changed dramatically, as groundwork has been done in theoretically relevant descriptions of many languages and theoretical points are more and more frequently settled on the basis of data from languages other than English. Knowledge of at least the basic structure of these languages is now required not just of the specialist in that language, but of the general theoretician as well. Some of these languages are Chinese (Huang (1982)), Japanese (Saito (1984)), Hebrew (Borer (1984)), Arabic (Aoun (1981a)), Warlpiri (Hale (1983)), Kru/Vata (Koopman (1984)), Irish (McCloskey (1979)), Hungarian (Kiss (forthcoming), Horváth (1985)), Scandinavian (Taraldsen (1983), Hellan (forthcoming)), German (Toman (1985)), Russian (Pesetsky (1982b)), Dutch (Evers (1975), Van Riemsdijk (1978b), Hoekstra (1984)), Italian

(Rizzi ·(1982)), Spanish (Jaeggli (1982)), and French (Kayne (1975), Obenauer (1976)).

We cannot, of course, acquaint the reader with this great wealth in a single chapter, or in an entire book for that matter. We will therefore restrict ourselves to five theoretical problem areas.

19.1 Generalized Binding

Under the theory outlined in chapters 6 and 7 *Wh*-Movement and its trace constitute a system quite different from the system of NP-Movement and its trace. For example, *wh*-trace is not governed by Opacity (principle A of the binding theory), whereas NP-trace is; furthermore, *wh*-trace, a variable, is subject to principle C of the binding theory, whereas NP-trace is not. *Wh*-Movement moves items to $\bar{\text{A}}$-positions, whereas NP-Movement moves items to A-positions. The binding theory concerns binding by A-positions only, not $\bar{\text{A}}$-positions. Thus, despite obvious similarities between the $\bar{\text{A}}$/variable system and the A/anaphor system—movement takes place in both, movement leaves a trace in both, Subjacency holds in both—the two are quite distinct in their properties.

Criticism has been leveled against this distinction since it first arose and has continued as more and more has come to depend on it. Notable among early (and sustained) criticisms is the work of Koster (1978a). A more recent effort to eliminate the dichotomy has been made by Aoun (1981a), whose proposals we will outline here.

Aoun notes a similarity between principle A of the binding theory, which requires that an anaphor (including NP-trace) be bound in its governing category, and the requirement of (a part of) the ECP that a *wh*-trace be bound to a local COMP. Nothing can be made of this similarity in the theory as developed so far, since principle A strictly involves binding of anaphors by A-positions, whereas the antecedent government required by the ECP involves binding by $\bar{\text{A}}$-positions. (The binding theory differs in this respect from the NIC, which links together anaphors and *wh*-traces.)

Aoun has devised a theory in which this similarity can be formally expressed. This involves analogizing $\bar{\text{A}}$-binding to A-binding in a certain way. According to Aoun, both are anaphoric relations; in other words, there is a common theory of anaphora that applies to both. This theory generalizes the binding theory, particularly principle A, to apply to both A-binding and $\bar{\text{A}}$-binding; Aoun calls the generalized binding

X-binding. The theory does not dissolve the difference between A- and Ā-binding, but in fact crucially relies on it.

First, following suggestions in Chomsky (1981c), discussed in chapter 17, Aoun suggests that the notion "governing category" as used in the binding theory must make use of the notion "accessible SUBJECT," because of the following data:

(1)
a. *John and Bill like Mary's pictures of each other
b. John and Bill like the pictures of each other

If (1a) is ruled ungrammatical because the anaphor *each other* is not bound in its governing category (the NP that contains it), then (1b) should be ungrammatical as well. Clearly, the only difference between (1a) and (1b) is that in (1a) the NP containing *each other* has a "subject," whereas in (1b) it does not. Thus, the proper definition of governing category will distinguish the two cases (see (20) of chapter 17):

(2)
Governing category: α is the governing category for X if and only if α is the minimal category containing X, a governor of X, and a SUBJECT accessible to X.

With this as background, Aoun seeks to replace the ECP with a generalization of binding principle A. In order to do this, *wh*-trace must be considered to be an anaphor—an Ā-anaphor (an anaphor bound to an Ā-position), but an anaphor nevertheless. Principle A is then rewritten as follows, where X means A or $\bar{A}$:

(3)
Generalized Binding Principle A
An X-anaphor must be X-bound in its governing category.

This generalization by itself does not accomplish the purpose of subsuming the ECP under the binding theory, but with some adjustments in the auxiliary notions of governing category, it will.

Consider the typical paradigm illustrating the ECP:

(4)
a. *Who$_i$ do you think (e_i) that [$_S$ e_i AGR left]$_S$
b. Who$_i$ do you think e_i [$_S$ e_i AGR left]$_S$
c. Who$_i$ do you think (that) [$_S$ Bill AGR saw e_i]$_S$

We might suppose that (4a) is ungrammatical because the subject trace is not bound in its governing category, the embedded S'. The embedded S' is the governing category for the trace, since it contains a governor for the trace (AGR) and a SUBJECT accessible to the trace (again, AGR); but the trace is not bound within the S', either because there is no trace in COMP to bind it, or because if there is a trace, the presence of *that* in COMP prevents the COMP trace from c-commanding the subject trace. In (4b), on the other hand, the COMP trace does bind the subject trace, so the generalized binding principle A is satisfied. Thus, it appears that the ECP can be subsumed under the generalized binding principle A, if *wh*-trace is considered an $\bar{\text{A}}$-anaphor.

A problem arises for (4c), however. The theory predicts that nonsubject traces should show ECP effects as well, which, as (4c) shows, they do not; the governor is the verb, the SUBJECT is the embedded subject, and so the governing category should be the embedded clause, just as before. Aoun avoids this conclusion by revising the notion "accessible," which has the result of changing the governing category for nonsubject *wh*-traces. The change depends on the fact that *wh*-trace is a variable—that is, an $\bar{\text{A}}$-bound element. If the *wh*-trace is coindexed with a subject NP (that is, with an A-position), the resulting structure will violate binding principle C, because variables must be A-free. But if A-position subjects are considered "inaccessible" to variables, then AGR will be inaccessible as well, even though it is not an A-position, since it is coindexed with the subject. The net result is that variables will not have governing categories at all. Hence, binding principle A will have no effect on variables, and no ECP effects will be expected.

The one exception will be a variable in subject position. Such a variable does have an accessible SUBJECT, AGR, since AGR is an $\bar{\text{A}}$-position and is not itself coindexed with any A-position other than the variable itself. Thus, ECP effects are predicted for subject position alone—the desired result. This reduction of the ECP to the theory of generalized binding, and the theory of generalized binding itself, have numerous consequences that we cannot examine here. We refer the reader instead to Aoun (1981a) and to Finer (1985), an application of the generalized binding theory (including a generalization of binding principle B) to the description of switch-reference languages, languages in which an embedded INFL is marked to indicate that the embedded subject is either coreferential with or disjoint from the matrix subject.

19.2 Phrase Structure

The nature of phrase structure is currently the subject of both interesting proposals and considerable controversy. The interesting proposals concern dismantling the phrase structure component and assigning many of its descriptive and explanatory functions to other components. The controversy concerns the treatment of *nonconfigurational,* or *free word order,* languages.

19.2.1 Reducing the Burden on the Phrase Structure Rules

The phrase structure component, as described in chapter 3, determines the identity and the ordering of the daughter constituents of every phrase type in the language. For example, the following rule for the English VP specifies the identity and underlying order of the daughters of VP:

(5)
VP → V NP PP AP S′

But perhaps this rule specifies too much information. For example, a language like English with postverbal objects will generally be prepositional and not postpositional (that is, in such a language prepositions will precede, not follow, their objects; see Greenberg (1963)), so there is some redundancy between (5) and the rule for PP, which specifies prepositionality:

(6)
PP → P NP

Early efforts to extract this generalization include Williams (1981a) and Jackendoff (1977).

Stowell (1981) proposes that the phrase structure rules of language are *category neutral,* in that the phrase structure rules of a given language are not rules for particular types of phrases, but instead rules governing the form of phrases in general in that language. Moreover, he seeks to show that the modules of Government-Binding Theory would make such a view of phrase structure tenable if they were formulated in the right way. For example, the phrase structure rule for English might be written as follows:

(7)
X′ → X NP PP S′

This rule is not particular to the phrase VP or PP, but says of both, among other things, that the head is on the left. (7) states that PPs can contain PPs and Ss, as indeed they can:

(8)
a. out [of the woods]
b. about [why John left]

But it also predicts that NPs can contain NPs, which of course they cannot:

(9)
*the destruction [the city]

But (9) does not affect the viability of (7) if there is some other reason why NPs cannot contain NPs—if, in other words, this explanation can be shifted from the phrase structure rules to some other component. And in fact it can—to case theory. If nouns are not case-assigners, then (9) will be generated by phrase structure rule (7) but will be ungrammatical because of the failure of case-assignment.

(7) may still contain too much information. For example, is it necessary to specify the order of the posthead constituents? Stowell proposes that it is not, and that the perceived order can be accounted for independently. If this is so, then it might be possible to reduce (7) to (10),

(10)
$X' \rightarrow X$ {NP, PP, AP, S}

where the material in brackets is unordered (that is, a phrase with any of these constituents, in any order, will satisfy (10)). Note that (10) still specifies that the head occurs to the left of the other constituents.

In order to account for the most salient problem raised by (10), the fact that the NP must immediately follow the verb (in English), Stowell proposes an Adjacency Condition on case-assignment, which says that a case-assigner must be adjacent to the NP to which it assigns case. If this condition is correct, then at least that one fact need not be specified in the phrase structure component. This proposal faces various problems (for example, the Germanic languages seem to keep the direct object distant from the verb) but this is exactly what one wants of a strong proposal: that it lead immediately to a great deal of empirical difficulty.

On the other hand, Stowell's proposal sharply reduces the burden to the child of acquiring the phrase structure component. Essentially, what must be learned is whether the phrases of a language are head-final or head-initial. Other features of phrase structure will follow from other facets of grammar. For example, the nature of the phrasal categories will follow from the nature of the lexical categories of the language, since the former are projected from the latter. And certain ordering restrictions will follow from case theory, as we have seen.

More recently, Koopman (1984) and Travis (1984) have suggested that even the phrase structural position of the head may not be an independent parameter of linguistic variation, but might reduce to other parameters of other subtheories, specifically case theory and θ-theory. They suggest that each of these theories has a parameter of directionality of assignment (of case in case theory, of θ-roles in θ-theory). In a language like English, these parameters coincide, since the verb assigns both its accusative case and its theme θ-role to the right, thus giving the illusion that in English the head is fixed to the left of the VP independent of these two theories. Koopman and Travis cite languages in which these parameters do not converge: for example, Chinese, where case-assignment is to the right, but θ-role assignment is to the left. Under this proposal, a clause in Chinese will look like this:

(11)

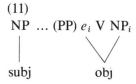

The object NP must be generated to the left of the verb, in order to receive a θ-role, and must be moved to the right of the verb, in order to receive case. One reason for positing this structure is that it is the object, and only the object, that appears to the right of the verb; all other θ-marked items appear to the left.

If this analysis is correct, clearly it is wrong to ask whether Chinese is head-initial or head-final; rather, we must decompose this question into questions about the directionality of case-assignment and of θ-role assignment. And if that is correct, then the linguistic variation that the phrase structure component allows is reduced to nothing, all perceived variation in phraseology being determined by parameters in other components.

19.2.2 Configurationality

The proper treatment of *free word order* (*nonconfigurational*) languages is currently the topic of considerable and very fruitful debate. On the one hand, Hale (1983) has proposed that languages like the Australian aboriginal language Warlpiri have the following type of phrase structure rule:

(12)
$$X' \rightarrow X'^* \; X$$

The * means that any number of X's may be generated. This rule is even more permissive than it seems, since it is meant to accommodate *discontinuous* constituents such as 'that kangaroo' in (13):

(13)
Wawirrikapi-rna   panti- rni   yalumpu
kangaroo   Aux spear   nonpast   that
'I will spear that kangaroo'

Warlpiri exhibits what may atheoretically be called "extremely free word order," in that the surface order of words does not determine their underlying constituency. If we think of S-Structure as containing, for example, the constituents necessary for assignment of θ-roles, then the phrase structure rule Hale proposes cannot be an account of S-Structure, since the phrases to which θ-roles must be assigned are not present in the level described by that rule. Rather, those phrases must be built up from the structures described by that rule, by "amalgamating," for example, 'that' and 'kangaroo' in (13). The level that results from all such amalgamations, which is not directly described by phrase structure rules, Hale calls *Lexical Structure*. Hale supposes that languages may differ in their ability to assign θ-roles in S-Structure— English can, but Warlpiri cannot. Warlpiri can assign θ-roles only in Lexical Structure. In other words, whether or not the Projection Principle holds beyond Lexical Structure is one dimension of parametric variation among languages. Other proposals in this vein are found in Mohanan (1982), Simpson and Bresnan (1983), Kiss (forthcoming), Zubizarreta and Vergnaud (1982), and Van Riemsdijk (1982).

On the other hand, there is the classical assumption made in generative grammar, adopted as well in more recent proposals, that the s-structures for such languages as Warlpiri are quite similar to the s-structures for languages like English, and that the diversity in surface word order derives from scrambling in the derivation of PF from

S-Structure. See Saito (1982), Saito and Hoji (1983), and Horváth (1985) for proposals in this spirit. Kiss (forthcoming) and Horváth (1985) are an especially interesting pair, since they respectively represent the two approaches applied to the same language, Hungarian.

Under the latter proposal, the s-structures of nonconfigurational languages are subject to the same conditions as the s-structures of configurational languages. Thus, for example, Saito (1982) demonstrates that the s-structures he hypothesizes for Japanese are subject to the principles governing weak crossover:

(14)
a. ?John$_i$no sensei ga [$_{VP}$ kare$_i$o syookaisita]$_{VP}$
   John's   teacher   him   introduced
   'John's teacher introduced him'
b. *John$_i$no sensei o kare$_i$ga syookaisita
   John's   teacher   he   introduced
   John's teacher, he introduced
   'He introduced John's teacher'

If Japanese were an "X'* X" language, generated by rule (12), there would be no reason for (14a) and (14b) to differ. However, if the Japanese clause has a VP containing its verb and object in S-Structure, as depicted in (14a), and the structure (14b) is derived from such an s-structure by scrambling, then the difference is accounted for: in (14b), but not (14a), the pronoun c-commands the NP antecedent.

Of course, the treatment of nonconfigurational languages cannot be resolved on the basis of such limited examples, nor do we believe that it is resolved in the extant literature. However, research to date has raised a theoretically important issue on which a good deal of progress may be expected.

19.3 Small Clauses

The notion "subject" has played a central role in the theory since Chomsky (1973) proposed the Specified Subject Condition, a role that remained unchanged until the notion "accessible SUBJECT" was introduced into binding theory. The actual definition of "subject" has received little attention until recently, the *Aspects* definition ("[NP,S]," or "the NP immediately dominated by S") having served the purpose.

An examination of what are known as *small clause* structures has brought the definition of "subject" into question, since these constructions contain a subject in an important sense, but it is not equally clear that a clause is involved:

(15)
a. John considers Mary proud of herself
b. Mary seems proud of herself
c. Mary strikes Bill as proud of herself
d. With Mary proud of herself, Joe left

In each of these cases it is quite easy to establish that *Mary* is a subject in the only sense that matters (that is, in terms of the binding theory); in each case *Mary* is the only available antecedent of the reflexive:

(16)
a. *John considers Mary proud of himself
b. *Mary seems to John proud of himself
c. *Mary strikes John as proud of himself
d. *With Mary proud of himself, John left

Thus, *Mary* is a subject—but subject of what? A plausible structure for (16a) is (17):

(17)

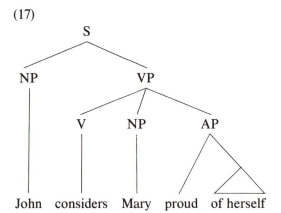

John   considers   Mary   proud   of herself

But in this structure *Mary* is not a subject in the sense of the *Aspects* definition [NP,S], and it would be inappropriate to generalize this definition (say, to [NP,X]) to include *Mary* in this case, since then objects in general would be included, and objects in general do not induce opacity—see for example (15c).

There are two ways out of this dilemma: to create a clausal node dominating *Mary* in these cases, or to change the definition of subject. The former is the *small clause solution* elaborated in such works as

Chomsky (1981c), Stowell (1983), and Kayne (1984). The latter is the *predication solution* elaborated in such works as Culicover and Wilkins (1984), Schein (1982), and Williams (1980).

The small clause solution posits a category (X in (18)) dominating the subject *Mary* and the phrase that follows, forming an embedded clausal structure:

(18)
John considers [$_X$ Mary proud of herself]$_X$

The identity of this X-node is a matter of debate. Stowell proposes that it is S, whereas Chomsky, noting that selectional restrictions hold between the matrix verb and the predicate (*proud of herself* in (18)), proposes that it is a projection of the predicate, a projection he labels X* (A* in the case of *proud of herself*) to distinguish it from a maximal projection, since government by the verb across its boundaries is possible (hence the case-assignment in (18)). In either case *Mary* can then be identified as a subject as in *Aspects,* as an instance of [NP,X], where X = {S,X*}.

Chomsky proposes that an extension of the Projection Principle ensures that this is the only solution to this problem, in the following way: if a verb like *consider* requires that its complement be clausal at any level, then the Projection Principle requires that it be clausal at every level, including of course S-Structure; furthermore, it is reasonable to insist that *consider* is a two-argument (or *diadic*) predicate, one of its arguments being *Mary proud of herself* in (18), and that this diadicity is a feature of the LF-representation.

The predication solution denies that there is an embedded clausal node in (15a–d); it says that *Mary* is a subject not by virtue of being dominated by a particular node, but rather by virtue of its relation to the predicate *proud of herself,* and that this relation can be established regardless of whether the subject-predicate pair is dominated by a clausal node or not. In Williams (1980) it is proposed that this relation is indicated by coindexing, so under the predication solution (18) would have the representation (19):

(19)
John considers [$_{NP}$ Mary]$_{NP_i}$ [$_{AP}$ proud of herself]$_{AP_i}$

The binding theory must be somewhat revised in the predication solution, because of the difference in the nature of subjects in that theory. Especially instructive are sentences with *strike:*

(20)

a. Mary strikes Bill as [AP proud of herself]AP

b. *Mary strikes Bill as [AP proud of himself]AP

Principle A of the binding theory says that the reflexive must be bound in some category containing a SUBJECT accessible to the reflexive. Clearly, this will not distinguish the two examples in (20). Because of (20a), the category in which the reflexive is bound must be the entire matrix S. But if so, then (20b) satisfies the binding theory as well—yet (20b) clearly violates the binding theory.

Since the predication solution defines "subject" in terms of "predicate," there is an alternative formulation of the binding theory, one that relies on the notion "predicate":

(21)

Binding Principle A'

An anaphor must be bound in the smallest predicate in which it occurs, or be bound to the subject of that predicate.

This immediately distinguishes the two cases in (20)—only in (20a) does the reflexive satisfy (21).

(21) handles the more ordinary cases that fall under the binding theory as well. For example:

(22)

*Mary$_j$ [VP wants [S John$_i$ to [VP like herself]VP$_i$]S]VP$_j$

The reflexive in (22) does not satisfy (21), since it is neither bound within the predicate *like herself* nor bound to the subject of that predicate.

Certain facts concerning quantifier scope seem to favor the predication solution. In truly clausal embeddings, quantifiers show scopal ambiguity:

(23)

a. Someone$_i$ seems [S e_i to have left]S

b. Seems [S someone$_i$ [S e_i to have left]S]S

c. Someone$_i$ [S e_i seems [S e_i to have left]S]S

(23b) represents the narrow-scope reading, derived by adjoining the quantifier to the embedded S, and (23c) represents the wide-scope reading, derived by adjoining the quantifier to the matrix S. Small clause constructions seem to systematically lack the narrow-scope reading:

(24)

a. Someone seems sick

b. John considers someone sick

(24a) seems not to mean "It seems that there is someone sick," and (24b) seems not to mean "John thinks that there is someone sick." Rather, they seem to mean "There is someone who is sick" and "There is someone that John considers sick," respectively. The absence of the narrow-scope reading would follow if there were no small-clausal node that could serve as the scope for the narrow reading; since the predication solution posits no such node, these facts favor it.

The above argument is far from conclusive, and many further details must be worked out in both solutions to the dilemma posed by (15). For example, note that the derivation of (23b) involves a lowering operation, and, technically speaking, an ungoverned trace is left in the subject position of *seems*.

19.4 Tree Geometry

Several recent proposals for revising the ECP depend on "geometric" or "graph-theoretic" properties of trees, most depending on some notion of a "path" through a tree, a notion introduced into current work by Kayne (1981d). These proposals include Kayne (1983), Pesetsky (1982b), Huang (1982), Longobardi (1985), and Baltin (1981).

19.4.1 G-Projections

Kayne (1983) supposes that in English the fact that left branches cannot be extracted from is somehow related to the fact that English is right-branching and, in particular, that lexical items seem to "govern" items to their right and not to their left. He revises the ECP so as to reflect this connection, a plausible place to begin, since the ECP already was stated in terms of government:

(25)

a. the book that it became difficult to talk about e

b. *the books that $[_S[_{NP}$ talking about $e]_{NP}$ became difficult$]_S$

Kayne proposes that the ECP should require not only that e be governed, but also that it be possible to trace a path from e to its antecedent in such a way that the path goes up only from right branches (or, at least, branches that are never to the left of the heads of phrases that the path passes through). The paths for (25a) and (25b) are marked by wavy lines in (26a) and (26b), respectively:

(26)
a.

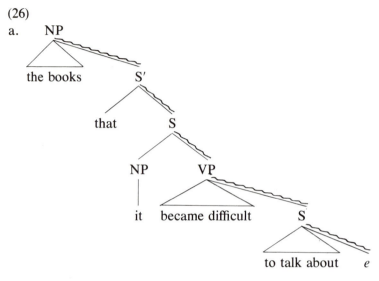

b.

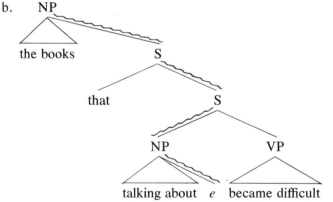

The path in (26b) is not a proper path, since it goes up a left branch. A *proper path* in a language will be one that goes up strictly left or right branches, depending on whether government in that language is to the left or to the right.

Though Kayne's proposal is stated not in terms of paths, but in terms of his notion "g-projection," "g-projection" can be stated in terms of "proper path":

(27)

G-projection: The g-projection of X is the largest proper path that starts at X.

Kayne's proposed extension of the ECP can then be stated as follows:

(28)

ECP

The antecedent of *e* must be immediately dominated by (one of the nodes of) the g-projection of X.

Actually, in Kayne's definition (28) is the whole of the ECP, since the proper path begins with the lexical governor of *e* and an item must therefore be governed in the first place in order to have a g-projection. This clearly distinguishes the two cases in (25): the g-projection of *e* in (25b) does not include the antecedent, whereas the g-projection of *e* in (25a) does.

It is of course possible that the restriction against extraction from a left branch is not properly seen as a part of the ECP, but is rather a restriction on the extraction in the first place. For this reason, it is of some interest that parasitic gaps, which do not arise through movement, show the same effects:

(29)
a. the books you should read *e* before it becomes difficult to talk about *e*
b. *the books you should read *e* before talking about *e* becomes difficult

Since parasitic gaps do not arise through movement, we cannot attribute these effects to bounding (movement) theory. This therefore confirms the idea that some extension of the ECP, which is indifferent to the source of the gaps (by movement or base-generation), is the appropriate way to treat the ungrammaticality of gaps on left branches.

Kayne shows that g-projections play a further role in the description of parasitic gaps, and a number of other constructions as well. To begin with, certain parasitic gaps on left branches are unexpectedly grammatical:

(30)

a person that people who read descriptions of *e* usually end up liking *e*

Compare (30) with the ungrammatical (31):

(31)

*a person that people to whom descriptions of *e* are read usually end up liking *e*

Both (30) and (31) have parasitic gaps on left branches. What is the difference?

(32)

a.

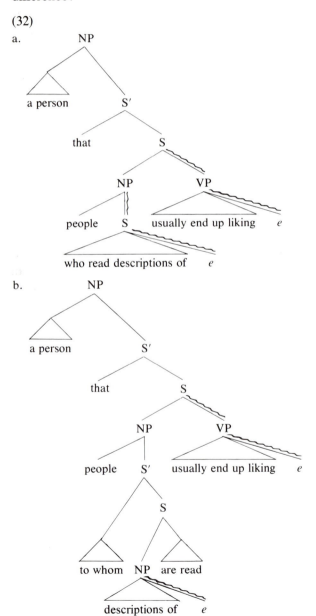

The difference is that in (32a), but not (32b), the g-projections are "connected." In (32b) the g-projection of the parasitic gap does not join the g-projection of the main gap—it stops inside the embedded relative. The problem then is not simply that the parasitic gap is on a left branch, which is the case in both (32a) and (32b), but that it is on a left branch too far removed from the g-projection of the real gap. Given this, the difference can be characterized in terms of the *union* of g-projections of traces:

(33)

a. *G-projection set:* A g-projection set is the union of the g-projections of a set of coindexed traces.

b. *ECP*

The g-projection set of a set of coindexed traces must

i. be "connected" (that is, form a full subtree), and

ii. contain the antecedent of the traces.

Note that only one trace must have a g-projection that reaches the antecedent; other traces, even on left branches, can "get a free ride" in case their g-projections form a full subtree with that trace. This distinguishes the two cases in (32).

Similar phenomena show up in other constructions. For example, multiple *wh*-questions show "connectedness" effects:

(34)

a.

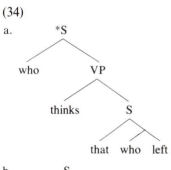

b.

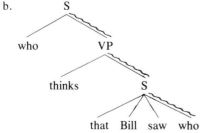

The g-projection of the unmoved *wh*-word in (34a) is short, because the unmoved *who* is on a left branch. These two cases can be distinguished by the following requirement:

(35)
The g-projections of a multiple question structure must (a) form a subtree and (b) contain the COMP at which it is interpreted.

In (34b), but not (34a), the g-projections form a subtree.

The correctness of this approach is confirmed by the following examples:

(36)
a. *Who thinks that who saw Bill
b. Who thinks that who saw what
c.

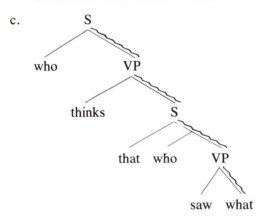

(36a) is just like (34a) in relevant respects and is also ungrammatical. (36b) is grammatical, however, despite being similar to (36a) in having a *wh*-word on a left branch. It is grammatical because adding the final *wh*-word "fills in" the g-projection set so that it constitutes a full subtree, as shown in (36c). This remarkable contrast follows directly from the use of g-projection sets. Kayne shows that similar facts obtain with multiple parasitic gap and multiple negation structures.

19.4.2 Path Containment

Adopting Kayne's notion of path, Pesetsky (1982b) has shown that the ECP, the prohibition against extracting from subjects, the "no crossing constraint" on double extractions (explained below), and the Coordinate Structure Constraint can all be derived in another way. That is, he shows that they all follow from a single constraint, the *Path Contain-*

ment Condition (PCC), so long as some auxiliary assumptions are made about phrase structure.

As has long been recognized (for example, by Fodor (1978)), double extraction structures seem to follow a "last in/first out" rule, as illustrated in the following examples:

(37)

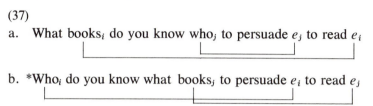

a. What books$_i$ do you know who$_j$ to persuade e_j to read e_i

b. *Who$_i$ do you know what books$_j$ to persuade e_i to read e_j

Technically speaking, both examples are ruled out by Subjacency. However, (37b) is clearly far worse, and the difference demands an account. Fodor proposed that the bindings must be nested in a certain way: if the material between the traces and the *wh*-phrases that bind them is underlined, one underlining must properly include the other, as in (37a); otherwise the sentence is ungrammatical, like (37b).

Pesetsky has shown that this *linear* nesting constraint can be reinterpreted as a *hierarchical* nesting constraint. So reinterpreted, its application becomes far broader. Instead of considering the linear stretch of material between the trace and the *wh*-phrase in (37a–b), we might instead consider the path from the trace to the *wh*-phrase:

(38)

a.

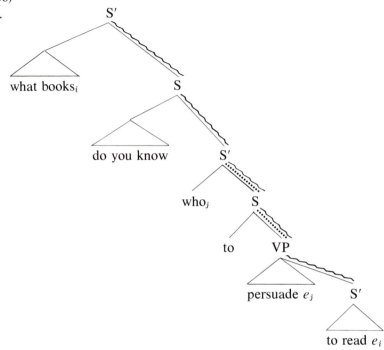

b.

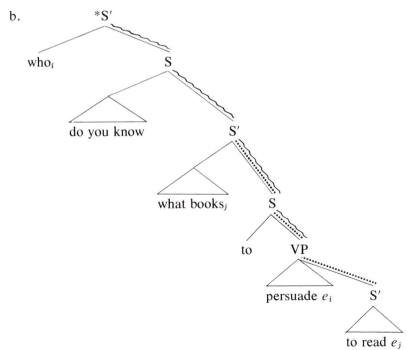

The paths in the grammatical (38a) are nested, whereas neither path in the ungrammatical (38b) is nested inside the other. If path formation is automatically associated with *wh*-binding, then the following condition will distinguish the two cases:

(39)
Path Containment Condition (PCC)
If two paths intersect, one must be nested inside the other.

In the examples given the linear nesting condition and the PCC yield the same result. In right-branching languages such as English the two conditions are indeed hard to distinguish. But consider a language just like English except that the sentential complement S' precedes rather than follows the object NP. This is a situation that can arise in left-branching languages. To see this, consider again (38b). If e_i and the most deeply embedded S' (*to read e_j*) were inverted, the linear nesting condition would predict the sentence to be grammatical, while the PCC would still rule this structure out. We will not pursue these empirical differences here.

As one application of the notion of path containment, Pesetsky proposes that the *that*-trace effects of the ECP can be reduced to the PCC. At first glance this would not seem possible, since the ECP rules out sentences with only one trace, and therefore only one path. The PCC would seem irrelevant in such cases. However, Pesetsky proposes that there is always another path, a path from INFL to COMP, and that this path interacts with the path of the *wh*-trace as predicted by the PCC. The INFL-COMP path arises from an LF movement of INFL to COMP, a movement motivated on the basis of the close connection between INFL and COMP; we will not discuss the motivation here, but refer the reader to Pesetsky's discussion.

But Pesetsky's suggestion alone will not suffice. Consider (40), a typical ECP violation. (In the remaining examples, we will use a more compact means of representing paths, equivalent to the trees given earlier: the nodes of a path will be underlined in the labeled bracketing of the examples. Specifically, the nodes of the trace path will be marked by straight underlining, and the nodes of the INFL-COMP path will be marked by wavy underlining.)

(40)
$[_{S'}$ Who$_i$ do $[_S$ you think $[_{S'}$ that $[_S$ e_i INFL left$]_S]_{S'}]_S]_{S'}$

Here, the trace path and the INFL-COMP path overlap but are nested; thus, the former properly contains the latter and the sentence is wrongly predicted to be grammatical. This prediction cannot be avoided by making INFL itself a part of the INFL path—if the item with which a path originates were made a part of the path, then clearly no two paths would ever be nested.

But the incorrect prediction can be avoided in another way—namely, by positing a slightly different phrase structure expansion for S. Rather than being daughters of S, perhaps INFL and VP are daughters of an intermediate node INFL′:

(41)
S → NP INFL′
INFL′ → INFL VP

With this new phrase structure, (40) will have the path structure (42):

(42)
[$_{S'}$ Who$_i$ do [$_S$ you think [$_{S'}$ that [$_S$ e_i [$_{INFL'}$ INFL left]$_{INFL'}$]$_S$]$_{S'}$]$_S$]$_{S'}$

Here, the paths intersect but are not nested—each has a node not contained in the other.

Now, what about a grammatical case of subject extraction, where a trace rather than *that* occupies the lower COMP? Here, the relevant path goes only to the lower COMP, since that is the location of the closest c-commanding binder of the trace:

(43)
[$_{S'}$ Who$_i$ do [$_S$ you think [$_{S'}$ e_i [$_{S|}$ e_i [$_{INFL'}$ INFL left]$_{INFL'}$]$_S$]$_{S'}$]$_S$]$_{S'}$

The trace path is nested in the INFL-COMP path, and the question is correctly predicted to be grammatical.

Under the assumptions made so far, nonsubject extractions (with or without *that*) are correctly ruled grammatical:

(44)
[$_{S'}$ Who$_i$ do [$_S$ you think [$_{S'}$ that [$_S$ Bill [$_{INFL'}$ INFL saw e_i]$_{INFL'}$]$_S$]$_{S'}$]$_S$]$_{S'}$

Here, the trace path will properly include the INFL-COMP path; moreover, this inclusion holds whether the trace path goes to the higher COMP (as in (44)) or stops at the lower COMP (as would be the case if trace appeared in (44) instead of *that*).

In sum, the basic ECP facts about subject extraction are predicted: subjects can be extracted only if trace appears in COMP instead of *that*, and nonsubjects can be extracted in either case.

Pesetsky shows that the facts pertaining to extraction *from* the subject (as opposed to extraction *of* the subject) also follow from the PCC. Consider a typical case of extraction from the subject:

(45)

*[$_{S'}$ Who$_i$ did [$_S$[$_{NP}$ pictures of e_i]$_{NP}$ [$_{INFL'}$ INFL upset Bill]$_{INFL'}$]$_S$]$_{S'}$

Here, the two paths intersect, but neither is nested in the other—the INFL-COMP path alone contains INFL', and the trace path alone contains the subject NP-node. All subject extractions will be of this form, and the PCC will uniformly reject them.

Assuming the phrase structure rule (41) and an INFL-to-COMP movement, then, a good deal follows from the PCC: the ECP, subject extraction, and the nested extraction constraint. For the derivation of the Coordinate Structure Constraint from the PCC and for more extensive discussion of the ideas treated here, see Pesetsky (1982b).

19.5 NP-Structure

The notion "reconstruction," which we have encountered several times, refers to a complex of problems involving certain details of the interaction among the modules of grammar, specifically the interaction of movement with the interpretive components of the grammar. (46) is a relevant example:

(46)
[Whose mother] do you think he likes *e*

At issue is not the disjointness between *he* and *whose mother* but that between *he* and *whose*. Principle C of the binding theory, which is responsible for this type of disjoint reference, seems to apply "as if" the phrase *whose mother* were in its original position, the D-Structure position in which *whose* is c-commanded by *he*. The Reconstruction rule discussed in earlier chapters is one way of implementing this "as if" relation. Here we will discuss another way of looking at this relation.

First, though, let us look at the scope of the phenomenon. It turns out that binding principles A and B involve reconstruction as well:

(47)

a. Which picture of himself$_i$ does John$_i$ like e
b. To him$_i$ we thought that John talked e
   (*him* and *John* disjoint)

If the moved phrases are in their D-Structure positions, then the principles apply correctly; they cannot apply correctly to these s-structures as they stand.

Besides principles involving "logical" relations of pronouns to antecedents, more purely structural or phonological rules also apply under "reconstruction." For example, the "Double-ing" Filter of Ross (1972) applies "as if" the moved constituent were in its D-Structure position:

(48)

a. The police began searching the car
b. *The police are beginning searching the car
c. my car, searching which the police have already begun e
d. *my car, searching which the police are beginning e today

Case-assignment also takes place "as if" unmoved *wh*-phrases were in their D-Structure positions:

(49)

Whom did you see e

The objective case on *whom* is licensed by its relation to the direct object position of the sentence.

Contraction also operates "as if" *wh*-phrases were in their D-Structure positions (section 9.2.2):

(50)

Who do you want e to die → *Who do you wanna die

Finally, even the correct interpretation of *wh*-structures would appear to require some sort of reconstruction. For example, in (51)

(51)

Whose mother did you see e

the trace does not correspond to the variable that the question turns on, since the trace is bound by *whose mother* and the question is about sons or daughters. From this point of view, a better representation would be the ungrammatical (52):

(52)

*Whose did you see [e mother]

In sum, it appears that a number of modules, including at least case, phonology, filters, the binding theory, and semantic interpretation, act as though *wh*-phrases were in their D-Structure positions. A more complete discussion of the range of cases in which reconstruction phenomena occur is presented in Van Riemsdijk and Williams (1981).

Now, how is the "as if" relation best accounted for? One account is based on the rule of *Reconstruction*. However, such a rule has a number of serious conceptual and empirical drawbacks. Conceptually, it is awkward to have a grammatical model in which the effect of such a central rule as *Wh*-Movement has to be undone. Empirically, one crucial problem is that a Reconstruction rule such as (18) in chapter 13 or (35) in chapter 17 cannot possibly be maintained for the phonological side of the grammar (i.e., for the "Double-ing" Filter and contraction), since it would affect the order of terminal elements in the string in unwanted ways, yielding wrong surface structures. For a more detailed critique of Reconstruction, see Van Riemsdijk and Williams (1981), where the alternative theory presented below is developed.

A second approach involves the notion of *layered traces*. This approach has no special rule of Reconstruction. Instead, it has a different view of traces: a trace is a phonologically null, but otherwise complete, copy of the moved constituent. For example, (46) would have the structure (53):

(53)

[$_{NP}$[$_{NP}$ Whose]$_{NP}$ [$_{N}$ mother]$_{N}$]$_{NP}$ do you think he likes [$_{NP}$[$_{NP}$ e]$_{NP}$ [$_{N}$ e]$_{N}$]$_{NP}$

Here, corresponding parts of the moved constituent and the trace are coindexed. Although only one movement has taken place—movement of the phrase *whose mother*—each part of this phrase has left its own trace. The binding theory can correctly apply between *whose* and *he*, since *he* c-commands a trace of *whose* in (53). This analysis has no advantage over the reconstruction analysis on the questions raised by case-assignment and phonology, so we will not consider these here. With regard to filters, the layered traces analysis would seem to require that the layered traces have sufficient information for the filters to apply in the absence of phonological information. For example, the "Double-ing" Filter must be construed as a filter blocking adjacent present participles, and the traces of verbs must be labeled with their participle status.

A third view of the reconstruction problem makes use of chains. In this view, various conditions and rules do not apply to the trace by itself, or to something in the position of the trace, but to the whole chain, including the *wh*-phrase and all traces that it binds. It requires that subjects be accessible to anaphors in the following way:

(54)
Accessible: A is accessible to B if A c-commands B or A c-commands a trace bound by a phrase containing B.

By this definition, *John* in (47a) (*Which picture of himself does John like e*) is the closest accessible SUBJECT to the reflexive and therefore may serve as its antecedent. Principle B of the binding theory will come out in a similar way. As in the previous analysis, the behavior of filters and case-assigners requires separate treatment.

We might seek a somewhat more abstract version of this theory, where instead of redefining *accessible* in terms of chains, we redefined *c-command* in terms of chains:

(55)
C-command: A c-commands B if A c-commands (in the old sense) B or A c-commands a trace of a phrase that contains B.

Under this redefinition, any condition that uses c-command will behave "as if" phrases were in their D-Structure positions. Suppose, for example, that a case-assigner assigns case to an NP that it c-commands (as was suggested in chapter 14); then the verb in the following sentence c-commands (in the new sense) the *wh*-word in COMP and thus may assign accusative case to it:

(56)
Whom did John see *e*

The principal difficulty with this view is that the revised definition of c-command has an artificial flavor, since it "reconstructs" prior stages of derivation without directly referring to them.

This leads immediately to the final analysis we will consider (as it happens, our own). In this view, all of the relevant rules (filters, binding theory, etc.) apply before *Wh*-Movement, in D-Structure. Clearly this will handle (47a), which has the d-structure (57), to which the binding theory can apply in the usual way:

(57)
John likes which picture of himself

Similarly, case-assignment, filters, and contraction can apply in the usual way, so long as they apply to D-Structure. This is a trivial conclusion—of course a rule will apply "as if" a phrase is in its D-Structure position, if the rule applies to D-Structure.

There are problems, however, if we mean *D-Structure* literally. Since D-Structure is the input not only to *Wh*-Movement, but also to NP-Movement, it is inappropriate for some rules or components to apply to D-Structure. Case theory obviously fails when applied to D-Structure. As we discussed in chapter 14, the derived subject of a passive verb must move to subject position *in order to receive case;* but if this is so, then case cannot be assigned prior to NP-Movement, as it would be if it were assigned in D-Structure.

Nor is the binding theory appropriately applied to D-Structure. Consider the following examples:

(58)
a. *It seemed to himself that Bob was the worst player
b.   It seemed to himself [Bob to be the worst player]
c.   Bob seemed to himself to be the worst player

If (58a) is any guide, the binding theory must not apply at D-Structure, since the d-structure of the grammatical (58c) is (58b), which is parallel to (58a) in structure and so should not allow the binding of the reflexive. Rather, the binding theory should apply to (58c) after NP-Movement.

Finally, there is evidence based on the raising use of *want* that the trace of NP-Movement does not block contraction (see section 9.2.2):

(59)
a. These papers want *e* to be finished by tomorrow
b. These papers wanna be finished by tomorrow

The dilemma, then, is this: in this approach to the reconstruction problem, binding theory, case theory, etc., must apply before *Wh*-Movement, but after NP-Movement. But there is no level of analysis that is the output of all NP-Movements and the input to all *Wh*-Movements. Rather, even in the pre-"Move α" version of the theory these two rules apply together, cyclically. However, it can be simply shown that NP-Movement "feeds" (that is, must apply before) *Wh*-Movement:

(60)
Who *e* was seen *e*

In this example, *Wh*-Movement had to apply after NP-Movement. However, there are no comparable cases to show the reverse—that *Wh*-Movement must apply before NP-Movement. In fact, it is possible to "prove" this, since *Wh*-Movement always moves to COMP and NP-Movement never moves from COMP. Therefore, it should be possible to rewrite all derivations in such a way that all NP-Movements precede all *Wh*-Movements. Going even further, we might declare that these are the only admissible derivations. Such derivations have the property that there is a level of structure to which all NP-Movements have applied, but to which no *Wh*-Movements have applied. We have called this level *NP-Structure*. NP-Structure is characterized by the rules and principles that have the reconstruction property:

(61)
Case theory, binding theory, contraction, the "Double-ing" Filter, etc., all apply at NP-Structure.

Needless to say, this proposal amounts to a wholesale reorganization of the T-model of grammar as presented in this book. On further motivation for and properties of the resulting model, which we call the *Linear Model* or *L-model* of grammar, see Van Riemsdijk and Williams (1981).

19.6 Conclusion

The survey of current research topics with which we close this book is admittedly selective and highly biased—biased, in fact, by our own work and research interests. We offer it not with any pretense of its being exhaustive, but as a window on the diverse and far-reaching types of questions that concern theoretical generative linguists of the 1980s. In a field as dynamic as linguistics is today, we hope that this book will serve not so much as a repository of facts but as a spark to urge readers to explore further on their own: to tackle the specialized literature, work through problems, and talk with others about them. In this way, the progress of the past decades will continue.

Bibliography

Akmajian, A. (1975). More evidence for an NP-cycle. *Linguistic Inquiry* 6, 115–129.

Akmajian, A., R. Demers, and R. Harnish (1984). *Linguistics: An Introduction to Language and Communication*. Second edition. Cambridge, MA: MIT Press.

Allen, C. L. (1977). Topics in diachronic English syntax. Doctoral dissertation, University of Massachusetts, Amherst. (Distributed by the Graduate Linguistics Student Association, University of Massachusetts, Amherst.)

Allen, C. L. (1980). Movement and deletion in Old English. *Linguistic Inquiry* 11, 261–323.

Allwood, J., L. G. Andersson, and Ö. Dahl (1977). *Logic in Linguistics*. Cambridge: Cambridge University Press.

Aoun, J. (1981a). The formal nature of anaphoric relations. Doctoral dissertation, MIT.

Aoun, J. (1981b). ECP, Move α, and Subjacency. *Linguistic Inquiry* 12, 637–645.

Aoun, J. (1985). *A Grammar of Anaphora*. Cambridge, MA: MIT Press.

Aoun, J., N. Hornstein, and D. Sportiche (1980). Some aspects of wide scope quantification. *Journal of Linguistic Research* 1, 69–95.

Aoun, J., and D. Sportiche (1983). On the formal theory of government. *The Linguistic Review* 2, 211–236.

Aronoff, M. (1976). *Word Formation in Generative Grammar*. Linguistic Inquiry Monograph 1. Cambridge, MA: MIT Press.

Bach, E. (1965). On some recurrent types of transformations. In C. W. Kreidler, ed., *Sixteenth Annual Round Table Meeting on Linguistics and Language Studies*. Georgetown University Monograph Series on Language and Linguistics 18. Washington, D.C.

Bach, E. (1971). Questions. *Linguistic Inquiry* 2, 153–166.

Bach, E. (1979). Control in Montague Grammar. *Linguistic Inquiry* 10, 515–531.

Bach, E. (1980). In defense of passive. *Linguistics and Philosophy* 3, 297–341.

Bach, E., and G. Horn (1976). Remarks on "Conditions on Transformations." *Linguistic Inquiry* 7, 265–299.

Bach, E., and B. Partee (1980). Anaphora and semantic structure. In J. Kreiman and A. Ojeda, eds., *Papers from the Parasession on Pronouns and Anaphora*. Chicago Linguistic Society, University of Chicago.

Baker, C. L. (1970). Notes on the description of English questions: The role of an abstract question morpheme. *Foundations of Language* 6, 197–219.

Baker, C. L. (1978). *Introduction to Generative-Transformational Syntax*. Englewood Cliffs, NJ: Prentice-Hall.

Baltin, M. R. (1981). Strict bounding. In C. L. Baker and J. McCarthy, eds., *The Logical Problem of Language Acquisition*. Cambridge, MA: MIT Press.

Baltin, M. R. (1982). A landing site theory for movement rules. *Linguistic Inquiry* 13, 1–38.

Belletti, A., and L. Rizzi (1981). The syntax of *ne:* Some theoretical implications. *The Linguistic Review* 1, 117–154.

Belletti, A., L. Brandi, and L. Rizzi, eds. (1981). *Theory of Markedness in Generative Grammar*. (Proceedings of the 1979 GLOW conference.) Scuola Normale Superiore, Pisa.

Besten, H. den (1978). On the presence and absence of *wh*-elements in Dutch comparatives. *Linguistic Inquiry* 9, 641–671.

Besten, H. den (1982). On the interaction of root transformations and lexical deletive rules. In *Groninger Arbeiten zur Germanistischen Linguistik*. German Department, Groningen University.

Bierwisch, M. (1967). *Grammatik des deutschen Verbs*. Fifth edition. Studia Grammatica II. Berlin (East): Akademie Verlag.

Borer, H. (1984). *Parametric Syntax: Case Studies in Semitic and Romance Languages*. Dordrecht: Foris.

Bouchard, D. (1984). *On the Content of Empty Categories*. Dordrecht: Foris.

Brame, M. K. (1976). *Conjectures and Refutations in Syntax and Semantics*. New York: Elsevier North-Holland.

Brame, M. K. (1978). *Base-Generated Syntax*. Seattle, WA: Noit Amrofer.

Brame, M. K. (1979). *Essays toward Realistic Syntax*. Seattle, WA: Noit Amrofer.

Bresnan, J. W. (1970). On complementizers: Toward a syntactic theory of complement types. *Foundations of Language* 6, 297–321.

Bresnan, J. W. (1972). Theory of complementation in English syntax. Doctoral dissertation, MIT. (New York: Garland, 1979.)

Bresnan, J. W. (1973). Syntax of the comparative clause construction in English. *Linguistic Inquiry* 4, 275–343.

Bresnan, J. W. (1975). Comparative deletion and constraints on transformations. *Linguistic Analysis* 1, 25–74.

Bresnan, J. W. (1976a). On the form and functioning of transformations. *Linguistic Inquiry* 7, 3–40.

Bresnan, J. W. (1976b). Evidence for a theory of unbounded transformations. *Linguistic Analysis* 2, 353–399.

Bresnan, J. W. (1976c). Nonarguments for raising. *Linguistic Inquiry* 7, 485–501.

Bresnan, J. W. (1977). Variables in the theory of transformations. In P. Culicover, T. Wasow, and A. Akmajian, eds. (1977).

Bresnan, J. W. (1978). A realistic transformational grammar. In M. Halle, J. Bresnan, and G. Miller, eds., *Linguistic Theory and Psychological Reality*. Cambridge, MA: MIT Press.

Bresnan, J. W. (1982a). Control and complementation. *Linguistic Inquiry* 13, 343–434. (Also published in Bresnan (1982b).)

Bresnan, J. W., ed. (1982b). *The Mental Representation of Grammatical Relations*. Cambridge, MA: MIT Press.

Bresnan, J. W., and J. Grimshaw (1978). The syntax of free relatives in English. *Linguistic Inquiry* 9, 331–391.

Brody, M. (1984). On contextual definitions and the role of chains. *Linguistic Inquiry* 15, 355–380.

Burzio, L. (1981). Intransitive verbs and Italian auxiliaries. Doctoral dissertation, MIT. (To be published by Reidel, Dordrecht.)

Chomsky, N. (1957). *Syntactic Structures*. The Hague: Mouton.

Chomsky, N. (1962). The logical basis of linguistic theory. In *Proceedings of the Ninth International Congress of Linguists*. The Hague: Mouton.

Chomsky, N. (1964). *Current Issues in Linguistic Theory*. The Hague: Mouton.

Chomsky, N. (1965). *Aspects of the Theory of Syntax*. Cambridge, MA: MIT Press.

Chomsky, N. (1966). *Cartesian Linguistics*. New York: Harper and Row.

Chomsky, N. (1968). *Language and Mind*. New York: Harcourt Brace Jovanovich.

Chomsky, N. (1970). Remarks on nominalization. In R. Jacobs and P. S. Rosenbaum, eds., *Readings in English Transformational Grammar*. Waltham, MA: Ginn & Co. (Reprinted in Chomsky (1972).)

Chomsky, N. (1972). *Studies on Semantics in Generative Grammar*. The Hague: Mouton.

Chomsky, N. (1973). Conditions on transformations. In S. R. Anderson and P. Kiparsky, eds., *A Festschrift for Morris Halle*. New York: Holt, Rinehart and Winston. (Reprinted in Chomsky (1977b).)

Chomsky, N. (1974). The Amherst lectures. Unpublished lecture notes. Distributed by Documents Linguistiques, Université de Paris VII.

Chomsky, N. (1975). *The Logical Structure of Linguistic Theory*. New York: Plenum.

Chomsky, N. (1976). Conditions on rules of grammar. *Linguistic Analysis* 2, 303–351. (Reprinted in Chomsky (1977b).)

Chomsky, N. (1977a). On *wh*-movement. In P. Culicover, T. Wasow, and A. Akmajian, eds. (1977).

Chomsky, N. (1977b). *Essays on Form and Interpretation*. New York: North-Holland.

Chomsky, N. (1980a). *Rules and Representations*. New York: Columbia University Press.

Chomsky, N. (1980b). On binding. *Linguistic Inquiry* 11, 1–46. (Reprinted in F. Heny, ed. (1981).)

Chomsky, N. (1981a). Markedness and core grammar. In A. Belletti, L. Brandi, and L. Rizzi, eds. (1981).

Chomsky, N. (1981b). Principles and parameters in syntactic theory. In N. Hornstein and D. Lightfoot, eds., *Explanation in Linguistics*. London: Longman.

Chomsky, N. (1981c). *Lectures on Government and Binding*. Dordrecht: Foris.

Chomsky, N. (1982a). *Some Concepts and Consequences of the Theory of Government and Binding*. Linguistic Inquiry Monograph 6. Cambridge, MA: MIT Press.

Chomsky, N. (1982b). *The Generative Enterprise: A Discussion with Riny Huybregts and Henk van Riemsdijk*. Dordrecht: Foris.

Chomsky, N., and M. Halle (1968). *The Sound Pattern of English*. New York: Harper and Row.

Chomsky, N., and H. Lasnik (1977). Filters and control. *Linguistic Inquiry* 8, 425–504.

Cinque, G. (1981). On Keenan and Comrie's primary relativization constraint. *Linguistic Inquiry* 12, 293–308.

Cinque, G. (1982). On the theory of relative clauses and markedness. *The Linguistic Review* 1, 247–294.

Cinque, G. (1983). Constructions with left peripheral phrases, "connectedness," Move α, and ECP. Ms., University of Venice.

Cooper, R., and T. Parsons (1976). Montague grammar, generative semantics, and interpretive semantics. In B. Partee, ed., *Montague Grammar*. New York: Academic Press.

Culicover, P., T. Wasow, and A. Akmajian, eds. (1977). *Formal Syntax*. New York: Academic Press.

Culicover, P. W., and W. Wilkins (1984). *Locality in Linguistic Theory*. New York: Academic Press.

Dougherty, R. (1969). An interpretive theory of pronominal reference. *Foundations of Language* 5, 488–508.

Dougherty, R. (1970). A grammar of coordinate conjoined structures: I. *Language* 46, 850–898.

Dowty, D. R., R. E. Wall, and S. Peters (1981). *Introduction to Montague Semantics*. Dordrecht: Reidel.

Emonds, J. E. (1970). Root and structure preserving transformations. Doctoral dissertation, MIT.

Emonds, J. E. (1976). *A Transformational Approach to English Syntax: Root, Structure Preserving, and Local Transformations*. New York: Academic Press.

Emonds, J. E. (1977). Comments on the paper by Lightfoot. In P. Culicover, T. Wasow, and A. Akmajian, eds. (1977).

Engdahl, E. (1983). Parasitic gaps. *Linguistics and Philosophy* 6, 5–34.

Evans, G. (1980). Pronouns. *Linguistic Inquiry* 11, 337–362.

Evers, A. (1975). The transformational cycle in Dutch and German. Doctoral dissertation, Utrecht University. (Distributed by the Indiana University Linguistics Club, Bloomington.)

Fiengo, R. W. (1974). Semantic conditions on surface structure. Doctoral dissertation, MIT.

Fiengo, R. W. (1977). On trace theory. *Linguistic Inquiry* 8, 35–61.

Fiengo, R. W., and H. Lasnik (1973). The logical structure of reciprocal sentences in English. *Foundations of Language* 9, 447–468.

Fillmore, C. J. (1963). The position of embedding transformations in a grammar. *Word* 19, 208–231.

Fillmore, C. J. (1968). The case for case. In E. Bach and R. Harms, eds., *Universals in Linguistic Theory*. New York: Holt, Rinehart and Winston.

Finer, D. (1985). The syntax of switch-reference. *Linguistic Inquiry* 16, 35–55.

Fodor, J. A. (1983). *The Modularity of Mind*. Cambridge, MA: MIT Press.

Fodor, J. D. (1978). Parsing strategies and constraints on transformations. *Linguistic Inquiry* 9, 427–473.

Fodor, J. D. (1979). *Semantics: Theories of Meaning in Generative Grammar*. Cambridge, MA: Harvard University Press.

Frege, G. (1980). *Translations from the Philosophical Writings of Gottlob Frege*. Edited by P. T. Geach and M. Black. Third edition. Oxford: Basil Blackwell.

Freidin, R. (1975). The analysis of passives. *Language* 51, 384–405.

Freidin, R. (1978). Cyclicity and the theory of grammar. *Linguistic Inquiry* 9, 519–549.

Freidin, R., and H. Lasnik (1981). Disjoint reference and *wh*-trace. *Linguistic Inquiry* 12, 39–53.

Gazdar, G. (1981). Unbounded dependencies and coordinate structure. *Linguistic Inquiry* 12, 155–184.

Gazdar, G. (1982). Phrase structure grammar. In P. Jacobson and G. K. Pullum, eds., *The Nature of Syntactic Representation*. Boston: Reidel.

George, L., and J. Kornfilt (1981). Finiteness and boundedness in Turkish. In F. Heny, ed. (1981).

Greenberg, J. (1963). Some universals of grammar, with particular reference to the order of meaningful elements. In J. Greenberg, ed., *Universals of Language*. Cambridge, MA: MIT Press.

Grimshaw, J. (1975). Evidence for relativization by deletion in Chaucerian English. In J. Grimshaw, ed., *Papers on the History and Structure of English*. University of Massachusetts Occasional Papers in Linguistics 1. Graduate Linguistics Student Association, University of Massachusetts, Amherst.

Grimshaw, J. (1979). Complement selection and the lexicon. *Linguistic Inquiry* 10, 279–326.

Groos, A., and H. C. van Riemsdijk (1981). Matching effects in free relatives: A parameter of core grammar. In A. Belletti, L. Brandi, and L. Rizzi, eds. (1981).

Gruber, J. S. (1965). Studies in lexical relations. Doctoral dissertation, MIT.

Gruber, J. S. (1976). *Lexical Structures in Syntax and Semantics*. Amsterdam: North-Holland.

Haaften, T. van, R. Smits, and J. Vat (1983). Left dislocation, connectedness, and reconstruction. In K. Ehlich and H. C. van Riemsdijk, eds., *Connectedness in Sentence, Discourse and Text*. Tilburg Studies in Language and Literature 4. Tilburg University.

Haïk, I. (1984). Indirect binding. *Linguistic Inquiry* 15, 185–223.

Hale, K. (1983). Warlpiri and the grammar of non-configurational languages. *Natural Language and Linguistic Theory* 1, 1–43.

Helke, M. (1971). The grammar of English reflexives. Doctoral dissertation, MIT.

Hellan, L. (1981). An argument for a transformational derivation of passives. In A. Belletti, L. Brandi, and L. Rizzi, eds. (1981).

Hellan, L. (forthcoming). *Reflexives in Norwegian and Theory of Grammar.* Dordrecht: Reidel.

Heny, F. (1979). Review of Chomsky (1975). *Synthese* 40, 317–352.

Heny, F., ed. (1981). *Binding and Filtering.* London: Croom Helm.

Higginbotham, J. (1980). Pronouns and bound variables. *Linguistic Inquiry* 11, 679–708.

Higginbotham, J. (1983). Logical Form, binding, and nominals. *Linguistic Inquiry* 14, 395–420.

Higgins, F. R. (1973). The pseudo-cleft construction in English. Doctoral dissertation, MIT. (New York: Garland, 1979.)

Hoekstra, T. (1984). *Transitivity.* Dordrecht: Foris.

Hoekstra, T., H. van der Hulst, and M. Moortgat (1980a). Introduction. In T. Hoekstra, H. van der Hulst, and M. Moortgat, eds. (1980b).

Hoekstra, T., H. van der Hulst, and M. Moortgat, eds. (1980b). *Lexical Grammar.* Dordrecht: Foris.

Hornstein, N., and A. Weinberg (1981). Case theory and preposition stranding. *Linguistic Inquiry* 12, 55–91.

Horváth, J. (1985). *Aspects of Hungarian Syntax.* Dordrecht: Foris.

Huang, J. C.-T. (1982). Logical relations in Chinese and the theory of grammar. Doctoral dissertation, MIT.

Hulst, H. van der, and N. S. H. Smith, eds. (1982). *The Structure of Phonological Representations.* Volumes I and II. Dordrecht: Foris.

Hyman, L. M. (1975). *Phonology: Theory and Analysis.* New York: Holt, Rinehart and Winston.

Jackendoff, R. S. (1972). *Semantic Interpretation in Generative Grammar.* Cambridge, MA: MIT Press.

Jackendoff, R. S. (1977). *X̄-Syntax: A Study of Phrase Structure.* Linguistic Inquiry Monograph 2. Cambridge, MA: MIT Press.

Jacobson, P. (1977). The syntax of crossing coreference sentences. Doctoral dissertation, University of California, Berkeley. (New York: Garland, 1980.)

Jaeggli, O. (1982). *Topics in Romance Syntax.* Dordrecht: Foris.

Jenkins, L. (1975). *The English Existential.* Tübingen: Niemeyer.

Jenkins, L. (1976). The COMP condition. In *Salzburger Beiträge zur Linguistik.* Tübingen: Gunter Narr.

Katz, J. J. (1972). *Semantic Theory*. New York: Harper and Row.

Katz, J. J., and J. A. Fodor (1963). The structure of a semantic theory. *Language* 39, 170–210. (Reprinted in J. A. Fodor and J. J. Katz, eds. (1964). *The Structure of Language: Readings in the Philosophy of Language*. Englewood Cliffs, NJ: Prentice-Hall.)

Katz, J. J., and P. M. Postal (1964). *An Integrated Theory of Linguistic Descriptions*. Cambridge, MA: MIT Press.

Kayne, R. S. (1975). *French Syntax: The Transformational Cycle*. Cambridge, MA: MIT Press.

Kayne, R. S. (1980). Extensions of binding and case-marking. *Linguistic Inquiry* 11, 75–96. (Reprinted in Kayne (1984).)

Kayne, R. S. (1981a). Two notes on the NIC. In A. Belletti, L. Brandi, and L. Rizzi, eds. (1981). (Reprinted in Kayne (1984).)

Kayne, R. S. (1981b). ECP extensions. *Linguistic Inquiry* 12, 93–133. (Reprinted in Kayne (1984).)

Kayne, R. S. (1981c). On certain differences between French and English. *Linguistic Inquiry* 12, 349–371. (Reprinted in Kayne (1984).)

Kayne, R. S. (1981d). Unambiguous paths. In R. May and J. Koster, eds., *Levels of Syntactic Representation*. Dordrecht: Foris. (Reprinted in Kayne (1984).)

Kayne, R. S. (1983). Connectedness. *Linguistic Inquiry* 14, 223–249. (Reprinted in Kayne (1984).)

Kayne, R. S. (1984). *Connectedness and Binary Branching*. Dordrecht: Foris.

Kayne, R. S., and J.-Y. Pollock (1978). Stylistic inversion, successive cyclicity, and Move NP in French. *Linguistic Inquiry* 9, 595–621.

Kean, M.-L. (1974). The strict cycle in phonology. *Linguistic Inquiry* 5, 179–203.

Kean, M.-L. (1975). *Theory of markedness in generative grammar*. Doctoral dissertation, MIT. (Distributed by the Indiana University Linguistics Club, Bloomington.)

Kean, M.-L. (1981). On a theory of markedness: Some general considerations and a case in point. In A. Belletti, L. Brandi, and L. Rizzi, eds. (1981).

Keenan, E. (1980). Passive is phrasal (not sentential or lexical). In T. Hoekstra, H. van der Hulst, and M. Moortgat, eds. (1980b).

Keenan, E., and B. Comrie (1977). Noun phrase accessibility and universal grammar. *Linguistic Inquiry* 8, 63–100.

Kempson, R. (1977). *Semantic Theory*. Cambridge: Cambridge University Press.

Kenstowicz, M. J., and C. Kisseberth (1979). *Generative Phonology: Description and Theory*. New York: Academic Press.

Keyser, S. J., and T. Roeper (1984). On the middle and ergative constructions in English. *Linguistic Inquiry* 15, 381–416.

Kiss, K. É. (forthcoming). *Chapters from a Generative Syntax of Hungarian*. Dordrecht: Reidel.

Klima, E. (1964). Negation in English. In J. A. Fodor and J. J. Katz, eds., *The Structure of Language*. Englewood Cliffs, NJ: Prentice-Hall.

Koopman, H. (1984). *The Syntax of Verbs*. Dordrecht: Foris.

Koopman, H., and D. Sportiche (1982). Variables and the Bijection Principle. *The Linguistic Review* 2, 135–170.

Koster, J. (1975). Dutch as an SOV language. *Linguistic Analysis* 1, 111–136.

Koster, J. (1978a). *Locality Principles in Syntax*. Dordrecht: Foris.

Koster, J. (1978b). Conditions, empty nodes, and markedness. *Linguistic Inquiry* 9, 551–593.

Koster, J. (1984). On binding and control. *Linguistic Inquiry* 15, 417–459.

Lakoff, G. (1968). Pronouns and reference. Distributed by the Indiana University Linguistics Club, Bloomington.

Lakoff, G. (1970). Global rules. *Language* 46, 627–639.

Lasnik, H. (1976). Some thoughts on coreference. *Linguistic Analysis* 2, 1–22.

Lasnik, H., and J. Kupin (1977). A restrictive theory of transformational grammar. *Theoretical Linguistics* 4, 173–196.

Lasnik, H., and M. Saito (1984). On the nature of proper government. *Linguistic Inquiry* 15, 235–289.

Lebeaux, D. (forthcoming). Locality and anaphoric binding. *The Linguistic Review*.

Lees, R. B. (1960). *The Grammar of English Nominalizations*. The Hague: Mouton.

Lees, R., and E. S. Klima (1963). Rules for English pronominalization. *Language* 36, 63–88.

Lightfoot, D. (1976). The theoretical implications of subject raising. *Foundations of Language* 14, 257–286.

Lightfoot, D. (1977). On traces and conditions on rules. In P. Culicover, T. Wasow, and A. Akmajian, eds. (1977).

Lightfoot, D. (1979). *Principles of Diachronic Syntax*. Cambridge: Cambridge University Press.

Longobardi, G. (1985). Connectedness and island constraints. In J. Guéron, H.-G. Obenauer, and J.-Y. Pollock, eds., *Levels of Syntactic Representation II*. Dordrecht: Foris.

Lyons, J. (1968). *Introduction to Theoretical Linguistics*. Cambridge: Cambridge University Press.

McCloskey, J. (1979). *Transformational Syntax and Model Theoretic Semantics*. Dordrecht: Reidel.

Manzini, M. R. (1983). On control and control theory. *Linguistic Inquiry* 14, 421–446.

Matthews, G. H. (1965). *Hidatsa Syntax*. The Hague: Mouton.

May, R. (1977). The grammar of quantification. Doctoral dissertation, MIT.

May, R. (1979). Must COMP-to-COMP movement be stipulated? *Linguistic Inquiry* 10, 719–725.

May, R. (1985). *Logical Form: Its Structure and Derivation*. Cambridge, MA: MIT Press.

Milner, J.-C. (1978). Cyclicité successive, comparatives, et Cross-over en français. *Linguistic Inquiry* 9, 673–693.

Milsark, G. (1974). Existential sentences in English. Doctoral dissertation, MIT. (New York: Garland, 1979.)

Milsark, G. (1977). Towards an explanation of certain peculiarities of the existential construction in English. *Linguistic Analysis* 3, 1–29.

Mohanan, K. P. (1982). Grammatical relations and clause structure in Malayalam. In J. W. Bresnan, ed. (1982b).

Montague, R. (1974). *Formal Philosophy*. Edited by R. Thomason. New Haven, CT: Yale University Press.

Montalbetti, M. M. (1984). After binding: On the interpretation of pronouns. Doctoral dissertation, MIT.

Muysken, P. C., and H. C. van Riemsdijk (1985a). Projecting features and featuring projections. In P. C. Muysken and H. C. van Riemsdijk, eds. (1985b).

Muysken, P. C., and H. C. van Riemsdijk, eds. (1985b). *Features and Projections*. Dordrecht: Foris.

Newmeyer, F. J. (1980). *Linguistic Theory in America*. New York: Academic Press.

Newmeyer, F. J. (1983). *Grammatical Theory: Its Limits and Its Possibilities*. Chicago, IL: The University of Chicago Press.

Obenauer, H.-G. (1976). *Etudes de syntaxe interrogative du français*. Tübingen: Niemeyer.

Partee, B. (Hall) (1971). On the requirement that transformations preserve meaning. In C. J. Fillmore and D. T. Langendoen, eds., *Studies in Linguistic Semantics*. New York: Holt, Rinehart and Winston.

Partee, B. H. (1975a). *Fundamentals of Mathematics for Linguistics*. Dordrecht: Reidel.

Partee, B. H. (1975b). Montague grammar and transformational grammar. *Linguistic Inquiry* 6, 203–300.

Perlmutter, D. M. (1971). *Deep and Surface Structure Constraints in Syntax*. New York: Holt, Rinehart and Winston.

Pesetsky, D. (1982a). Complementizer-trace phenomena and the Nominative Island Constraint. *The Linguistic Review* 1, 297–343.

Pesetsky, D. (1982b). Paths and categories. Doctoral dissertation, MIT.

Peters, P. S., and R. W. Ritchie (1971). On restricting the base component of transformational grammars. *Information and Control* 18, 483–501.

Postal, P. M. (1969). Review of A. McIntosh and M. A. K. Halliday, *Papers in General, Descriptive and Applied Linguistics*. *Foundations of Language* 5, 409–439.

Postal, P. M. (1970). On coreferential complement subject deletion. *Linguistic Inquiry* 1, 439–500.

Postal, P. M. (1971). *Cross-over Phenomena*. New York: Holt, Rinehart and Winston.

Postal, P. M. (1972). On some rules that are not successive cyclic. *Linguistic Inquiry* 3, 211–222.

Postal, P. M. (1974). *On Raising*. Cambridge, MA: MIT Press.

Postal, P. M., and G. K. Pullum (1982). The contraction debate. *Linguistic Inquiry* 13, 122–138.

Reinhart, T. (1976). The syntactic domain of anaphora. Doctoral dissertation, MIT.

Reinhart, T. (1979). Syntactic domains for semantic rules. In F. Guenthner and S. J. Schmidt, eds., *Formal Semantics and Pragmatics for Natural Languages*. Dordrecht: Reidel.

Reinhart, T. (1983). *Anaphora and Semantic Interpretation*. London: Croom Helm.

Riemsdijk, H. C. van (1978a). On the diagnosis of *Wh* Movement. In S. J. Keyser, ed., *Recent Transformational Studies in European Languages*. Linguistic Inquiry Monograph 3. Cambridge, MA: MIT Press.

Riemsdijk, H. C. van (1978b). *A Case Study in Syntactic Markedness: The Binding Nature of Prepositional Phrases*. Dordrecht: Foris.

Riemsdijk, H. C. van (1982). Locality principles in syntax and phonology. In I.-S. Yang, ed., *Linguistics in the Morning Calm*. Seoul: Hanshin.

Riemsdijk, H. C. van (1983). The case of German adjectives. In F. Heny and B. Richards, eds., *Linguistic Categories: Auxiliaries and Related Puzzles I*. Dordrecht: Reidel.

Riemsdijk, H. C. van, and E. S. Williams (1981). NP-structure. *The Linguistic Review* 1, 171–217.

Rizzi, L. (1978). Violations of the *Wh*-Island Constraint in Italian and the Subjacency Condition. In C. Dubuisson, D. Lightfoot, and Y. C. Morin, eds., *Montreal Working Papers in Linguistics* 11. (Reprinted in Rizzi (1982).)

Rizzi, L. (1982). *Issues in Italian Syntax*. Dordrecht: Foris.

Rizzi, L. (1983). On chain formation. Ms., MIT.

Rosenbaum, P. S. (1967). *The Grammar of English Predicate Complement Constructions*. Cambridge, MA: MIT Press.

Ross, J. R. (1967). Constraints on variables in syntax. Doctoral dissertation, MIT. (Distributed by the Indiana University Linguistics Club, Bloomington.)

Ross, J. R. (1972). Double-ing. *Linguistic Inquiry* 3, 61–86.

Rouveret, A., and J.-R. Vergnaud (1980). Specifying reference to the subject: French causatives and conditions on representations. *Linguistic Inquiry* 11, 97–202.

Safir, K. (1982). Syntactic chains and the definiteness effect. Doctoral dissertation, MIT. (To be published by Cambridge University Press, Cambridge.)

Saito, M. (1982). Case marking in Japanese: A preliminary study. Ms., MIT.

Saito, M. (1984). Some asymmetries in Japanese and their theoretical implications. Doctoral dissertation, MIT.

Saito, M., and M. Hoji (1983). Weak crossover and Move α in Japanese. *Natural Language and Linguistic Theory* 1, 245–260.

Schein, B. (1982). Small clauses and predication. Ms., MIT.

Selkirk, E. (1972). The phrase phonology of English and French. Doctoral dissertation, MIT.

Selkirk, E. (1982). *The Syntax of Words*. Linguistic Inquiry Monograph 7. Cambridge, MA: MIT Press.

Simpson, J., and J. W. Bresnan (1983). Control and obviation in Warlpiri. *Natural Language and Linguistic Theory* 1, 49–64.

Smith, N. V., and D. Wilson (1979). *Modern Linguistics*. London: Penguin.

Sportiche, D. (1981). On bounding nodes in French. *The Linguistic Review* 1, 219–246.

Sportiche, D. (1983). Structural invariance and symmetry. Doctoral dissertation, MIT. (To be published by Foris, Dordrecht.)

Stowell, T. (1981). Origins of phrase structure. Doctoral dissertation, MIT.

Stowell, T. (1983). Subjects across categories. *The Linguistic Review* 2, 285–312.

Taraldsen, K. T. (1978a). The scope of *Wh* Movement in Norwegian. *Linguistic Inquiry* 9, 623–640.

Taraldsen, K. T. (1978b). On the Nominative Island Condition, vacuous application, and the *That*-Trace Filter. Distributed by the Indiana University Linguistics Club, Bloomington.

Taraldsen, K. T. (1981). The theoretical interpretation of a class of "marked" extractions. In A. Belletti, L. Brandi, and L. Rizzi, eds. (1981).

Taraldsen, K. T. (1983). Parametric variation in phrase structure: A case study. Doctoral dissertation, University of Tromsø.

Toman, J., ed. (1985). *Issues in the Grammar of German*. Dordrecht: Foris.

Torrego, E. (1984). On inversion in Spanish and some of its effects. *Linguistic Inquiry* 15, 103–129.

Travis, L. (1984). Parameters and effects of word order variation. Doctoral dissertation, MIT.

Vat, J. (1978). On footnote 2: Evidence for the pronominal status of *þær* in Old English relatives. *Linguistic Inquiry* 9, 695–716.

Vergnaud, J.-R. (1974). French relative clauses. Doctoral dissertation, MIT.

Vergnaud, J.-R. (1982). *Dépendances et niveaux de représentation*. Thèse de doctorat d'état, University of Paris. (To be published by John Benjamins, Amsterdam.)

Wall, R. (1972). *Introduction to Mathematical Linguistics*. Englewood Cliffs, NJ: Prentice-Hall.

Wasow, T. (1972). Anaphoric relations in English. Doctoral dissertation, MIT.

Wasow, T. (1977). Transformations and the lexicon. In P. Culicover, T. Wasow, and A. Akmajian, eds. (1977).

Wasow, T. (1979). *Anaphora in Generative Grammar*. Ghent: E. Story-Scientia.

Williams, E. S. (1974). Rule ordering in syntax. Doctoral dissertation, MIT.

Williams, E. S. (1977). Across-the-board application of rules. *Linguistic Inquiry* 8, 419–423.

Williams, E. S. (1978). Across-the-board rule application. *Linguistic Inquiry* 9, 31–43.

Williams, E. S. (1980). Predication. *Linguistic Inquiry* 11, 203–238.

Williams, E. S. (1981a). Language acquisition, markedness, and phrase structure. In S. Tavakolian, ed. (1981). *Language Acquisition and Linguistic Theory*. Cambridge, MA: MIT Press.

Williams, E. S. (1981b). Argument structure and morphology. *The Linguistic Review* 1, 81–114.

Williams, E. S. (1984). *There*-insertion. *Linguistic Inquiry* 15, 131–153.

Yang, D.-W. (1983). The extended binding theory of anaphors. *Language Research* 19, 169–192.

Zubizarreta, M. L., and J.-R. Vergnaud (1982). On virtual categories. In A. Marantz and T. Stowell, eds., *Papers in Syntax*. MIT Working Papers in Linguistics 4. Department of Linguistics and Philosophy, MIT.

Name Index

Subject Index